EUROPE AND THE COLLAPSE OF YUGOSLAVIA

The Role of Non-State Actors and European Diplomacy

Branislav Radeljić

I.B.TAURIS
LONDON · NEW YORK

Published in 2012 by I.B.Tauris & Co Ltd
6 Salem Road, London W2 4BU
175 Fifth Avenue, New York NY 10010
www.ibtauris.com

Distributed in the United States and Canada
Exclusively by Palgrave Macmillan
175 Fifth Avenue, New York NY 10010

Copyright © 2012 Branislav Radeljić

The right of Branislav Radeljić to be identified as the author of this work has been asserted by the author in accordance with the Copyright, Designs and Patent Act 1988.

All rights reserved. Except for brief quotations in a review, this book, or any part thereof, may not be reproduced, stored in or introduced into a retrieval system, or transmitted, in any form or by any means, electronic, mechanical, photocopying, recording or otherwise, without the prior written permission of the publisher.

Library of International Relations, vol. 61

ISBN 978 1 84885 989 0

A full CIP record for this book is available from the British Library
A full CIP record for this book is available from the Library of Congress

Library of Congress catalog card: available

Typeset by Newgen Publishers, Chennai
Printed and bound by CPI Group (UK) Ltd, Croydon, CR0 4YY

For My Parents

CONTENTS

Acknowledgements ix
List of Abbreviations xi

Introduction 1
Chapter One—Writing the Collapse of Yugoslavia:
   Existing and Potential Arguments 13
   Internal Factors 15
   Economics: Factor of Connectivity 18
   External Factors 21
   What Is Yet to Be Examined? 33
   Conclusion 36

PART ONE: EUROPEAN COMMUNITY
RELATIONS WITH YUGOSLAVIA 39

Chapter Two—The European Community and Yugoslavia
   from Unofficial to Official Relations 41
   Getting to Know Each Other 43
   Communication 47
   The 1960s: Closer or Looser Ties? 53
   1968: The Establishment of Official Relations 56
   New Dynamics 61
   Conclusion 65

Contents

**Chapter Three—The European Community and Yugoslavia
from Integration to Disintegration**   68
Introducing New Debates and Greater Concerns   70
The 1980s: New Agreement and New Challenges   73
'A Slight Cooling in EEC-Yugoslavia Relations'   77
The End of the 1980s   81
Yugoslavs in the European Community   88
Conclusion   91

PART TWO: THE ROLE OF NON-STATE ACTORS   93

**Chapter Four—Calling Diaspora and Diaspora Calling:
Impact of Diasporas on European Community Policy**   95
Slovenian Activism   97
Croatian Activism   100
Diaspora Strategies within the European Community   105
Diasporas and Individual European States   110
Conclusion   119

**Chapter Five—Media Power: Media Influence on
European Community Policy**   121
Yugoslav Media and the Public   123
Awakening of the Western Media   126
European Community Reactions   130
Media Relevance for European Decision-Making   136
Conclusion   144

**Chapter Six—With the Blessing of the Vatican:
The Catholic Church and European Community Policy**   146
Between the Yugoslav Leadership and the Vatican   148
Religious Aspects of the Yugoslav Crisis   154
From Churches to the Brussels Officials   158
Conclusion   167

Conclusion   169
Notes   175
Bibliography   222
Index   247

ACKNOWLEDGEMENTS

It is appropriate to acknowledge that the work on this book was possible, primarily, thanks to the Overseas Research Student award provided by Goldsmiths College, University of London, and the British Government.

I owe my gratitude to numerous individuals who offered endless support from the very beginning to the very end. My supervisor, Dr Jasna Dragović-Soso, provided exemplary encouragement, guidance and insightful comments which altogether contributed to the timely completion of my thesis. Special thanks are also due to the personnel in various institutions across Europe whom I consulted and who kindly agreed to talk to me about my topic, share their ideas and offer material that I found of great use.

I offer sincere thanks to some dear people around me who understood when I preferred staying at home in order to produce another line or paragraph, instead of joining them for a good night out. Amongst them, Marco Salaorno, Mary Louise Wardle, Nebojša Dmitrović, Pádraig O'Connor and Scott Stensland deserve particular recognition. At the same time, I thank my colleagues from the University of East London, who, already being in academia, knew exactly how I felt at various stages. I appreciated their interest in the topic and readiness to contribute, whenever possible.

I am indebted to I.B.Tauris and especially Tomasz Hoskins who accepted and supported this book from the very beginning and helped bring it to the finish line. Also, I offer sincere thanks to anonymous reviewers for their useful comments on the earlier draft of the manuscript.

Last, but never least, I wholeheartedly thank my family back in Belgrade: my parents, Jelena and Bogdan Radeljić, and my brother Zoran, for having always been there for me. Their love and belief that I had selected the right path for myself made work on this project so much easier.

B. R.
London

LIST OF ABBREVIATIONS

CAC	Croatian American Congress
CDU	Christian Democratic Union
CDUCE	Christian Democratic Union of Central Europe
CFSP	Common Foreign and Security Policy
CNN	Cable News Network
COMECON	Council for Mutual Economic Assistance
CSCE	Conference on Security and Co-operation in Europe
CSU	Christian Social Union of Bavaria
EC	European Community
EC-COY	EC Conference on Yugoslavia
ECSC	European Coal and Steel Community
ECU	European Currency Unit
EEC	European Economic Community
EFTA	European Free Trade Association
EIB	European Investment Bank
EP	European Parliament
EU	European Union
FAZ	Frankfurter Allgemeine Zeitung
HDZ	Hrvatska demokratska zajednica / Croatian Democratic Union
ICFY	International Conference on the Former Yugoslavia
IMF	International Monetary Fund
JNA	Jugoslovenska narodna armija / Yugoslav People's Army

List of Abbreviations

LCY	League of Communists of Yugoslavia
MEP	Member of the European Parliament
NATO	North Atlantic Treaty Organization
NFCA	National Federation of Croatian Americans
SAA	Stabilization and Association Agreement
SANU	Sprska akademija nauka i umetnosti / Serbian Academy of Sciences and Arts
SDS	Srpska demokratska stranka / Serbian Democratic Party
SFRY	Socialist Federal Republic of Yugoslavia
TVL	Television Ljubljana
TVS	Television Slovenia
UK	United Kingdom
US	United States
USA	United States of America
ZDF	Zweites Deutsches Fernsehen

INTRODUCTION

This book is about the Socialist Federal Republic of Yugoslavia (SFRY) and its collapse – an investigation of a complex issue that can be approached from many different perspectives. In fact, the variety of hypotheses makes any academic project on Yugoslavia an active, on-going investigation, as anyone who has conducted research on its disintegration must surely know. In analysing the break-up of the Yugoslav state, Mihailo Crnobrnja, its ambassador to the European Communities (1989–1992) and an academic, rejects the idea of a 'single cause or explanation for the Yugoslav drama', stating that 'dissolution ... happened as a result of a myriad of forces and events as well as mutually linked disruptive moves'.[1] Such complexity encouraged diametrically opposing points of view among academics, politicians, the media, and accordingly, various general and scholarly writings have emerged, often raising as many questions as they answer and, more importantly, inviting new contributions to the field.

At the same time, this book is about the then European Economic Community (EEC) and the present European Union (EU). The EEC officially became the EU on 1 November 1993, with the coming into force of the Treaty on European Union, also known as the Treaty of Maastricht. Throughout the book, the terms 'European (Economic) Community', 'Community', 'Europe' or 'Europeans' will be employed interchangeably, whereas the term 'European Union' is primarily used when talking about the present (post-Maastricht) period. Thus, both Yugoslavia and the Community are placed at the core of the project: Yugoslavia is a particularly interesting case because of its tragic destiny and lessons learnt here can only serve as a valuable example with regard to the subsequent challenges faced by the EU, although some scholars argue that '[t]he world is slowly learning the lessons of the Balkan crisis even if Western leaders remain doggedly determined to ignore them and to turn a blind eye'.[2] To be precise, the following text examines the involvement of the European Community in the catastrophic fall of the Yugoslav state; it is an inquiry into the very nature of the relations that developed between the two parties from the establishment of the Community, the complexity of those relations and the overall mismanagement that contributed to and resulted in the collapse of the Balkan state.

To date, there are several books discussing the Community's recognition policy and a number of academic articles focusing on the eve of Yugoslavia's break-up and therefore the Community's reactions, but none of them considers relations between the Community and Yugoslavia prior to the collapse of the state or what went wrong and how particular decisions on behalf of the Community were affected. In order to fill the gap, this book sets out primarily to offer substantial empirical analysis while bearing in mind the relevance of different theoretical approaches.[3] Furthermore, it examines the relations between the two parties and positions the Yugoslav state within both the European and world political frameworks, while bearing in mind the effect of international affairs. Conversely, it does not ignore the role played by Yugoslavia within the international arena during the second half of the twentieth century as any omission of Yugoslavia's role on the world stage might cast doubts on the objectivity of the present investigation.[4]

This volume sets out to complement the interpretations concentrating on macro-structural factors (economic problems, the geopolitical position of Yugoslavia, ethnic diversities within the state), specific individuals (Josip Broz Tito, Slobodan Milošević or Franjo Tudjman), republics (Serbia, Croatia or Slovenia) or states (Germany or the United States of America). In light of these studies, this volume does not intend to reject the relevance of the existing material in the field or question the seriousness of the authors who have contributed to the intellectual puzzle. However, it argues that both the nature of the relations between the European Community and the Yugoslav federation and the Community's subsequent confusion over how to approach the outbreak of the Yugoslav crisis minimized the efficiency of the Community as a decision-making body, allowing specific non-state actors (diaspora members, the media and Churches) to take advantage of this deficiency. In this sense, the European Community is understood as a vital player with a very specific role due to its 'failure to fully anticipate the consequences of [the] collapse and the lasting impact it would have on local, regional, global and humanitarian security', all closely linked to its 'lack of common purpose and interest in addressing the collapse of Yugoslavia'.[5]

Main Arguments

Relations between the Socialist Federal Republic of Yugoslavia and the European Economic Community were often problematic. Indeed, from an economic perspective, the creation of the European Common Market threatened Yugoslavia's own position and therefore undermined their relationship. From a political perspective, while mistakenly considering Yugoslavia equal to other Eastern-bloc countries, the Community perceived that their relationship lacked solidity – a position that was slightly modified towards the end of the 1970s. Finally, from a social perspective, the presence of Yugoslav guest-workers within the Community represented a matter of serious concern. Thus, my first argument is that, more often than not, relations between the Community and Yugoslavia were rather questionable. According to one study, such an impression derives from a relationship of mutual benefit: 'Just as Belgrade was opportunistically seeking to gain Western support in return for its neutrality in the east-west conflict, so the West, under no illusion about the political nature of this regime, cultivated Yugoslav [economic] dependency, hoping to sustain its independence in the event of renewed hostilities in Europe'.[6] Therefore, the West's shift of perception, from first cultivating Yugoslav dependency to then supporting Yugoslav dismemberment in 1991, requires deeper investigation.

The second argument goes one step further and, while confirming the complexity of the first, examines how the establishment of official relations between the European Economic Community and the Yugoslav federation in 1968 did not have a substantial impact on the existing situation between them. While the official letter expressed Yugoslav 'thankfulness to the Directorate General for External Relations of the Commission of the European Communities ... for the offer to enter into official relations with the Communities',[7] at the same time the Yugoslav leadership was determined to develop the optimum strategies for obtaining Western aid without actively doing a great deal to build on their interdependence. Although Yugoslavia was the first Eastern European country to accredit an ambassador to the European Communities,[8] and the establishment of diplomatic relations meant that Yugoslavia finally had a direct connection with the Community and thus 'the opportunity of being kept informed of the contents of the decisions and of all the available data relating to the problems which they dealt with',[9] (which in practical terms meant greater transparency), both parties had different goals: for the Community it was sufficient that Yugoslavia remained where it stood ideologically and Yugoslavia was happy to receive financial aid from the Community.

While the 1970s were supposed to be a period of economic cooperation, due to numerous agreements signed between the European Economic Community and the Yugoslav federation, the success of such agreements was in fact very limited. Once the European Commission 'endeavored to reinforce economic cooperation with Yugoslavia',[10] extremely positive on paper, it immediately endorsed certain reservations: for example, the third chapter regulating the commercial agreement between the two parties stipulated that 'whenever it proves that the European Market is or will be threatened by greater import deriving from Yugoslavia ... the Community can immediately suspend its facilitating measures'.[11] This protectionist and at the same time discriminatory regime became an additional cause for mistrust. Another factor to be taken into consideration was that of the Yugoslav guest-workers in the Community whose presence led to the introduction of restrictive measures aimed at regulating the influx of Yugoslav immigrants.

Thirdly, the 1980s confirmed the lack of a clear position over relations between the Community and Yugoslavia: in Viktor Meier's words, the Community's advocacy of Yugoslav unity 'was unrealistic for Slovenia and Croatia, insofar as it did not at all take into account the entire intra-Yugoslav course of events which had driven Slovenia and Croatia to decide on independence'.[12] Thus, on one hand, there was the Community, an international organization with its ambition of providing Europe with a stable and secure future, while, on the other, there was the Yugoslav federation, a state with a questionable future due to the growing disagreements (political, economic, cultural) within the SFRY itself. At this point, the importance of the hitherto ignored historical perspective in the literature becomes clear. The relations of the past structure the present, and therefore history should not be ignored – overlooking history can affect our understanding of the present or contribute to a manipulation of the future.[13] This is why the understanding of the whole set of relations (the Community vis-à-vis Yugoslavia, the Member States vis-à-vis the Community and Yugoslavia, the non-state actors vis-à-vis their possible partners) is facilitated if we provide a deeper insight into their origins.

The initial lack of European Community competence in addressing the outbreak of the Yugoslav crisis, avoidable if well-grounded relations based on mutual dependence had been exercised, played a decisive role in allowing certain non-state actors to become involved in the situation. Meier points the finger at the Western diplomatic corps in Belgrade, 'most of whom went beyond the city limits of the capital only with great reluctance', and therefore 'misunderstood the realities' of Yugoslavia.[14] In this period the European Community's attention switched from the Yugoslav federation as a whole to its constituent republics.[15] However, regarding signals from the Community, while 'encouraging Yugoslavia's unity and strongly discouraging Slovenia's and Croatia's planned unilateral dissociation from the existing federation ... [they] may have actually encouraged the Yugoslav federal government and the JNA [Yugoslav People's Army] to employ force against the country's two breakaway republics'.[16]

Finally, this book investigates the European Community's reaction to the crucial question of what was to be Yugoslavia's future, in other words, its collapse. Accordingly, it will show that both Slovenia and Croatia gained enormous support from the Brussels officials at decisive moments – a close link that has been subject to various interpretations. In fact, the most frequently asked question is: Why and how did the EC decision-makers change their position from supporting Yugoslav unity to supporting Slovenia and Croatia on their way to independence? Decisions are often made under unclear circumstances. In their analysis of decision-making, Werner Kroeber-Riel and Jürgen Hauschildt distinguish between collective and individual decisions and warn that '[t]he participants in the decision-making process may have specialized functions, which enhance productivity, but since the co-ordination of these specialists requires planning and adjustment, collective decision-making may be a long drawn-out process'.[17] This model can be used to examine decision-making processes during the Yugoslav crisis where the Community represents the 'collective' element and a Member State can be viewed as an 'individual'.

However, while ignorance over the Yugoslav situation was open to manipulation, this book investigates the tools used by the two republics to achieve their objectives. It argues that links between diaspora members, the media and the Catholic Church in the Community and the republics of Slovenia and Croatia facilitated their path towards dissociation. Here, rather than blaming any of these groups, this volume seeks to demonstrate their strength at times when bigger actors such as governments and institutions of the Community lacked it. Although the literature on the activism of non-state actors during the Yugoslav crisis has been very limited, their role is of strategic significance. One author clearly confirms their capacity to contribute to 'the fragmentation of political responsibility' and suggests '[t]he more successful non-state actors are in affecting political outcomes, the more responsibility they should be asked to take for those outcomes'.[18]

The role of the diaspora as facilitating the achievement of independence for Slovenia and Croatia is key to understanding the involvement of the European Community in the Yugoslav crisis. The process of the 'political socialization of diaspora' was swift and well-defined.[19] Each party used its diaspora members to influence Western decision-makers. According to some accounts, during the Yugoslav conflict 'the Croatians were the big winners of the diaspora influence, as their large lobby in Germany decidedly influenced the German government's decision to recognize Croatia's bid for independence'.[20] More precisely, in 1990 they commenced 'to lobby the Christian Social Union of Bavaria (CSU) to push for Germany's support of Croatia's interests'.[21] Although some authors insist that it was Belgrade's political elite who manipulated Western perception of the Yugoslav crisis and at the same time controlled the information reaching Western embassies in Belgrade, thus raising the question of lobbying,[22] this book will outline the way in which close links between home-grown movements in Slovenia and Croatia and their representatives in the Community established close ties at crucial moments and worked on a joint project: independence.

The mass media, both domestic and international, encouraged and sustained the Yugoslav conflict.[23] With regard to the Slovenian and Croatian representation of the processes in question, they managed to create their own interpretation of events, a narrative that reinforced their distinct positions within the Yugoslav federation and was also adopted as the dominant vision within the Western media, and thus across the European Community. Having presented the information surrounding the process in such a way as to justify their intentions, the facts presented in the national broadcasters' reports were picked up by the media in Western Europe as something alarming and requiring action. In Slovenia and Croatia, such practice was greeted with approval, considering their dissatisfaction with the federation. Although Serbia was equally involved in the political process, information disseminated by the Serbian media did not resonate with the Western media: this was a result of domestic control imposed by the party in power which primarily concentrated on Serbian victimization and on accusation of the Slovenes and Croats, and thus contributed to Serbia's voice remaining virtually unheard abroad.[24]

Lastly, with the outbreak of the Yugoslav crisis, religion came to occupy a vital role, with membership of one religious organization rather than another becoming an increasingly important factor. In this respect, as observed elsewhere, 'religion was a social component of the forces that helped dismember the Yugoslav "experiment"'.[25] On the eve of the conflict, churches became active interest propagators: religion proved to be a powerful tool in strengthening identity and therefore accentuated national or ethnic diversity. While the Serbian Church turned towards the Orthodox Greeks who openly supported the idea of Serbian expansionism,[26] Slovenian and Croatian Churches sought support from the Western Catholic Church. One study, while understanding religion as 'the catalyst of the crisis in the 1980s and 1990s', points out that it was the Church that helped President Tudjman come to power and that subsequently 'the Vatican led several Western countries to recognize Croatia as an independent state'.[27] The highly politicized involvement of the Church had an impact on European involvement in the crisis. Understandably, the Catholic Church was more powerful due to the denomination of the countries deciding upon Yugoslavia's destiny.

In conclusion, the analysis of the aforementioned relations is aimed at offering a fuller understanding as to how European Community involvement in the collapse of the Yugoslav federation was first challenged and then constructed by the non-state groups and it should not, ultimately, provoke surprise but rather be viewed as a foregone conclusion. While 'the Community partners acted collectively but within an ill-defined institutional framework',[28] other, non-state actors were given an opportunity to reconfirm their power at decisive moments for the Balkan state.

A Note on Methodology

While aware of the importance of the examination of events within their appropriate context, I have adopted an interdisciplinary approach including political science and history. Keeping in mind that the relationship between the European Economic Community and the Yugoslav federation has received little academic attention to date, the value of such an approach lies in its capacity to demonstrate that relations characterizing certain periods contributed to the outcome, in this case the collapse of the state. At the same time, I am fully aware of the unexpected consequences that may result from historical analysis, meaning that my point of view is informed by the serenity of the present situation, when the outcome is well-known.[29] This is something I bore in mind when conducting my research and working on this book.

The present text has benefited from numerous secondary as well as primary sources. Chapter One will examine only a selection of secondary sources – the vast number of written contributions in the field, along with space limitations, do not allow presentation of all the relevant scholarship. In order to collect primary sources, I moved between London, other European capitals that played an important role during Yugoslavia's disintegration, and the former Yugoslavia's cities, once capitals of the country's constituent republics and today capitals of independent states. First of all, the archives were of considerable use as they offered valuable information and encouraged in-depth analysis of the historical material necessary for a greater understanding of the relations that developed between the two parties.[30] Notwithstanding certain restrictions existing at the time (in terms of confidential material drafted for official purposes only), I benefited from its public disclosure once the period of confidentiality had expired: indeed, some of these documents were collected and published in different edited volumes as this research was being carried out.[31]

Diaspora organizations, media agencies and religious organizations provided relevant materials that were primarily used to write Chapters Four, Five and Six. In this respect, the Slovenes seemed to be well ahead as they decided to make public whatever material they found: for example, the *Viri o demokratizaciji in osamosvojiti Slovenije*[32] represent a valuable collection of official correspondence and transcripts related to the disintegration of Yugoslavia. In the meantime, some media agencies have made their archives available on-line – another advantage for time management. While the Churches remain rather difficult to approach, a number of personal contacts have allowed me to approach a variety of individuals and collect information that proved of significant use. Here, I refer primarily to the Vatican, which is considered to have notably influenced EC decision-makers.

Interviews represented another source of information and helped crystallize some ideas. Although their methodological soundness is questioned in some quarters,[33] interviews were chosen for a number of reasons. First, there is always something new to be said on such a complex topic, as proved by most of the interviewees, especially when speaking off the record. Second, most of the actors directly involved in the Yugoslav state crisis offered new perspectives and raised fresh questions requiring fresh answers. Finally, some of the informants consulted have never produced written documentation of the issues they are familiar with, and their contribution can thus be seen as a useful source, necessary for value-relevant knowledge, that would otherwise have remained unexplored. As to the different structures, I have opted mostly for semi-structured or guided interviews. As explained by Tom Wengraf, these interviews 'are ones where research and planning produce a session in which most of the informant's responses can't be predicted in advance and where you as interviewer therefore have to *improvise* probably half – and maybe 80% or more – of your responses to what they say in response to your *initial prepared* question or questions'.[34] This ploy proved to be an effective way of collecting relevant and, at the same time, detailed information. In addition, having a similar set of questions and repeating them to different respondents was a necessary tool, allowing as it did the comparison of answers and the identification of the most appropriate responses.

The interviewees were selected according to the following criteria: their direct involvement in events and policy-making both within the European Community and the Yugoslav federation, their indirect involvement as government officials, diplomats, advisors, academics, journalists, clergy members, or their extensive writings that at times appeared as published memoirs. They all contributed to my understanding of relations between the Community and Yugoslavia as well as how important non-state actors were in shaping the Community's decision-making processes during the Yugoslav crisis. Moreover, I came across a surprising amount of criticism still surrounding discourses about certain decisions. In fact, most of the diplomats representing former Yugoslav republics – now states – offered often dramatically opposing interpretations of leaders, the crisis and consequent wars. As a result, I heard the worst and the best about the Slovenes, Milošević, Tudjman, the Germans, etc. However, there was a general consensus among respondents that the art of diplomacy was rather weak during the Yugoslav state crisis and that diplomatic efforts served to fulfil the basic concept that there should be some kind of diplomacy, rather than actively contributing to the solving of the crisis.

Chapter Outline

Chapter One examines the existing literature making the distinction between different schools of thought and their views of the Yugoslav crisis in general. While distinguishing between internal factors (Milošević, Slovenian and Croatian leaderships, economic performance) and external factors (Western powers) as contributing factors in the collapse of the Yugoslav state, it outlines those areas that have not as yet been sufficiently dealt with in scholarship, and explains why it is hoped that the present study into this field will prove a valuable contribution.

Chapter Two provides a detailed reading of relations between the European Economic Community and the Yugoslav federation and, within the timeframe it encompasses (from the early 1950s to the late 1970s, thus including the first decade after official relations between the two had been established), it points out the strengths and weaknesses with regard to both sides and concludes that the nature of their relationship was rather problematic, characterized by constant oscillations within primarily economic and, consequently, political and social segments. Chapter Three addresses the 1980s – an important period as it defined Yugoslavia's destiny – and gives a picture of the Community's relations with Yugoslavia by showing major misunderstandings deriving from their relationship. While understood as the period of the last throes of Tito's Yugoslavia, the main causes and consequences and the EC's reactions in relation to this are examined. In particular, this chapter will identify the non-state actors and their developing strategies which appeared to play a leading role in protecting their respective republics' interests abroad and therefore secured the aim of the Yugoslav wars: secession.

The three chapters that follow will detail the involvement of non-state actors inside and outside Slovenia and Croatia, and their ability to secure the European Community's support in order to secede from the Yugoslav federation. All of them investigate the facilitating tools these actors adopted (in synergy with the ambitions of the two republics' leaderships) to influence the Community's decision-makers. The non-state actors addressed did not appear out of the blue and this is why each chapter on these powerful players will pay some attention to their activism during the decades preceding the Yugoslav crisis. Chapter Four discusses diaspora groups, whose readiness to coalesce and protest complemented the sentiments the media were trying to provoke, Chapter Five investigates the media and their undeniable power, and Chapter Six concentrates on the Catholic Church and its remarkable capacity to intervene in political decisions, which somehow validates the discourse of the undeniable presence of religion in politics. The examination of these actors will allow a clearer understanding of how the Community accepted another act of secession without really considering its impact on the remaining republics: the Community's decision to recognize Croatia meant that the war was then transferred to Bosnia-Herzegovina.

Finally, the Conclusion will provide a brief summary of the main arguments and try to place them into a broader context for future research. The book follows my central point: due to the nature of relations between the European Community and the SFRY, and moreover, because of lack of proper strategy at critical times, specific non-state actors came to react at the key stages of Yugoslavia's development, and influence decision-making within the European Community in favour of recognizing the independence of the republics of Slovenia and Croatia.

CHAPTER ONE

WRITING THE COLLAPSE OF YUGOSLAVIA

Existing and Potential Arguments

This chapter provides an overview of the existing scholarship and debates within the field of the social sciences closely related to the disintegration of the SFRY. Even if some observers understood the Yugoslav state as an artificial and non-permanent entity, others believed in its structure as it stood, without questioning its future. As one author puts it, Yugoslavia was 'a rare bird in Europe: Communist, yet moderately tolerant, open to trade with the West, and politically independent of both Cold War blocs'.[1] When the country started facing economic, political and social problems, academics turned their attention to the area, trying to establish the causes and possible outcome of these problems. The wars in the former Yugoslavia 'shocked the civilized West'[2] and encouraged an endless debate about the Balkans:

> Today, the very word "Balkans" conjures up images of intrigue, war, and human suffering on a scale abhorrent to Western society. To some people, the Balkan countries lack a clear Western orientation and carry far too much cultural baggage to belong in the European club. Western leaders refer to the region as the back door to Europe, the Balkan powder keg, or Europe's

doorstep. What these euphemisms hide is, perhaps, the wish that the Balkans were located anywhere other than in Europe.[3]

While opposing this at one point rather fashionable understanding among Western authors of the Balkans as incapable of Westernizing, I argue that the Yugoslav wars sparked a debate over credibility and capability not only with regard to the international community as such,[4] but also with regard to individual states and actors who were assigned important roles in the handling of the devastating situation.

What the scholarship immediately did was to point the finger at one or more actors, most commonly at specific individuals, while at the same time shielding a number of crucial contributing factors from serious criticism.[5] In his analysis, Robert Hayden comments:

> Academic debates on the Former Yugoslavia are as polarized as those surrounding the creation of Israel or the partitioning of Cyprus, with criticism of a study often depending more on whether the work supports the commentator's predetermined position than on the coherence of its theory or the reliability and sufficiency of its arguments. When one side in such a conflict wins politically, it usually also wins academically, because analyses that indicate that a politics that won is, in fact, wrong tend to be discounted. Political hegemony establishes intellectual orthodoxy.[6]

Hayden's statement is a warning on how to approach investigations in the field. Today, when the SFRY does not exist any more and some of the actions perpetrated have become well-known, scholarship continuously extends its interest with the purpose of re-examining the contributing factors, what could have been done to prevent the four Yugoslav wars,[7] and what remains to be done in order to ensure that a similar disaster is never repeated, at least in Europe. I agree that the collapse of Yugoslavia was stimulated by numerous causes, and that most of them were interlinked and jointly contributed to the actual state disintegration. Before I present my own ideas and what remains to be examined, I will reflect upon the existing causes, and while broadly dividing them into two main categories (internal and external), link them to the main arguments of the book.

Internal Factors

Even though this book is about one specific external factor and its role in the Yugoslav crisis, internal elements are worthy of consideration for two reasons: first, due to their undeniable presence in any debate regarding the collapse and, second, because they are linked to external factors on a mutually inclusive and influential basis. The internal factors presented here primarily discuss individuals (Milošević,[8] Tudjman[9] and Kučan[10]) and the republics they represented (Serbia, Croatia and Slovenia). Less influential, but still remarkably present in academic research, three additional factors deserve quick mention: ancient hatreds, nationalism and cultural diversity.[11] Although some studies examine possible links between these factors and violence that subsequently led to the disintegration of Yugoslavia,[12] their relevance for this study is limited due to their own limited capacity to directly affect policy-making processes both in Belgrade and Brussels. Therefore, these factors are rather understood as background components in the discourse often used to justify certain domestic policies across the Yugoslav federation.

To begin with, Slobodan Milošević remains one of the most controversial political figures of the 1990s. His name is rarely found without accompanying modifiers or 'clarifying' phrases: while for Francis Fukuyama he was 'a semi-fascist demagogue',[13] for David Owen he was somebody ready 'to regard individuals as disposable: to use them and then discard them',[14] and *The Observer* dubbed him 'the Butcher of the Balkans'.[15] Many scholars would agree that Milošević and his regime were the driving force behind the process of Yugoslav destruction,[16] although a number of them fall into the error of assimilating the ex-banker-turned-politician with Belgrade and Serbia in general, a debatable association when the numerous demonstrations in Belgrade against his regime are taken into account.

Once the socialist Yugoslavia had become a failure, many authors undertook a deeper analysis of human agency and while looking at the decades that preceded the disintegration, blame Josip Broz Tito[17] for creating an unrealistic system and Milošević for triggering the war. Tito had remarkable power: he was in effect the state. He was irreplaceable and in charge of the main state policies. But, in his analysis, Bogdan Denitch blames Tito for being 'a perverse coda of the dead Habsburg era', uninterested in 'the development of close ties with the democratic-socialist parties and the labour movement of Western Europe', but rather 'maintaining a sentimental ideological link with the Soviet-run Communist world'.[18] Indeed, chapters covering relations between the European Economic Community and Yugoslavia will confirm the relevance of Denitch's standpoint. Still, however, linking Tito to Milošević has to be done cautiously as they were products of different timeframe: Tito emerged from the post-war period and thus settlement, and Milošević from the Yugoslav drama. In addition, Tito's approach was supra-national with a focus on national identification, while Milošević's aim was to subsume Yugoslavia within a nationalist discourse – his intention was that of a Serbia-dominated Yugoslavia, serving the interests of the 42 per cent of Serbs living outside the republic of Serbia.[19]

Alongside studies of Tito and Milošević, some scholars investigate the role played by another human agent: Franjo Tudjman. Here, Siniša Malešević, while pointing out that actually all three of them 'had control over the most important sections ... that had an influence on popular attitudes' notes that '[t]he only difference was that [Tudjman] would also make an appeal through his extensive knowledge of the history of southern Slav relations and on that basis would patronize his followers'.[20] Indeed, when considered within the discourse of disintegration, his involvement is usually analysed within the context of actions carried out on behalf of the republic of Croatia, with individual ambitions and responsibilities broadly ignored.

Going further, some writings do not even distinguish between Croatia and Slovenia when talking about their ambitions. For them, the seceding republics appeared to seek foreign support regardless of the possible outcome of the Yugoslav state's crisis. As Denitch puts it:

> In unleashing their destruction of Yugoslavia – whether for the stated purpose of maintaining the status quo or for unconditional,

absolute, and immediate sovereignty of their own nations – the political elites of the individual Yugoslav states have sharply reduced the actual independence of their peoples and have created a situation in which their nations must in the long range become protectorates to be jointly overseen by the UN and the European Community.[21]

In contrast, other contributors approach the question of the objectives of the two secessionist republics, Slovenia and Croatia, in a different manner. When talking about divided responsibility, Slovenia is often accused of being self-centred and disrespectful towards Belgrade. In fact, as Warren Zimmermann, the ambassador with 'a lack of sympathy for Slovenia and Croatia',[22] notes: 'While the Slovenes hated Slobodan Milošević, they built no ideology against him ... They just wanted to be left alone. Their virtue was democracy and their vice was selfishness. In their drive to separate from Yugoslavia they simply ignored the twenty-two million Yugoslavs who were not Slovenes. They bear considerable responsibility for the bloodbath that followed their secession'.[23]

This book accepts the existence of self-centred behaviour within Titoist Yugoslavia. Therefore, apart from Milošević, a malefactor bent on turning Yugoslavia into a Serb-dominated country or Tudjman, who desired a Croatian state for Croats without guaranteeing equal rights to the Serbs living in Croatia, Slovenia deserves criticism for being self-centred within the Yugoslav federation and not being interested in finding an appropriate solution for all the parties concerned.[24] In order to secure its position, Slovenia decided to pass amendments to its own constitution in 1989 and determine the future of the SFRY. The main objective of the amendments was 'to transform what had until then been a working (if clumsy) federation into an unworkable confederation, and this change is important for understanding the dynamics and trajectory of the collapse of the Yugoslav state'.[25] This understanding complements what Mario Nobilo, advisor to President Tudjman, later described as the principal approach of both Croatia and Slovenia – 'to paralyze the federal institutions as much as [they] could, so that their reaction to the ever widening independence of certain parts of Yugoslavia was weaker and more confused'.[26]

Finally, from a diametrically opposed standpoint, some contributors offer their full support for the policies adopted by the two republics. Here, scholarship discussing the political circumstances, in order to comprehend the Slovenian attitude, very often concludes that it had to choose between taking on the role of victim of a totalitarian regime dictated by Belgrade and orienting itself towards a democratic future. Only the second option proved acceptable within the European Community framework. With regard to Slovenia, the smallest and wealthiest Yugoslav republic, Viktor Meier expresses 'sympathy for the aspirations of the Slovenian people'.[27] In his opinion, the Slovenian leadership was the most rational of all the Yugoslav groups affected by the ongoing chaos. While clearly stating his position, Meier argues that the Yugoslav state collapsed due to its multinational architecture and insists that the main problem was a democratic deficit largely reflected by the struggle between two factions: one supporting market liberalization and a multiparty system, and the other opposing reform.[28]

By the late 1980s, both Slovenia and Croatia started seeking ever closer relations with Western Europe, with the aim of securing additional support for future secession (Chapter Three). For example, within the economic field, both republics adopted an autonomous foreign policy through the Alps-Adriatic Working Community, a regional association aimed at fostering cooperation between Austria, Italy, Bavaria, Slovenia and Croatia.[29] Later, it was the Brioni Agreement that allowed the Slovenian dream of achieving independence to come true.[30] And Croatia followed. Still, it is academically accepted that the international recognition of both represents 'the most debated question of the whole European response to the Yugoslav conflict'.[31]

Economics: Factor of Connectivity

The economic argument can be approached both from internal and external perspectives. If analysed within the Yugoslav state borders, the economic crisis in the late 1970s is what most academic writing concentrates on as it became evident that Yugoslavia's future would be conditioned by its economic performance.[32] According to Susan

Woodward, the economic crisis caused constitutional conflict and thus the crisis of the Yugoslav state as such. In order to understand the specific situation at that time, she points out that growing unemployment pushed the political elite to implement certain policies, thus challenging 'the system's capacity to adapt to ... new economic and social conditions' and 'the country's ability to continue to manage unemployment itself' further eroding the 'balance in constitutional jurisdictions of the federal system'.[33]

In addition, regional economic disparities characterizing the state, where Slovenia, Croatia and northern Serbia performed well, while Bosnia-Herzegovina, Macedonia, Montenegro and Kosovo constantly faced economic underperformance, affected perception of the SFRY and encouraged attachment to individual republics rather than to the federation.[34] In the post-war communist federation the imbalance between the republics 'could only be rectified by massive state control of the economy'.[35] The communist leaders were aware of this circumstance, but when it became obvious that their attempts to phase it out had failed, a new set of complaints emerged. The underperforming republics blamed the federation for not being sufficiently involved in solving their problems while authorizing delayed payments for more advanced republics. In contrast, the more advanced republics complained that their growth was being restricted and that their funds were being reallocated in favour of the less developed regions.[36] As is often the case, such conditions raise the question as to whether the situation is being manipulated by the system itself, with citizens expected to adapt to the rules imposed by their leaders. In the SFRY the potential for economic instability increased both social and national tensions.[37]

As will be shown in Chapters Two and Three, the validity of economic argument can be better understood if relations between Yugoslavia and the West (including the European Economic Community) are examined. Without going into detail over the ties between the two entities, Ann Lane explains how their connection was cultivated: 'At the heart of Tito's foreign policy was the notion of sustaining a balance in Yugoslavia's relations with both East and West, achieving ideological sustenance from a relationship with the communist movement as a whole, while benefiting from Western economic aid and (if need be) military support'.[38] The response from the West was its 'policy of "keeping Tito afloat", a phrase ... which led the West to underwrite Yugoslav economic development until the end of the 1980s'.[39] The cost of economic dependence was paid by the SFRY in a number of different ways: it affected its reputation in the West, undermined its non-aligned position and deepened domestic frustration due to possible social problems.

The economic changes the Yugoslav state was required to implement came from external sources, mostly international organizations, rather than domestic bodies. When the International Monetary Fund (IMF) imposed policies on Yugoslavia in the 1980s,[40] bringing unemployment and double-digit inflation with them, central state policies shifted from protecting the people and the standard of living in general to attacking them.[41] Such a circumstance 'turned Yugoslavia into the West's worrisome child [and] Washington and Brussels started to fear that Yugoslavia's economic breakdown might have unforeseeable political consequences'.[42] Thus, at a certain point it became 'fashionable in the West to be pessimistic about Yugoslavia's future after Tito', an approach justified by the re-emergence of the national issue that was always going to be difficult to solve peacefully.[43] In his attempt to explain Yugoslavia, John Allcock defines Yugoslav socialism as rigid and incapable of adjusting itself to market demands and the control of the distribution of credit, and observes that it was this complex system that prevented Yugoslavia from undertaking the necessary modernization process.[44] Later, the death of Tito and the collapse of the Yugoslav debt-ridden economy put the hegemony of Yugoslav ideology to the test.[45] Reforms were necessary to accommodate the changes required, and Slovenia and Croatia were the only two republics ready to cooperate, while stipulating more inclusive structural changes, a process that consequently encouraged more obvious decentralization that resulted in the break-up of the state.

Further scholarship notes that economists did propose solutions regarding the federation as a whole but not the specific requirements of the individual republics.[46] Such a situation clearly demonstrated unequal distribution of resources, and a perception of 'economic injustice' became 'crucial in perpetuating interethnic competition'.[47] As to the

European Economic Community's involvement, which for a long time remained unclear, its 'conditional development assistance' sometimes included issues related to political and social matters.[48] Moreover, the Community, in early 1991, began to mention considering united Yugoslavia for membership, and the day before Slovenia and Croatia declared independence, it offered Yugoslavia a five-year loan. Once the fighting commenced, the Community required both republics to suspend their move toward independence, threatening to cut off all aid.[49] Indeed, the Community was too focused on the economic component in its relationship with Yugoslavia, whereas the political component gained its full relevance only after it had become clear that it was not possible to remedy the crisis with economic incentives.

External Factors

Whose lack of interest?

As will be argued in Chapter Three, in the late 1980s when the collapse of the Yugoslav federation turned from being a possibility into a probability, the European Community decided to leave the initiative to local actors. Literature discussing this period points out that both the United States of America and the Community opted for preventive diplomacy – an approach that 'revealed one of the weaknesses that subsequently hindered the mediations – the inability of the intervening states and the international organizations to speak in a single voice and convey a clear message to the disputing parties'.[50] In short, as far as the US position is concerned, they had no clear standpoint with regard to the Yugoslav crisis. Lenard Cohen assesses 'Washington's historic policy of supporting Yugoslav unity' as having become even more evident once Lawrence Eagleburger, Deputy Secretary of State, 'had reconfirmed the US view that Yugoslavia should remain united' while considering Milošević 'a reasonable man with whom Washington could do business'.[51] However, this rhetoric changed as soon as doing business with the Serbs no longer seemed possible, in the late 1980s.[52] Finally, *The New York Times* reported the opinion of US intelligence that the Yugoslav experiment had failed and 'that federated Yugoslavia will break apart, most probably in the next 18 months, and that civil war in that multinational Balkan country is highly likely'.[53]

In his attempt to trace Yugoslavia's break-up, Raymond Duncan does not distinguish initial disengagement of the United States of America from the European Community, but rather attacks their decision-makers for their incapacity to coordinate military, political and economic intervention in order to prevent violence. In his words, the USA unnecessarily stayed 'on the sidelines during the early stages', ignored the Yugoslav problem due to other international events and cared about 'Gorbachev's mounting problems in Moscow', whereas the EC on its own was powerless as far as foreign policy was concerned, concentrating more on integration, without considering the use of military force, and therefore creating the impression that the 'EC decisions lacked teeth'.[54] Other scholars interpret both US and European reluctance to intervene as the general tendency characterizing the post-Cold War era: 'the governments of liberal democracies are extremely reluctant to place members of their armed forces in situations where their lives may be at risk'.[55]

With regard to the European position, what is interesting is the Community's apparent unawareness of the circumstances. It was the USA who informed the EC about the deteriorating situation in the SFRY. Instead of advocating a tight federation or loose confederation, once US policy opted to remain neutral, it left space for the Yugoslav federation to decide its future.[56] However, the US policy of waiting on the sidelines was supported in Europe. In Zimmermann's terms,

> the Europeans simply couldn't believe that Yugoslavia was in serious trouble. There had been too many cries of wolf in the decade after Tito's death in 1980, when practically everybody had predicted that the country would fall apart. When it didn't, Europeans blinded themselves to the cataclysm that was now imminent ... their approach to Yugoslavia was without any of the urgency with which they acted fourteen months later, when the breakup they said couldn't happen was upon them.[57]

Thus, the scholarship is in agreement that the international community appeared bewildered. However, not enough attention has been paid to the nature of the relations that developed between the West, in particular the European Community, and Yugoslavia prior to 1991. For example, in the early 1980s, one author briefly reflected upon relations between the two: 'Political cooperation has so far been isolated, remarkably, from the bureaucratic politics of national administrations; but it is unlikely that it can remain isolated for much longer'.[58] Although Yugoslavia was absent from regular Western debate, Stevan Pavlowitch insists that while the West was enthusiastic about the first Yugoslavia 'as the new state seemed to fit a new European order', it supported Tito from the beginning 'as he was deemed the best chance for a united Yugoslavia, before it turned his regime into a bastion against Soviet advance in the Cold War and a hoped-for model for the development of the rest of Eastern Europe', but still concludes that 'the West's understanding of Yugoslavia was illusory [as it] went on supporting Yugoslavia's communist leadership to the very end, thus enabling Tito's heirs to avoid real reforms'.[59]

Later, when Milošević was elected leader of the Serbian League of Communists in May 1986, he 'presented himself at the time rather as a young technocrat who, in the view of many Western diplomats stationed in Belgrade, wanted to set Yugoslavia on a modern foundation'.[60] Therefore, it is important to comprehend the relevance of Milošević and his perception in the West at the time. As Woodward puts it:

> Milošević's victory over the Serbian League of Communists is often cited, because of the war and Western policy in 1991–94, as the beginning of the end of Yugoslavia. But this view was not shared by Western banks and governments ... They supported him because he appeared to be an economic liberal ... who might have greater authority to implement the reform. Although Western governments were later accused of complicity, or foolishness in the extreme, Milošević was an economic liberal ... It was common at the time (indeed into the 1990s) for Westerners and banks to choose "commitment to economic reform" as their prime criterion for supporting East European and Soviet leaders

... and to ignore the consequences that their idea of economic reform might have on democratic development.[61]

What is evident here is that both Pavlowitch and Woodward perceive the West as not stating any clear objections to the Yugoslav establishment.

Furthermore, other writings question Western familiarity with Yugoslavia at the time. Chapters Two and Three will demonstrate that apart from being a trading partner[62] and labour exporter, Yugoslavia did not enjoy much EC attention prior to the actual outbreak of the state crisis. According to Meier, the Western diplomats stationed in Belgrade, who had little interest in understanding the state of affairs outside the Yugoslav capital, bear their share of responsibility for Western policy with regard to the Yugoslav tragedy. Meier himself 'had never before encountered such a colossal jumble of political error, lazy thinking, and superficiality as [he] encountered then among the Western diplomatic corps in Belgrade'.[63] Thus, the general discourse stating that Western powers are partly responsible for the Yugoslav crisis is acceptable because of their poor knowledge of the area and diplomatic ignorance and this would explain why the West was initially sympathetic toward a united Yugoslavia, thus postponing the recognition of Slovenia and Croatia.

Still, in addressing the question as to the origins of this initial lack of interest, some scholars look into other events. For example, Christopher Bennett argues that 'since the demise of the Eastern bloc, the West has decided that it no longer has any strategic interests in the former Yugoslavia. While the international community undoubtedly wanted Yugoslavia to remain a single entity, the great powers were not prepared either to invest in democracy there or to intervene to avert tragedy'.[64] By saying this, the author identifies two strong reasons for blaming the leading Western powers: first, for trying to stop Slovenian and Croatian secession, thus supporting Milošević and his warmongering Yugoslav People's Army, and second, for not seriously seeking a peaceful solution.[65] In addition, Peter Radan examines circumstances and sees the international community as 'more preoccupied with other major international problems', precisely the fall of the Soviet Union and the Gulf War, and it was only after Slovenia and Croatia had declared independence, in late June 1991, that 'any significant steps were taken' to confront both political and military crises.[66] Once the break-up of the SFRY had become a reality, it was deemed necessary to define exactly what had happened and who the perpetrators had been.

'The hour of Europe has come'

This book rejects the argument that some internationally recognized problems had primacy over the Yugoslav one, but rather maintains that the confusion surrounding the outbreak of the Yugoslav problem and how to tackle it and anticipate the fall of the state played a decisive role in its disintegration. In fact, the Yugoslav crisis was a European problem from the beginning: this despite the fact that, for Europeans, the Yugoslav federation became a matter of interest only when the conflict seemed easy to deal with, thus, according to Barry Buzan and Ole Wæver, 'boosting the EU foreign policy profile – as expressed in the infamous statement by Jacques Poos that "the hour of Europe has come"'.[67] The paradox of this statement was twofold: first, it demonstrated how powerful the Europeans were by claiming that 'if one problem can be solved by the Europeans, it is the Yugoslav problem. [Yugoslavia] is a European country and it is not up to the Americans',[68] and second, it was pronounced in a moment of complete ignorance and lack of serious strategy as to how to approach the Yugoslav problem. Obviously, the EC policy did not manage to resolve the crisis in the Balkans or prevent the spread of violence.

As will be argued in Chapters Four, Five and Six, the initial period – 'the period without decisive external action'[69] – meant that each of the local actors hoped for the support of their influential friends abroad. The Slovenes and Croats sought support in Austria, Germany and Italy, while the Serbs had a degree of consensus with the Russians. Once the conflict attracted global attention, the European players decided to step in. Indeed, an opt-out strategy was no longer possible. Zimmermann is critical of the approach: 'The European Community leapt into the accelerating maelstrom with a pedagogical rather than a political approach. Without much understanding of the nationalist forces at play, the Europeans lectured the Yugoslavs as if they were all unruly schoolchildren whose naughtiness would deprive them of the sweets only Europe could provide'.[70]

Although not voluminous, the scholarship discussing the EC's involvement fits into two subgroups: one, which concentrates on the Community's recognition policy, and a second, which examines specific Member States and their undisputable power to influence decision-making at the EC level. The recognition policy was a turning point during the Yugoslav state crisis. Again here, arguments somehow take both the USA and Europe into consideration. While rejecting terms such as 'fall', 'disintegration', 'collapse' or 'tragedy', Raju Thomas insists that the Yugoslav federation was 'dismembered' and this was achieved by a selective international recognition policy of its internal republics. According to him, the Yugoslav state was not destroyed 'because of domestic struggles and militant Milošević-led Serbian nationalism', but due to a Western *ad hoc* recognition policy which violated the 1975 Helsinki Accords Final Act guaranteeing territorial integrity of European state frontiers.[71] Thomas attacks two men in particular for the Yugoslav collapse: Warren Zimmermann, the last US ambassador to Yugoslavia before the fall and Hans-Dietrich Genscher, the German Foreign Minister, and thus divides external involvement in two, US and European.[72] As mentioned earlier, placing blame on the USA for the policy adopted by the EC is rather pointless, especially if the Community's statement of being ready to approach the Yugoslav crisis is the reference point.

In his analysis of the European Community and its initial involvement, John Pocock notes that European policy-makers found themselves facing 'a choice between encouraging the devolution of sovereignty as a means of creating larger market economies, and maintaining existing centralizations of sovereignty as a means of preventing endemic inter-ethnic warfare – war having become a means less of asserting the interests of states than of posing ethnic challenges to their authority'.[73] However, more present than this are the arguments focusing on the EC's and its Member States' overall capacity to address the crisis. In this respect, the outbreak of war in Yugoslavia 'demonstrated Europe's weakness, even as a regional power. German diplomacy may have contributed to raising the temperature of the conflict but, once the small-scale wars broke out, Germany and the EU contributed significantly neither to the military outcome nor to the ... settlement'.[74]

It may be worth recalling that official involvement of the European Community began with the establishment of the EC Conference on Yugoslavia (EC-COY) in September 1991.[75] While the EC Troika was already actively engaged,[76] the EC-COY was replaced by the International Conference on the Former Yugoslavia (ICFY).[77] Here, the Community failed to confront the Yugoslav problem which it had initially marked as European: bearing in mind that the EC adopted the *Declaration on Yugoslavia* in December 1991 – a document which allowed republics to apply for independence – the replacement of the EC-COY by the ICFY meant greater legitimacy for the policy of recognition.

The Badinter Commission, an arbitration body established by the EC on a French initiative and on the basis of very broad terms,[78] was expected to assess the republics' applications for recognition. The logic of adopting the policy of recognition offers various interpretations. In his study, Richard Caplan identifies three valuable reasons for recognition: first, recognition was perceived 'as a tactical measure', aimed at preventing Belgrade's policy of violence against the secessionist republics; second, recognition was a medium for transforming an internal conflict into an interstate war and thus approving the third-party engagement; and finally, recognition let republics adopt a set of policies 'that might eliminate or at least mitigate one of the presumed causes of the conflict'.[79] Indeed, the policy of recognition decided the future of Yugoslavia, as it allowed recognition of two secessionist republics while ignoring possible consequences. As one author observes:

> The greatest defect of the recognition policy pursued was that it operated in the absence of an overall agreement for Yugoslavia. If none of the former Republics had been recognized in the absence of such an agreement, then the carrot of recognition would have been an important element of pressure to moderate behaviour

and to reach agreements respecting minority rights. The practical effect of the recognition policy was to try to predetermine the outcome of the military and political crisis. Conflict could continue in the Former Yugoslavia but the end result would be six new states. Claims to statehood by units within the former Republics would not be accepted even if they were militarily successful. So claims to statehood by the Krajina region of Croatia were not accepted, nor those of Kosovo in Serbia, or of the Republika Srpska in Bosnia.[80]

After the Badinter Commission had given its opinion that the Yugoslav federation was falling apart and called for the use of the principle of *uti possidetis juris* whereby republics keep their previous borders as new international borders,[81] the existence of the SFRY came to an end. What some scholars find surprising when evaluating the work of the Arbitration Commission is the fact that even though in 1991 Bosnia-Herzegovina fulfilled 'the criteria for a state in the process of a dissolution', the Commission 'failed to apply its own criteria ... and instead recommended its international recognition', thus it used international law 'selectively to legalize some secessions but not others'.[82]

Based on the previously mentioned arguments, other authors are right when pointing out that the EC decision to recognize Slovenia and Croatia 'seemed to intensify the Serbian threat to Bosnia'.[83] While being without a clear strategy with regard to the immediate future, Judge Robert Badinter opened the debate and indirectly encouraged the spread of conflict. Thus, contrary to the expectations of its supporters, the EC's policy of recognition made no difference to the violence that had already begun to spread. In fact, what appeared to be the real problem was not recognition itself, but the fact that recognition was not accompanied by military intervention to protect the borders of Croatia and Bosnia-Herzegovina.

Equally important is the argument that questions Member State relations within the European Community. Initially, the Community spoke on behalf of the Twelve. However, while facing what Stanley Hoffmann identifies as four main issues, 'preventive action, a choice of principles, the problem of recognition, and the problem of coercion', the EC's 'main consideration was not the future of Yugoslavia, or even the effectiveness of the EC in this first major post-war crisis in Europe; it was the preservation of the appearance of unity among the 12 members'.[84] Considering that 'the EC was almost willy-nilly sucked into the crisis',[85] the voices of the Member States therefore began to carry more weight. By mid-1991 the EC faced a split over the Yugoslav problem. As Cohen summarizes it: 'German, Austrian and Italian political leaders, for example, were generally more sympathetic to the views advanced by the governments of Slovenia and Croatia for a confederation of sovereign states, whereas Serbian advocacy of a remodeled federation — though not necessarily according to the highly centralized perspectives of Milošević — were received more sympathetically in London and Paris'.[86]

Therefore, the emergence of different points of view demanded a switch from a supranational to an inter-governmental approach in order to tackle the crisis. Moreover, the confusion characterizing Western behaviour, according to Woodward's *Balkan Tragedy*, demonstrated that Western powers had no clear idea regarding 'the relation between states and nations and the meaning of national self-determination'.[87] Apart from stating that EC involvement in the Yugoslav crisis aimed to prove its ability to develop a common foreign policy, she argues that prior to the signing of the Treaty of Maastricht 'the EC had not yet recognized the need for a policy of self-determination and ... could not fully confront the necessary link between a cease-fire and a political settlement'.[88] This is where the argument regarding German actions finds its place. Woodward criticizes the EC states for all becoming 'increasingly vulnerable to German assertiveness'[89] and the 'German maneuver' that pressured other EC members to recognize Slovenia and Croatia: 'The precedent set by the German maneuver was that the principle of self-determination could legitimately break up multinational states, that EC application of this principle was arbitrary, and that the surest way for politicians bent on independence to succeed was to instigate a defensive war and win international sympathy and recognition'.[90]

Germany was committed to the process of strengthening foreign-policy cooperation within the European Community. Accordingly, it is German policy towards the SFRY, initially perceived by its EC partners as a 'case of defection from international cooperation', which is examined by Beverly Crawford in her study.[91] She attempts to explain German behaviour based on the initial idea that Germany 'had agreed to cooperate in the indefinite future ... and the value of continued cooperation should have outweighed the benefits of any one defection'.[92] While rejecting the pressure of public opinion, lobbying, or the media as possible driving forces — contrary to this book — she argues that German unification and its growing power, unstable multilateral regimes and lack of synchronized international norms 'lowered the costs of unilateralism and provided the permissive conditions for defection'.[93] Furthermore, in order to understand German behaviour, while drawing attention to foreign economic policy in which policies are shaped by domestic preferences, Crawford argues that Germany's position within Central Europe and its 'expanded economic interests' in the East could better be served by an independent Croatia and Slovenia; in her words, 'Germany was attempting a modern version of a divide-and-conquer strategy in the Balkans'.[94]

The debate about Germany and its decision to recognize Slovenia and Croatia (approved by Austria and the Vatican) is further complemented by explanations noting that the whole process was a complex deal, buying off British reservations with an opt-out clause on key aspects of the European Community harmonization policy and rewarding Greek acquiescence with the power of veto over the recognition of the republic of Macedonia.[95] International organizations which supported the break-up of Yugoslavia based on national self-determination opened up two immensely dangerous problems: the first was related to the number of nations in Yugoslavia, and the second tackled the issue of the relationship between designated nations and territory which could have led to another war and consequently to the creation of new states.[96]

Nonetheless, the argument about German tactics has also had its supporters. In his attempt to underplay German responsibility, Norbert Both writes that when EC ministers met in November 1990, Germany insisted on human rights having priority over the Yugoslav unity question, an issue that was disregarded by most ministers. Four months later, the German Foreign Ministry stressed its concerns again after the Serbian forces had suppressed anti-war protests in Belgrade on 9 March 1991.[97] Both clarifies that it was the Netherlands who criticized Serbia's attitude most vehemently, thus supporting the Slovenian and Croatian drive toward independence. Surprisingly, when Hans Van den Broek, the Dutch Foreign Minister, together with the EC president for the summer of 1991, announced a forceful resolution, Germany withdrew and supported the French in advocating a weaker option.[98]

As some authors insist, the German attitude towards Yugoslavia should be understood as a 'unique combination of situational factors, personal idiosyncrasies, inexperience, and misperceived domestic pressures'.[99] For example, Daniele Conversi justifies German policy and thus the recognition of the two republics: 'The idea that the German attitude expressed a deliberate will to "dismember Yugoslavia" was easily invalidated ... First, the German government acted in response to public pressure. Second, this pressure was shared by other European countries. Third, Germany acted only after initial hesitancy and considerable distress. These three factors alone can dispel the idea of a "deliberate plan to dismember Yugoslavia"'.[100] Indeed, here I accept Conversi's argument about the role public pressure played in the process of the disintegration of Yugoslavia. As will be discussed in the book, diaspora groups, the media and churches all contributed to decision-making processes. In this sense, German policy was shaped as a 'human rights' response to the growing conflict and further outbreak of war. However, Conversi's overall and less convincing argument about German policy is supported by other scholars who say that any discourse aimed at blaming Germany for its allegedly premature behaviour with regard to the recognition of Slovenia and Croatia is misplaced. In their view, it was not Germany that supported armed Serbs, but France and the United Kingdom, both 'in effect prepared to see Croatia, and later Bosnia-Herzegovina be defeated by Serbia'.[101] At this point, it is worth recalling that the Community had agreed in July 1991 to postpone recognition of Croatia and Slovenia until October, until the three-month moratorium on independence relating to the secessionist republics had expired.

In September 1991, Genscher, together with Gianni de Michelis, the Italian Foreign Minister, agreed that they would recognize Slovenia and Croatia if the negotiations failed. Later, during the meeting at Stuyvenberg, a multilateral Christian Democratic Initiative confirmed the readiness of Germany, Italy, Benelux and Greece to recognize Slovenia and Croatia, by Christmas at the latest.[102] The Netherlands did have second thoughts because of possible problems that recognition itself might have on the situation in Bosnia.[103] However, Germany's involvement, although not entirely clear, reconfirmed its power within the EC. Indeed, when Germany started pressing for the recognition of Croatia and Slovenia in the autumn of 1991, other EC Member States considered such an idea inappropriate and dangerous. It was only after the meeting in December and a ten-hour debate that criteria for the recognition of new states in Yugoslavia were established and the German plan was approved, resulting in the recognition of Slovenia and Croatia in January 1992. As summarized by Alan Hanson, the main effects of this recognition were as follows: 'it (i) formally established Yugoslav federal dissolution, (ii) eliminated Croatia's interest in participating in ongoing negotiations about Yugoslavia's constitutional future, (iii) shifted the focus of the crisis from Croatia to Bosnia-Herzegovina, and (iv) precluded any further efforts for a general settlement to the Yugoslav crisis by the EC'.[104]

The Slovene issue was, for example, 'admittedly the one political problem which could be solved in isolation', but the European Community interpreted the Brioni Agreement as a success, bringing peace to the Yugoslav crisis – a colossal mistake.[105] It is true that François Mitterrand, the French President, and John Major, the British Prime Minister, were both against German pressure to recognize the two republics. Although initially successful, they were pressured again during the European Community foreign ministers' meeting in Maastricht in December 1991, when the voting led to the following outcome: eight to four against recognition. The German Foreign Minister insisted on unanimous support.[106] Here, although a subject of controversy, the question of whether Germany used the negotiations over the Maastricht Treaty in order to blackmail other EC members and obtain their support for recognition of Slovenia and Croatia remains open.[107]

What Is Yet to Be Examined?

Although some of the existing and probably yet-to-come arguments are quite exclusive in their nature, it is more appropriate to examine Yugoslavia's disintegration through the conglomerate of various factors and their interconnectedness. Therefore, this book will complement the arguments focusing on the links between internal and external factors. Indeed, the Yugoslav example illustrates the relevance of the interaction between internal and external factors where non-state actors managed to challenge and shape decision-making processes. So far, the role of non-state actors in influencing the policies of EC states, that soon after became the official policy of the Community, has not been adequately explored. Therefore, while bearing in mind the complexity of the relations between the Community and Yugoslavia prior to the crisis, my interest is focused on the role played by non-state actors such as diaspora groups, the media and churches.

Debate over diaspora groups has not been studied to sufficient extent. Both politically and economically they play a significant role in contemporary social mechanisms.[108] Some authors discuss their role during the Yugoslav crisis, but without dedicating much attention to the actions adopted on the eve of the disintegration of the state and more importantly what impact they had on EC policies. For example, James Gow and Cathie Carmichael point out that the 1990 Slovene World Congress brought Slovenian émigrés around the world together with a common goal: independence. As they put it:

> While it was important to spread the word everywhere and anywhere, it was quickly realized that an independent Slovenia would be in no position to establish links with all the eighty-four states with which the Yugoslav federation had diplomatic relations, let alone the eighty or so with which it had no link. Efforts were therefore concentrated on the shaping of foreign policy. This meant, among other things, secretly contacting as many of the small number of Slovenes in the Yugoslav diplomatic service as could be trusted, forging links with the larger Slovene émigré communities, and building links with neighbouring

countries and especially with those capitals judged to be the most "interesting" for Slovenia in its current situation – most notably Washington, Bonn and Prague.[109]

However, in their analysis, the authors do not focus on what exactly the Slovenian leadership did and how the contacts were developed and their activities coordinated – something this book seeks to address in Chapter Four.

The discourse about the Croatian diaspora has more space in the literature. Apart from focusing on the economic assistance and the target countries,[110] some authors concentrate on the evolution of both formal and informal contacts. In his discussion of exile patriotism, Paul Hockenos looks at the Croatian diaspora in Canada and the United States of America and clearly shows its greater involvement after 1987, first in backing President Tudjman's electoral campaign and subsequently in supporting the country's fight for independence.[111] However, he remains somewhat silent about diaspora activism in Europe – a topic worthy of consideration, as the Croatian diaspora in Germany actively participated in the overall developments during the crisis and thus tried to contribute to the decision-making processes. In fact, Hans Stark claims that some 470,000 Croat workers residing in Germany influenced Bonn to recognize their homeland.[112] Thus, based on one author's argument that '[a] sense of solidarity and attachment to a particular locality can generate a common identity without propinquity, where territorially defined community and spatial proximity are decoupled', diaspora groups present powerful components in conflict-affected societies.[113]

The manipulative power of the media has been one of the most controversial issues in regard to the Yugoslav crisis and, as will be argued in Chapter Five, its bias characterized the crisis from its very beginning. Discussing the link between media and politics, Diana Mutz says: 'Media influence politics in subtle but powerful ways by informing beliefs about social reality that in turn shape political attitudes and behaviour'.[114] However, most authors adopt an impartial position when discussing the media. For example, Branka Magaš criticizes the media in Yugoslavia for being 'the exclusive property of the ruling party',[115] while ignoring the fact that, even before the conflict, governments of individual republics did their best to place their people in top positions in order to control and influence the media. Furthermore, such behaviour by the executives managed to provoke enmity among the ethnic groups who for so long had shared the same territory.[116] Thus, during the crisis, propaganda demonstrated its importance by managing to create confusion and contribute to the intensification of inter-ethnic hatred – an aspect overlooked by the EC establishment. In fact, Marina Blagojević goes into depth by assigning the media two different roles: one related to 'the slow but steady deconstruction of former Yugoslav commonalities and the promotion of divisive ethnic cultures' and the other, aimed at 'creating demands that "something must be done" to justify concrete political acts and military actions'.[117]

Thus, what happened? During the crisis, the wider perception of events depended rather on what exactly the media had to say than what the actual situation was. This was further accentuated by the emergence of independent media. With the beginning of hostilities, Slovenia and Croatia, on one side and, Serbia, on the other, adopted two different strategies. While the first two republics focused above all on Western audiences by attacking the Community for its incapacity to prevent a conflict that threatened European security, thus insisting on narratives about how the crisis was going to affect the EC, Serbia primarily concentrated on its domestic audience by justifying the policies adopted. In this, the coverage of the Yugoslav crisis in the West was directed against the Serbs. By contrast, Conversi tries to argue that the Belgrade political elite manipulated Western perception of the Yugoslav crisis and at the same time controlled the information reaching Western embassies in Belgrade, thus raising the question of lobbying.[118] Even if this had been the case, it could have not lasted for long considering the strategy Slovenia and Croatia had opted for.

However, the literature briefly questions the role that Slovenian and Croatian media played within the SFRY, but fails to answer how they gained support among Western media, which at one point commenced to advocate independence for the two republics. This study will show that, by insisting on European responsibility for the spread of conflict and the idea that the conflict itself represented a potential threat to European stability, reporting from both republics gained attention from various EC Member States that further influenced EC policy. For example, the influential *Frankfurter Allgemeine Zeitung* attributed pro-European values to Croatia, in contrast to their treatment of Serbia.[119] Thus, by being 'open and friendly with the foreign press' from the beginning of the conflict,[120] Slovenia and Croatia secured support in their struggle towards independence.

Finally, the scholarship discussing religion often focuses on its internal dimension and disagreements arising from ethnic heterogeneity within the state. As will be noted in Chapter Six, in the former Yugoslavia, and especially once the conflict had commenced, denomination played a critical role and belonging to one religion rather than another was a matter of importance.[121] Usually, in war-torn territories, multiple identities disappear leaving only the identity most closely related to the conflict: this identity is often outlined by religion.[122] Indeed, this proved to be the case during the Yugoslav crisis. Based on this understanding, some authors argue that '[a]s Serb-Croat polemics heated up in the course of the period 1989–1990, the Catholic Church was ineluctably drawn into the fire',[123] and therefore conclude that 'religion was a social component of the forces that helped dismember the Yugoslav "experiment"'.[124] I argue that a more complete understanding of the Yugoslav experiment is possible only if the external dimension of religion is also taken into consideration. The cross-border power of Slovenian and Croatian Catholic churches to secure support among respective Catholic organizations within the European Community meant gaining a powerful ally in their fight for independence. While the Serbian side enjoyed support for its expansionism from the Greek Orthodox Church,[125] the two Catholic republics communicated with the Vatican which openly lobbied for them.[126] However, the literature has not demonstrated yet how the communication between them was handled, what strategy was adopted and to what degree their activism influenced decision-making processes.

Conclusion

In general, lack of academic research concerning specific elements might affect the complete understanding of any important issue, and this is also true in the case of the disintegration of Yugoslavia. This study aims at examining the interaction between the European Community and the Yugoslav federation via non-state actors – an interaction that should provide deeper insights into both sides' actions. Having consulted the extensive literature on the collapse of Yugoslavia and European Community involvement, I understand the conflict to have been almost inevitable, but have not found any 'good' reason as to why it was so devastating and long-lasting.

The Community was expected to do its utmost in order to keep the Yugoslav state together, but once the conflict commenced the EC should have redirected its policies to prevent the spread of violence. While of vital importance, mediation was ineffective. Thus, incapable of reacting swiftly and identifying the correct approach, all the parties concerned fought for or against the war of secession and enclaves. The main questions this book raises relate to the consequences of the reaction of the Community and its Member States to the initial Yugoslav crisis and their behaviour towards the collapsing state. It also asks how non-state actors cultivated contacts necessary to influence the EC's positions and the extent to which decision-makers were influenced by actors such as diaspora groups, mass media and churches. While answering these questions, an inevitable question arises regarding the credibility of the EC, which eventually supported the collapse of Yugoslavia, thereby encouraging further fighting and, once the wars had ended, started discussing how to assist the Western Balkans.[127]

PART ONE

EUROPEAN COMMUNITY RELATIONS WITH YUGOSLAVIA

CHAPTER TWO

THE EUROPEAN COMMUNITY AND YUGOSLAVIA FROM UNOFFICIAL TO OFFICIAL RELATIONS

This chapter examines the connections between the European Economic Community and Yugoslavia from their earliest interaction until the late 1970s. Keeping in mind the period it covers, the chapter is broadly divided into two parts: while the first focuses on relations until 1968, the year when official links between the two parties were established, the second part investigates whether, and to what extent, the establishment of diplomatic relations influenced further developments among them. In his writing, Adam Watson notes the diplomatic capacity of the European society of states: 'When a group of states forms a closely knit system, the involvement of many self-willed political actors imposes upon each state a continuous awareness that the others have interests and purposes distinct from its own, and that the things other states do or may do limit and partly determine its own policies'.[1] Accordingly, the main questions of this chapter are: How knowledgeable were the Community and socialist Yugoslavia about each other and what kind of cooperation characterized their relationship? If a lack of attentiveness existed for one reason or another, when did the Community or Yugoslavia, or both, modify their position and begin considering the other party within its future policy-making framework? Answering these questions is of crucial importance as it would offer a broader understanding of the Community's behaviour vis-à-vis the Yugoslav crisis in the early 1990s.

In spite of the fact that the second half of the twentieth century was characterized by a great interest in securing multifaceted cooperation through a number of regulatory bodies,[2] the relations between the European Community and Yugoslavia did not follow this pattern, but were rather fraught and, in fact, difficult to define. The period before 1968 was problematic for both actors; a mutual lack of substantial interest dominated the relations between them and thus no particular connection existed. This was a result of differently positioned objectives, where each party was primarily concerned with its own performance rather than being significantly involved in direct relations with the other: Yugoslavia was a country without a clear standpoint towards the EEC due to domestic miscalculations, while the Community was focused on its integrationist project and less interested in the Yugoslav federation. Further, once the Community had decided to play the role of sponsor and Yugoslavia accepted to play that of beneficiary, insufficient attention was paid to the negative consequences of such an arrangement. The growing dependence on the Community's aid allowed Yugoslavia to ignore the seriousness of its economic mismanagement and postpone any significant steps to secure its own future.

After 1968, a greater opportunity for official communication and reconsideration of further policies presented itself. However, in practice relations between the Community and Yugoslavia did not become remarkably different from the ones characterizing the previous years. Again, both sides continued along their parallel lines lacking any serious interaction inspired by mutually beneficial cooperation, thus allowing ignorance and misinterpretation of one another. In fact, the parties continued with their roles of benefactor and beneficiary – a situation to be reconsidered only after the Community had labelled the Yugoslav problem as political in its nature and agreed that political cooperation was a fundamental tool for generating stable economic relations, thus diverting its attention from economics to politics.

Getting to Know Each Other

According to the first Five-year plan (1947–51), aimed at changing post-war Yugoslavia from an agricultural to an industrial economy, the country was supposed to take part in international economic relations focused primarily towards the socialist bloc, therefore ignoring the West.[3] Despite its initial success, the economic plan proved overambitious and therefore unrealistic. Shaping Yugoslavia's economy on the Soviet model 'was conceptually flawed owing to the differences between the two states as economic entities'.[4] In fact, there was no evident similarity between the two that might have served as a model to follow. Thus, for the sake of its own survival, Yugoslavia's leadership decided to position the country between the East and the West and embark on a policy which would benefit the country by representing the midpoint between the two opposing sides.

For the Yugoslav leadership it was important to approach Western powers in order to obtain financial aid and sign trade agreements. Nevertheless, issues regarding Western assistance served to inspire further political discord. Such an atmosphere was the product of Western judgement which 'strongly opposed communism in principle and in practice', and for both the United States of America and Western Europe 'it seemed ludicrous to support the "containment" policy with one hand and to assist an isolated and weak Communist state with the other'.[5] In their examination of Yugoslavia's policy, some scholars correctly conclude that initially, 'there was no Yugoslav intention to abandon Soviet-style planning, despite results that were already unsatisfactory before the interruption of economic relations with the Soviet Union and its Eastern European allies'.[6] This observation clearly demonstrates how the Yugoslav leadership approached the West: its self-centred ambition to secure financial support dominated the discourse, rather than development of closer cooperation and therefore stronger links at other levels.

To sum up the initial period of assistance, it can be noted that the benefits for Yugoslavia were remarkable: without general Western aid, the country would not have been capable of defending its independence against Soviet pressure. As observed from the outside, 'Yugoslavia not only survived, but it became one of the most prominent and significant "neutral" states in the world, playing a role far beyond what its military and economic power position apparently justifies'.[7] But, what proved to be the case is that the first half of the 1950s shaped its further development: Yugoslavia became a dependent state – a dependence that characterized almost the whole period of the Cold War and therefore allowed the Yugoslav leaders to avoid introducing the necessary economic reforms. In her study, Ann Lane criticizes the West for its policy towards Tito's Yugoslavia: by offering 'a choice of losing control of the state or bartering with the West', Tito opted for the latter, and therefore provided the West with 'an advantage in strategic terms of a foothold in the communist camp'.[8] Thus, Western aid sustained the state but at the same time encouraged dependency 'which militated against necessary economic reform, permitting economic mismanagement to be disguised until after Tito's death'.[9]

Along with economics, which represented a key point in Yugoslavia's post-war development, the political situation of the time also requires attention. The break with Stalin in 1948 gave birth to Yugoslav socialism or Titoism as it was known in the West – a unique phenomenon that proved to be a test of the state of national relations in Yugoslavia.[10] According to one account, '[w]ithout the framework of the material and cultural circumstances of Yugoslavia, the inertia of the socialist illusions of the people, and the new social relations/conflicts, there is fertile ground for conflict in the political movement'.[11] This argument suggests that the situation in socialist Yugoslavia was not stable due to the lack of coordination among its constituent parts. Thus, the break with the Soviets implied the creation of a new Yugoslav model based on 'the cohesiveness of the political system', a model which made the Yugoslav leadership decide 'to further de-emphasize the federative and multi-national features of the political system and society ... and to concentrate on the creation of closer social bonds among citizens based upon the allegedly similar position and common interests of "producers" in all groups and sections of the country'.[12]

But, in complex systems (of which Yugoslavia was an example), successful political changes require a new set of people, otherwise it is difficult to achieve noticeable change. When analysing the political atmosphere in the country, it can be concluded that the Yugoslav issue 'remained very sensitive, especially in reaction to the different phases in the Cold War, for Yugoslavia's exposed position between East and West both geographically and ideologically, was uniquely vulnerable'.[13] In fact, the country's domestic situation determined its international standing. In his analysis of the situation at the time, Stevan Pavlowitch notes that the '[c]ircumstances had already put limits to Tito's foreign policy ambitions', and any attempt to approach one or the other side would have had significant consequences.[14] Yugoslavia's geographical vulnerability was understood as a product of non-alignment, and therefore it reflected the international aspect of its performance, whereas ideological vulnerability was a domestic concern. Still, in the West, the federal system of Yugoslavia enjoyed a good reputation and the country was appreciated for its highly unitary structure. While it was not possible to predict which path socialist Yugoslavia was to follow in the forthcoming years, the insecure domestic situation 'was aggravated by the deterioration in Yugoslavia's relations with the outside world' provoking condemnation of everything capitalist and Western: 'cultural relations were with other communist states [while] all contacts with the capitalist West were reduced to a minimum'.[15]

This Yugoslav reluctance was in opposition to the ideas promoted by the first European Community,[16] which advocated greater interdependence between its Member and non-Member States being brought about not by a single force, but by different converging and mutually sustaining elements. Later, it proved that these elements constituted what Jacques Delors, the eighth President of the European Commission, defined as Europe: 'A grouping that is unique in the density and quantity of its commercial exchanges, a comparative oasis of monetary order and even of financial equilibrium, and a considerable reserve of internal growth. It possesses a demographic, historical and cultural wealth, homogeneous even in its extreme diversity, which, doubtless, no other region of the world can claim'.[17]

Thus, it was envisaged that the Community would develop external relations and cooperation with non-Member States. For example, the 1953 *General Report of the High Authority* stated that 'the relations with the other European countries were also further developed', but without naming Yugoslavia among those countries.[18] This omission was a consequence of Yugoslavia's international position at the time, which consisted of charting a path that permitted it not to join either of the blocs, while maintaining bilateral relations with both blocs' members.[19] However, although the Yugoslav federation was not cited in the 1953 report, it is difficult to argue that the Community did not intend to consider it at some point in the future as its mission stipulated: 'The European Coal and Steel Community is an open-to-all community. From its earliest days, it has set out to develop its relations with the countries which do not belong to the Community, and to co-operate with the international organizations'.[20]

Nonetheless, the enthusiasm about the Community's own development was very often accompanied by criticism. While being a major work in progress, the Community encouraged numerous analyses in regard to its sustainability. One of them is offered by Richard McAllister for whom the Community was 'an animal in motion', without 'fixed' destination and 'not something quite separate from and independent of the states that set it up'.[21] While arguing the EEC evolution to be a puzzling business and describing the Community as 'a strange creature, a kind of hybrid', the author underlined: 'The world of the Community is full of paradox and irony'.[22] This understanding obviously questions the ideal of European solidarity – a restricted concept at the time. In fact, only countries then having a delegation in Luxembourg were fortunate enough to be informed with regard to decisions taken: 'Through such exchanges of views, the High Authority is in a position to ascertain the repercussions of its actions in the international sphere and to keep itself informed on the interests, wishes, and at times even the apprehensions, of the non-member countries'.[23] Accordingly, the Community was operating, intentionally or not, as an exclusive club that decided whether anyone not holding a delegation in Luxembourg should have access to information or not and even whether to marginalize individual states. This behaviour surely explains one of the central points for this period related to the lack of deeper interests with regard to the Yugoslav federation: the non-existence of appropriate Yugoslav representation in the Community's headquarters.

Communication

The reluctance towards the Western world seemed to diminish once the Yugoslav leadership began to pay more attention to relations with the European Community and be present in so-called European issues through its active involvement. In fact, Leo Mates, one of the architects of the Yugoslav policy, explained that that approach was not one-sided, or directed towards the two superpowers in order to generate benefits depending on what they could have offered. He insisted that Yugoslavia made no distinction between the states and sought rather serious connections with its former enemies and potential collaborators in the future: 'This is why Yugoslavia represented an active partner with clear positions about its goals and intentions even when its relations with some countries had not been normalized'.[24] More importantly, Mates's standpoint on European integration at the time, which affected Yugoslavia negatively, deserved attention. In fact, he noted that economically-driven integration of Europe encouraged further divisions of the European continent and therefore undermined Yugoslavia's position: 'The combination of noticeable political tensions between the East and the West and economic disturbances created by the establishment of different economic divisions [ECSC/EEC, European Free Trade Association (EFTA) and the Council for Mutual Economic Assistance (COMECON)], marginalized and slowed the development of Yugoslavia's pro-European politics'.[25]

While the Community was concentrated on its own economically-driven performance and international position, Yugoslavia was 'a small, semi-developed country' distracted between the East and the West:

> [the Yugoslavs] sent up a series of signals to Moscow indicating their desire to maintain normal and expanding economic relations with the East despite deteriorating political relations. As a reserve line, they accelerated efforts to increase trade and credit arrangements with the West, including in particular a commercial agreement with the EEC, already by far their most important trading partner, and new credit lines to the World Bank and the US Export-Import Bank.[26]

It was not until the late 1960s that Yugoslavia's primary concerns consisted of 'bilateral and economic relations with neighbours and important trading partners, particularly including a commercial treaty with the EEC, and with attracting foreign investment'.[27] The provisions in regard to aid show that the Community was indirectly involved (via some of its Member States) in Yugoslavia from shortly after its establishment. In general, Western backing included not only economic aid, but diplomatic and military assistance. With regard to politics, there was no evident intention by the Western powers to affix political condition to their aid, and the Yugoslav government was careful not to trigger such an outcome.[28] Here, the argument that posits that the Community and Yugoslavia followed two separate ways becomes exact: the Community was unfamiliar with the problems Yugoslavia was facing, while Yugoslavia was exempted from any concerns linked to the Community.

Understandably, apart from previously mentioned economic aid, there is not much left to be said about Yugoslavia's position or interference within the European context or vice-versa. Although initially condemning Western behaviour, Yugoslav foreign policy continued to maintain amicable relations with both the communist and capitalist worlds. Tito's foreign policy focused on balancing its relations with both East and West, thus 'achieving ideological sustenance from a relationship with the communist movement as a whole, while benefiting from Western economic aid ... [which] provided a safety net for the fragile Yugoslav economy and kept Tito afloat during the most critical period of Yugoslavia's international isolation'.[29] Therefore, major Western powers opted to support Yugoslavia while ignoring its economic mismanagement simply in order to dissociate it from the Soviet bloc – an approach that contributed to the worsening of its international reputation.

The Community was not familiar with Yugoslavia's domestic setting and, notwithstanding the fact that the relations between the two existed out of economic necessity, the Community remained silent when domestic changes started shaping the Yugoslav system. Still, it is worth mentioning that the Western powers considered Yugoslavia for their plans for European defence: after Greece and Turkey had officially joined the North Atlantic Treaty Organization (NATO) in 1951, separated from Western Europe directly by the Yugoslav federation, the Western powers insisted on Yugoslavia improving its bilateral relations with Greece, Turkey and Italy,[30] and forging some kind of link with NATO – an illusory project at the time.[31] Even when the most important obstacles were overcome, the Yugoslav leadership began to move away from such a form of association and opted for the establishment of closer links with other independent states, for example in Asia and Africa. In his study, Pavlowitch identifies two main reasons for this policy: first, these destinations 'appeared as a field in which [Yugoslavs] could promote their new brand of independent and progressive democratic socialism', and second, 'by associating with the states of the "third world" Tito could hope to reduce his increasing dependence on the West'.[32]

With or without Yugoslavia, European optimism with regard to further integration was not allowed to expire. For Jean Monnet, one of the founding fathers of European unity, 'the essential thing is to hold fast to the few fixed principles that have guided us since the beginning: gradually to create among Europeans the broadest common interest, served by common democratic institutions ... This is the dynamic that has never ceased to operate'.[33] Moreover, during the twelfth session of the Committee of Ministers held in May 1953 in Strasbourg, 'the Ministers reaffirmed that the Council of Europe remained open to the accession of all European nations "which, as the Statute requires, acknowledge the rule of law and the sanctity of fundamental freedoms"'.[34] The concept of membership, while lacking a well-defined basis, allowed acceding states to 'vary their membership; countries could take part in some schemes and perhaps not in others, whereas in any particular arrangement such divided choice would obviously not be tolerable'.[35] Moreover, the Committee expressed its willingness to conclude association agreements with countries unwilling or unable to become full members of the Council and, according to press commentators at the time, Yugoslavia might have been one of the countries the Council referred to.[36]

As a consequence, the Community recognized the importance 'to close the phase in which the problems of the underdeveloped countries are a matter of discussion and to draw up a practical program of aid'.[37] This controversial decision of the Community not to deal with its neighbouring countries in need of aid first, but to devote itself to negotiations for the expansion of international trade with less-developed countries, such as Cambodia and Tunisia,[38] certainly questions the Community's initial interests and intensions concerning European non-members, Yugoslavia in particular. Due to their substantially different paths, the Community appeared ignorant about Yugoslav domestic affairs. Very often, Western commentators stationed in Belgrade were receiving manipulated information that resulted in superficial reporting, which was insufficient to transmit reality.[39] The only viable reason for such Yugoslav behaviour was its ambition to maintain good, aid-inspired relations with the West, while negotiating additional aid in the East. By playing such a role, it secured substantial resources enabling the Yugoslav government to return interest payments on a short-term basis from the West. What the majority of documents point out is that the 1950s were a difficult period. The complexity derived from the involvement of the Yugoslav leadership in securing an amicable relationship vis-à-vis Moscow, thus enjoying immediate interests, while maintaining 'a tricky relationship with the West, one which could help it when it was left isolated on the doorstep of the Communist camp'.[40] As summarized by Pavlowitch, the Yugoslav authorities were determined 'to switch from intimidation to persuasion, but to carry on in leading the fight for socialism, and against Western ideas, at a time when friendship with the West was fostered, and the Soviet Union denounced for practices which had been their own'.[41]

If the Yugoslav federation was specific and 'a rare bird in Europe', then why did the Community behave as it did at this particular stage? Possibly due to its incapacity to gain a clear picture of Yugoslavia, a country administered by political actors who had been granted jobs usually because of their wartime performance; but another cogent and more influential argument is the modification of the economic policy of the COMECON, which left the Community bewildered about its future relations with the Yugoslavs. According to one report, the Soviet Union's new position with regard to Yugoslavia actually reflected

President Khrushchev's position, advocating 'the establishment of Soviet-Yugoslav trade based on equality and mutual benefits'.[42] Due to Yugoslavia's policy aimed at avoiding alignment with either bloc, relations with the Soviets deteriorated as a consequence of *The Program of the League of Communists of Yugoslavia*,[43] a document viewed by Tito as 'of historic importance',[44] submitted to the Ljubljana Congress in March 1958, which advocated close bilateral or multilateral cooperation with other countries, regardless of their political standpoint or bloc alignment.[45]

Once again, the Community remained confused and silent. The decision to stand aside encourages discussion even today as to how the interest of the West, and of the Community in particular, was conceptualized. In this regard, I identify two possible reasons: first, the EEC itself was a developing organization and avoiding additional involvement in the affairs of non-Member States might have seemed to be a good idea and, second, although Yugoslavia had already enjoyed diplomatic relations with each of the founding members of the Community, official relations between the Community and Yugoslavia were not yet established, thus making the whole interconnectedness rather voluntary. In his analysis, Pavlowitch correctly asks: 'The Yugoslav government had been able to obtain Western aid when it needed it, and to reject it when it preferred to do without it, because its Western creditors believed that they could help it financially to remain at some distance from the Soviet Union; but for how long would it be considered worth aiding'?[46]

Towards the end of the decade, economic, diplomatic and cultural contacts with the Community were opening Yugoslavia to the Western world, and that seemed to be promising for the future of the Balkan state. However, once the idea that such contacts might have undermined the reputation of the Communist Party appeared, Tito changed his strategy by issuing 'warnings against the danger to socialist development of infiltrations from the West'.[47] Another two Yugoslav speakers, Edvard Kardelj, the Yugoslav Vice-president, and Aleksandar Ranković, Minister of the Interior, fully supported their president and labelled growing Western influence as highly problematic for the SFRY as well as for EEC–SFRY relations. As a response to this understanding, in their secret report submitted to the Council, the Community representatives residing in Yugoslavia in 1959 described the federation as upset solely with regard to the Common Market.

In fact, considering that the concept of a 'common market' had not been precisely defined,[48] the Community's officials must have expected to hear European non-Member States complain and question their future relations with the Community. As stipulated in the interview Kardelj gave to the French *Observateur*: 'We have been surprised by the creation of the European market, possibly less than other countries, because of our export policy, but still we have felt a number of negative effects. Our country needs a solution which will eliminate any discriminatory clause, but still benefit both parties. Thus, the Yugoslav federation does hope that our cooperation will continue in that direction'.[49] At the time, Western Europe remained the most significant single trading area, although Yugoslavia's trade balance was increasingly negative,[50] while a positive trade balance with the Eastern bloc and the Third World was useless, due to the fact that it was tied down by long-term credit arrangements or strict bilateralism.

With regard to Community-Yugoslav cooperation, the Ljubljana Program noted the risk of creating economic blocs and further exclusion: 'Seclusion, within national frontiers, autarchy, as well as discrimination, which stem from ideological or political motives, are contrary to the needs of the economic development of the world, as well as damaging, not only to individual countries, but to the world as a whole'.[51] This is what inspired Kardelj to clearly express Yugoslavia's opposition to the existence of supranational bodies deciding upon economic cooperation and his endorsement of equality among the states. As he put it: 'I am afraid that inequality in economic relations discourages integration, and thus fosters disintegration. I have already perceived such a tendency'.[52] Kardelj's point reflected the Yugoslav standpoint of the time, perceiving regional integration as being marked by 'a number of negative features, which are impressed upon [it] by the existing sharp division of the world into blocs, as well as by the influences of imperialism and hegemony of the strongest capitalist states'.[53] This Yugoslav approach, criticizing the Community's *modus operandi,* could hardly have been appreciated within the Community as such: Yugoslavia might have been perceived only as a direct Soviet affiliate aimed at undermining the European project. As William Nicoll and Trevor Salmon summarize, 'the total opposition of the Soviet Union ... regarded the European Communities as part of the war-making plot against it'.[54]

What proved to be a valuable component with regard to subsequent EEC–SFRY linkage was the awareness of the following: the Community acknowledged the importance of considering its external relations more seriously.[55] In addition, while the Community was examining whether an economic Europe should be the prelude to a political Europe, a strategy advocated by Monnet, or not, as preferred by President de Gaulle, Yugoslavia's authorities were preoccupied with a different reality. In his assessment, Dobrica Ćosić, a Serbian writer, political and national theorist, notes: 'In Titoist Yugoslavia, like in any other totalitarian state, two different political realities coexisted – an official one, presented in the media and public, and an illegal one, intimate in its nature, discussed in restaurants and at home'.[56] While usually used for manipulative purposes, the two realities clashed during the 1960s, followed by inflation, unemployment and social dissatisfaction.

The 1960s: Closer or Looser Ties?

Most of the European integrationists optimistically presented the period from 1958 to 1962 as a 'honeymoon' for the Community. There was some truth in this, considering that during the 1960s the Community faced numerous problems regarding its nature, its potential and membership. In fact, one scholar writes that 'as the 1960s proceeded, there were crises in plenty', and on several different occasions 'it looked as if the Community might reach a breaking point'.[57] Thus, again, busy with its own affairs, the Community hardly considered its neighbouring countries.

With regard to Yugoslavia, a number of reforms introduced in the early 1960s and aimed at helping the Yugoslav economy become competitive in foreign economic relations had both positive and negative outcomes.[58] In his discussion of the changes, Pavlowitch points out that '[t]he reforms of 1961 were a half-hearted attempt to remedy the country's economic ills, an experiment which the government wanted to be able to control, so that it should not detract from the long-term aims'.[59] In Yugoslavia, protecting favoured industries meant protecting particular regions. Therefore, in order to help poorer ones, Macedonia and Kosovo in particular, the government decided to subsidize each of them – a strategy that irritated better performing republics obliged to contribute to the General Investment Fund. These republics argued that their own resources were wasted and obliged the government to reconsider its strategy. In addition, criteria regulating investment policies were more political, and as such in the hands of central government, than economic and this atmosphere led to over-production, expansion of under-utilized capacities, and stock-piling of unsold goods.[60] Unemployment grew, caused by poor agricultural production, which forced surplus agricultural labour to seek work in industry, at home or abroad, after the government had decided to open the borders to the West. With regard to this, the Community's reaction is worthy of consideration: notwithstanding the fact that the majority of its official documents tended to classify Yugoslavia as a Mediterranean country, the 1962 EEC report did not name Yugoslavia or any other country specifically when stipulating the following: 'The working out of the common agricultural policy has given rise to numerous approaches by agricultural countries, more particularly Mediterranean countries'.[61] Avoiding naming any state in particular reflected the Community's awareness of discriminatory effects its customs union might have had with regard to non-Member States.

Within the Community's official agenda, Yugoslavia was named for the first time later in 1962 when the Yugoslav leadership approached the Community to discuss technical measures with regard to trade between them.[62] During its meeting, the Council pointed out that the Yugoslav authorities had complained both to the Community's Member States separately and the Commission, requesting that negotiations open in regard to the reciprocal trade exchange.[63] On a positive note, the EEC Member States were in favour of seeing Yugoslavia approaching the Community in general, but at the same time, they wanted to see Yugoslavia fostering its position vis-à-vis the Eastern bloc. On a more negative note, while facing the economic crisis and the population's growing dependence on consumer goods, the Community unconsciously opted to assist Yugoslavia by feeding its appetites, 'seeking to detach the Yugoslavs once and for all from the Soviet bloc'.[64]

As far as Yugoslavia's domestic situation was concerned, its alarming aspects were dealt with in the context of a transparent debate, as by the mid-1960s, 'strikes and unemployment were openly discussed among Communists, in the press and in parliament'.[65] This critique of the Yugoslav situation was heard within the Community. Accordingly, foreign correspondents identified two *chefs de file*: Kardelj, representing the reformists, and Ranković, representing the conservatives.[66] Having them both active represented an opportunity for the Community to commence paying greater attention to the political component of the Yugoslav crisis. However, at this particular point, when the economic cooperation enjoyed priority, this did not become the case.

Having examined the beginning of the 1960s and looking back to the perception of Yugoslavia within the Community framework, it can be noted that the early 1960s general reports commenced considering the Yugoslav federation separately, but under a newly coined subtitle: *Relations with the Eastern bloc countries*. This was not a straightforward misunderstanding, but rather an EEC reaction to the ambiguous attitude deriving from both Yugoslavia and the Soviet Union. As for Nikita Khrushchev as someone who shaped the Soviet position with regard to the Yugoslav federation, the Council quoted his words revealing that 'trade between the Soviet Union and Yugoslavia should be based on equality and mutual interests'.[67] Thus, concerned about Yugoslavia's orientation, the Community's position about the bloc was not optimistic: 'The relations between the Community and the Eastern bloc countries continue to lack any formal basis. While continuing their violent attacks on the Community, to which the Commission has suitably replied, the Eastern bloc countries have shown a growing interest in the Community, and their reactions to its development seem to reflect a certain fundamental change of attitude'.[68] In practice, this meant that future cooperation between the East and the Community was not pursued due to the Community's continuous rejection of the Eastern bloc countries' requests to extend intra-Community tariff concessions by virtue of the most-preferred-nation clause.[69] But, another international organization aimed at facilitating non-communist international linkages – the Danube Commission – which at one point during the Cold War proved to be as much a communist organization as COMECON itself was, 'in the 1960s became a vehicle through which small states could pursue policies designed to reduce the isolation of the East European regional system because its membership included Yugoslavia and, after December 1959, Austria, as well as West Germany as an associate member'.[70]

1968: The Establishment of Official Relations

After the Community had chaired a meeting regarding trends in trade between the Yugoslav federation and the EEC in 1965 – thus examining prospects for economic cooperation[71] – significant moves with regard to diplomatic cooperation were made in 1968 when the Community and its institutions expressed interest in establishing official relations with Yugoslavia.[72] In practice, this was supposed to be an important step, as Yugoslavia was the first East European country to accredit an ambassador to the European Communities.[73] The establishment of diplomatic relations finally meant that Yugoslavia could benefit by having a direct link with the Community and therefore 'the opportunity of being kept informed of the contents of the decisions and of all the available data relating to the problems which they dealt with. Through such exchanges of views, the High Authority is in a position to ascertain the repercussions of its actions in the international sphere and to keep itself informed on the interests, wishes, and at times even the apprehensions, of the non-member countries'.[74] In addition, both sides' enthusiasm regarding the establishment of diplomatic relations was accompanied by the opening of formal trade negotiations particularly aimed at addressing the problems of exporting agricultural products to the Community.[75] Thus, again, the accent remained on economic cooperation, whereas political cooperation lagged behind.

After having entered into official relations with the European Community, Yugoslavia and its leadership, while given a chance to become closer and take pro-active part in the developments of the Community, did not seem to abandon their Eastward direction completely. In her analysis, Lane acknowledges: 'Eastward looking politically, but westward looking economically, Yugoslavia seemed to outside observers to be poised to capitalize on its rising international status among the non-aligned'.[76] Although the Community seemed to be ready to aid Yugoslavia economically and thus support the only buffer state, it disregarded Yugoslavia's economic mismanagement and its further consequences: inflation, unemployment and social discontent,[77] which altogether inflamed nationalism and caused a political crisis the Community could never have been able to mitigate.

Patrick Artisien and Stephen Holt examine the establishment of diplomatic relations between Belgrade and Brussels and identify three reasons why such an association might have been important. Their first argument concentrates on Yugoslavia's active membership within the non-aligned movement where it played a significant role in 'the creation of a new international economic order which would meet the needs of less developed nations,' thus being considerate towards underperforming countries.[78] The second argument is related to the geopolitical position Yugoslavia held: 'Her geographical position – at the intersection of the markets of the Community and Communist countries – and her political ambivalence – embodied in a delicate balancing act aimed at reconciling ideological principles with conflicting economic exigencies – are constant reminders to the Belgrade politicians of the uneasy balance of power between the Western and Eastern blocs'.[79] Finally, the authors discuss Yugoslavia's concern with regard to further Community enlargement. With particular emphasis on the accession of Greece, Yugoslavia feared that the Community might introduce additional restrictions on its exports and therefore 'as a "spokesman" for the Mediterranean countries, Yugoslavia wants a long-term assurance from Brussels that the traditional trading relations between the Member States of the Common Market and the Mediterranean nations will not suffer from the Community's enlargement'.[80]

The three arguments are clearly dominated by an economic dimension: while the first two deal with ambition and potential, the third discusses the actual situation – Yugoslavia's concerns about its further treatment by the Community. The validity of these concerns is justified even more if the lack of solid political cooperation, at the time, is taken into consideration. Alongside this, Ross Johnson examines some important developments that led to a general deterioration in relations between Belgrade and the Community after 1971: first, an incursion of Croat émigré terrorists into Yugoslavia from Austria in mid 1972 reinforced Yugoslav fears as to the threat to the country from émigrés in the West; second, driven by international events in 1973 in Chile and the Middle East, some Yugoslav leaders opposed Western 'progressive and revolutionary forces'; and finally, Yugoslavia's connection with non-aligned countries was re-emphasized.[81] Once again, this decade, while being influenced by economic, political and social circumstances, opened a number of questions related to the position of Yugoslavia at that time as well as its future perspective.[82]

At this point, it can be said that, notwithstanding initial uncertainties accompanying relations between the Community and Yugoslavia, from an economic aspect, the new decade offered a positive sign. A new trade agreement signed in February 1970 was aimed at providing the Yugoslav federation with new trade benefits and additional political cooperation with the Community.[83] While accentuating the Yugoslav government's favourable position for developing external economic relations, and in particular with the Community, Toma Granfil, Federal Executive Council member, advocated the importance of 'a long-term integration within the international economy while maintaining a non-aligned status'.[84] Moreover, the Yugoslav delegation insisted that advantages deriving from bilateral agreements signed with the Member States could not be compromised by the agreement signed with the Community.[85]

Documents reveal that after the Joint Committee, established by the 1970 Commercial Agreement, met in Belgrade and 'noted that there had been a substantial expansion of trade between the Community and Yugoslavia', the Commission 'endeavored to reinforce economic cooperation with Yugoslavia' – a positive trend confirmed by another decision to help Yugoslavia even more, this time by the application of the generalized preferences system.[86] Although this might have seemed extremely positive, the Community maintained some very strict reservations: for example, the third chapter regulating the commercial agreement between the two parties stipulated that 'whenever it proves that the European Market is or will be threatened by greater import deriving from Yugoslavia ... the Community can immediately suspend its facilitating measures'.[87] Having stipulated this, Yugoslavia was not in a position to imagine its future relations with the Community. On two occasions, the Yugoslav leadership reconfirmed the importance of looking towards the East: first, the East was acknowledged to be the most important trading partner,[88] and second, cooperation with the East never implied uncertainty and restrictions in the same way as the EEC did.[89] Understandably, any state without a clear perspective is prone to self-undoing and lack of sufficient involvement can very often lead to negative results. In fact, most probably the result will be negative. This was confirmed by the report of the Economic Research Institute which perceived certain distortions being lessened, while stating that investment expenditure decreased and the growing industrial production showed stagnation in favour of agricultural production.[90]

Furthermore, the documents in relation to the period examined above lead to the following conclusion: the Community approached Yugoslavia in a rather particular way, playing both the role of lawyer and of judge. The federation was encouraged to 'specify the problems it would like to see discussed in the future negotiations and indicate the possible guidelines of commercial and economic cooperation with the EEC'.[91] So far, the SFRY had signed six cooperation agreements while at the same time taking part in the administrative committees established under them.[92] Later, a new non-preferential trade agreement on cotton products signed in June 1973 and valid for five years was 'intended to consolidate and extend the economic and trade relations between the two parties with due regard for their respective development, and to promote the development of mutually advantageous economic cooperation'.[93] In its communication to the Council, the Commission pointed out that during its confidential negotiations of the agreement with Yugoslavia, 'the Yugoslav delegation drew the Community's attention to the fact that its content could jeopardize the ratification of the agreement by the Yugoslav Government'.[94] Its second letter underlined:

> If any difficulties should arise which could not be solved with reasonable speed to the mutual satisfaction of the parties concerned,

and if the serious nature of the problem should be established during the consultations ... the importing country would have the facility of regulating the imports of the products in question, provided always that this is an exceptional arrangement and strictly limited to temporary remedial measures'.[95]

Apart from stipulating that 'the two parties will grant each other most-preferred-nation treatment and maximum liberalization for their imports and exports', this agreement provided a mechanism to examine the situation with regard to Yugoslav guest-workers in the Community – a necessary examination in order to understand the influx of immigrants and whether any kind of restrictions would need to be imposed in the future.[96]

In 1974 Yugoslavia acquired a new constitution[97] and Europe was hit by an unexpected energy crisis that affected the Community's trade deficit considerably. Although the *General Report* confirmed the EEC's positive engagement in other fields, especially with regard to its external policy – 'both in its bilateral aspects and in the context of the multilateral negotiations in which the Community continued to play an important part',[98] with regard to Yugoslavia, there were two concerns that undermined the relations between the two: first, safeguarding measures implemented by the Community affecting Yugoslav beef and veal exports,[99] major Yugoslav export commodities, and second, the problem of Yugoslav citizens employed in the Community, leading to the EEC opening talks with the Yugoslav authorities.[100] With regard to the first matter, Artisien and Holt criticize the Community's embargo as 'directly responsible for Yugoslavia's endemic trade deficit'.[101] It led to an application submitted to the European Commission to enjoy the same special treatment as that enjoyed by other Mediterranean countries such as Cyprus and Morocco. However, the authors note that the EEC restrictions also had their supporters for whom Yugoslavia's trading behaviour 'betrays her old habits of thinking in terms of centrally planned bilateral trading'.[102]

The second concern regarded the presence of the Yugoslavs in the Community, as the Common Market countries were 'the principal recipients of the Yugoslav migrant labour force ... and the chief source of workers' remittances, private transfers and foreign tourism ... [all together creating] the largest source of Yugoslavia's invisible earnings'.[103] However, the large-scale return of Yugoslavs working abroad, which was expected to occur due to the outcome of the 1973 oil crisis in Western Europe, did not materialize. As a result, while the introduction of restrictive measures on additional foreign labour by Western countries attempted to close 'an important outlet for Yugoslav labour', the growing influx of Yugoslav guest-workers continued due to the growing unemployment rate in the federation. This itself was a consequence of the 1965 Reforms launched during the previous decade.[104] In their writing, Artisien and Holt observe:

> The social status of Yugoslav workers temporarily employed in the EEC ranks high on the Yugoslav agenda. The growing trend of returning migrant labour prompted the Yugoslav authorities during the recent negotiations to press for a clause in the agreement which would abolish discrimination by the host country in its employment and social security policies towards foreign labour. However, it would be unfair both to Brussels and Belgrade not to balance the difficulties of the negotiations against the jointly-held belief that further cooperation is desirable.[105]

Although stressing the above mentioned concerns, at the time the Community's policy towards Yugoslavia seemed encouraging as well: it supported its transport services,[106] it recognized the importance of Yugoslavia as being 'a non-aligned country lying at the crossroads between the industrialized and the developing countries' and its will to strengthen and extend the cooperation established by the new non-preferential agreement.[107]

New Dynamics

The European Economic Community claimed to be ready to support the Yugoslav federation.[108] However, the mid 1970s demonstrated how the relations and future cooperation between the two parties were highly questionable. First, Yugoslavia was heading towards the end of Tito's era; in Johnson's terms it was 'in a state of political flux'. According to the author, 'internationally Yugoslavia maintains reasonably good relations with all the major Western and communist states ... yet perceives potential and implicit threats from various quarters ... Casting a shadow over everything is Tito's 82nd birthday and the certainty that – whatever the future – Yugoslavia without Tito will be a new international quantity'.[109]

Second, there was a noticeable switch of attention by both parties: once set aside, the validity of the political dimension was acknowledged. In their attempt to link politics and economics, Artisien and Holt conclude:

> It is clearly in the political interests of the EEC to arrest the trend of Yugoslavia's growing trading dependence on COMECON countries. Yugoslavia herself does not want to be dependent on either bloc, particularly in a world without Tito. Indeed it is on the economic rather than the military front that Yugoslavia may feel more threatened by the Soviet Union. The military repercussions of a Soviet intervention have been made crystal clear by the Yugoslavs themselves from the moment when Tito's illness began. Besides this, Yugoslavia does not have a Treaty of Friendship with the Soviet Union.[110]

Furthermore, the *Memorandum* of the Yugoslav Mission to the European Communities communicated: 'The prevailing condition characterizing commercial and other economic relations between Yugoslavia and the Community's Member States preoccupies the Yugoslav government more and more, and has a tendency of gaining a bigger political dimension'.[111] While mostly aimed at criticizing the Community's policy towards the federation as discriminating, this seven-page document also asked the Member States to define their policies vis-à-vis Yugoslavia. It stipulated that any further cooperation, while aimed at mutual benefits, was expected to be complemented by an appropriate political approach deriving both from the Community and its Member States. Moreover, the memorandum emphasized that 'if a non-aligned and a developing country at the same time were exposed to certain economic difficulties and limitations, such treatment would inevitably influence the Yugoslav foreign policy'.[112] This concern was justified on two fronts. First, Yugoslavia was conscious of the significance of its stable and long-term relations both with the Community and its Member States, and thus it believed that any economic disturbance might seriously affect it, and second, while showing domestic self-awareness in regard to the state's possibilities and objectives, and thus an overall position at the time, the memorandum was an open attack on the Community's policy towards the Yugoslav federation. Still, what was surprising from the present perspective is the EEC's unwillingness to mention and comment on the memorandum openly in its 1975 annual report and give its clear standpoint with regard to it, instead of simply saying the following: 'Contacts between Yugoslav and Community officials developed during the year'.[113]

In fact, official visits between Brussels and Belgrade did proliferate, followed by continuous dialogue at the meetings of the EEC–SFRY Joint Committee which confirmed the existence of mutual interest and shared goals. For example, Džemal Bijedić, President of the Federal Executive Council of Yugoslavia, visited Brussels and exchanged views with the Community officials,[114] while representatives of the subcommittees on agriculture and industry travelled to Belgrade.[115] In the Council's view, both parties expressed readiness to reinforce cooperation via joint ventures pointing out 'interdependence and compatibility' to be prerequisites for mutual progress.[116] Moreover, once the new areas of cooperation included the financial sector, the Yugoslav leadership understood it as an EEC offer and demanded loans. This was an important point regarding the existing relations between the two: as soon as the Belgrade authorities realized that their expression of interest in strengthened relations would actually generate financial support, they were ready to modify their reluctance toward the Community. However, the Community's *General Report* summarized that 'the Council agreed that the guarantees for the loans to be granted to Yugoslavia by the European Investment Bank as a result of a decision taken in January should be covered by the Community budget'.[117]

Whether the Community's decision to assist the Yugoslavs was wise, it was certainly not a clear-cut issue at the time. In general, when a country is affected by economic disturbances, solving economic problems does not neglect the political factor. In this scenario, cooperation which is basically an economic plan, turns into a political plan. Accordingly, in April 1977 both the Commission and the Council on one side, and the Yugoslav government on the other, 'confirmed their basic political resolve to extend and strengthen the present links between the Community and Yugoslavia'.[118] Further to this, other documents demonstrate the Community's enthusiasm for closer cooperation with Yugoslavia in different fields, including transport, environment, social and financial affairs, thus 'outside the context of traditional trade in industrial and agricultural products'.[119] What became noticeable was the perception of the other side: on the one hand, there was the Community considering expanded cooperation with Yugoslavia, but on the other hand, there was the Yugoslav delegation expressing its government's concern about the trend in trade towards a trade deficit.[120] However, busy with its domestic problems, 'the Community's negotiating directives did not make it possible to translate into practical terms the political will expressed in the Belgrade Joint Declaration to strengthen economic and trade ties between the two partners'.[121] In their analysis, Artisien and Holt argue that the Commission's attempt to advocate a broader agreement

> was not well received in Belgrade, where it was felt that the preferential and non-reciprocal nature of the plan contravened Yugoslav interests in at least two respects: Yugoslavia's close association with the non-aligned movement barred her from entering into preferential agreements with Western European nations; furthermore, the lack of reciprocity was declared incompatible with the 1976 Belgrade Joined Declaration, which expressed a determination to diversify mutual economic, financial and social cooperation.[122]

Thereafter, as a consequence, the Community measures included facilitated access of Yugoslav products to the Community market based on 'the abolition of custom duties and quantitative restrictions for industrial products, specific concessions in the agricultural sector and a financial protocol to correspond in amount and degree of liberalization to the criteria adopted in this field for the other Mediterranean countries'.[123]

Again here, political aspects of cooperation were given attention when they became a necessary means to tackle trade distortions. For example, the European Parliament (EP) debate expected the Commission to 'state what measures it proposes to correct the imbalance in trade between the EEC and Yugoslavia'.[124] According to Enzo Bettiza, an Italian politician and member of the EP, the Community needed to define what kind of relationship it sought to establish with Yugoslavia, a country with a strategically significant position for the Community itself: 'If it does not want to become a thorn in the side of Europe, the Community, while prudent, must open its doors to non-member European states'.[125] In his statement, Bettiza opposed the idea of relations with Yugoslavia being based on financial aid only, but advocated the urgent creation of a complementary political approach in order to facilitate solving the Yugoslav problem. For him, financial assistance, while being an 'excellent means', if not accommodated within a political framework, did not necessarily lead to problem-solving, but rather to problem-deepening. Financial help excluding a political component could easily turn into 'failure for both parties'.[126] This opinion was an open call for the Community to reconsider its policy towards the Yugoslav federation due to the presence of new circumstances characterizing their relationship.

Conclusion

In order to justify its overall argument about the problematic nature of relations between the European Economic Community and the Yugoslav federation, this chapter examined the most important developments – an approach that allows a full understanding of the complexity of the issue. With regard to the period prior to 1968, the analysis here outlines two substantial conclusions. The first is that Yugoslavia and the Community were two separate works in progress, with differently positioned objectives, so that any serious linkage between them was slow in coming. Due to its non-aligned position, Yugoslavia was a country that strongly believed in endless balancing between the East and the West. By using its own mechanisms to manipulate both of them, it managed to generate financial assistance. Linked to this situation, the second conclusion regards the initial relationship when the West, and consequently the Community, demonstrated its readiness to support Yugoslavia economically and therefore become indirectly responsible for the country's domestic mismanagement. In addition, Yugoslavia's domestic problems were never acknowledged and discussed within the Community (in fact, the EEC was not familiar with them to the necessary extent), and at various times keeping Yugoslavia afloat was considered the right option no matter what the consequences.

The establishment of official relations in 1968 did not significantly improve the relations between the parties. The dynamics that ensued, apart from allowing Yugoslavia to gain a better insight into the Community's affairs by its direct presence, meant greater communication. Indeed, various documents were drafted with the aim of expressing the parties' opinions towards each other and about their relationship. More importantly, some issues that previously had not been a matter of discussion now emerged and, at times, put further cooperation into question. Here, for the first time it was possible to make a clear distinction between economic, political and social elements with regard to the EEC–SFRY relationship. Accordingly, I offer three conclusions. The first one focuses on the economic aspect which emerged as the most important connection between the two bodies. The Community decided to support Yugoslavia, sign new agreements and when necessary impose restrictions upon their relationship – a position that the Yugoslav authorities welcomed and criticized by turn. However, frequently, signing a new agreement implied new problems. The second conclusion concerns the political dimension of the relations. Towards the end of the 1970s, the relevance of political dialogue as a prerequisite for long-term success of the EEC–SFRY relationship was acknowledged. In the words of the Community, 'without an independent and stable Yugoslavia, the hope for cooperation and security in Europe would just be an illusion'.[127] Finally, the third conclusion confirms the importance of the social factor, both within the

Community where the Yugoslav guest-workers all of a sudden became a serious threat to host countries, and within Yugoslavia, which lacked an adequate strategy in the case of their return.

Bearing in mind the complexity characterizing the relations between the European Community and the Yugoslav federation, it is the following decade and the following chapter that will address both parties' commitments. The chapter will also discuss their positions during the crucial periods determining further cooperation and integration or, more importantly for this book, the disintegration of the SFRY. Although the proliferation of official correspondence might have been expected to bring the Community and Yugoslavia closer together, the next chapter will show that the emergence of discord regarding various economic, political and social segments led to a switch of attention by the Brussels officials from the Yugoslav federation to its constituent republics – an aspect that gained its full relevance with the outbreak of the crisis in 1991.

CHAPTER THREE

THE EUROPEAN COMMUNITY AND YUGOSLAVIA FROM INTEGRATION TO DISINTEGRATION

This chapter focuses on the relations between the European Economic Community and the Yugoslav federation during the 1980s. This period, as was already clear towards the end of the previous decade, was in need of a clearer distinction and interconnectedness among the most relevant aspects characterizing the EEC–SFRY relationship. In fact, at some points, a more explicit discourse about economic, political and social performance dominated their correspondence and meetings. However, their relationship did not progress to the extent that could have offered mechanisms to prevent the violence in 1991.

By the end of the 1970s some fierce debates over Yugoslavia had become a frequent feature within the EP. Most of the parliamentarians expressed appreciation for Slovenian and Croatian economic advancement which had nothing in common with that in less developed areas of the Yugoslav federation – an argument that had already been made by the two republics themselves.[1] For example, while recognizing Slovenia to be 'the most prosperous among the six constituting republics of the federation', Enzo Bettiza, member of the EP, insisted that this was the area that might have become an 'experimental zone of big interest for the Community' to test its new technical norms possibly applicable across other Yugoslav regions later on: 'It is exactly between Trieste, Gorizia, Rijeka and Ljubljana where the Community might want to experiment with its new technical achievements expected to be extended to other areas, in the future'.[2] This ambitious idea, including Italy, Croatia and Slovenia, represented an excellent basis for cooperation between the Community and Yugoslavia: a place to experiment and improve institutional functioning connecting both sides, and thus allow Yugoslavia to maintain its international reputation.

Once the Yugoslav state entered a phase in which a new set of difficult economic conditions were accompanied by equally difficult political decisions, the Community took on an even more fundamental role. According to Mario Zagari, another MEP, the Europeans had to approach the Yugoslav problem as political in nature and see political cooperation as a necessary tool for generating stable economic relations and vice versa. In relation to this, the Yugoslav problem represented 'an important test for the Community itself'.[3] This is a valid reason why the relations between the Community and Yugoslavia deserve to be analysed from every relevant perspective – economic, political and social – as this analysis will clarify the overall argument about the problematic relationship between the two parties and its impact on the later crisis.

During the 1980s, numerous meetings, powerful statements and disputable promises served to bring both parties' authorities together in order to test their readiness to cooperate. Often erroneously, financial assistance was understood as the only prerequisite for Yugoslavia's successful recovery no matter the field and, accordingly, the Community agreed to continue to support its Mediterranean partner. But despite this, relations between the two did not improve significantly. Growing concerns in relation to the political situation in Yugoslavia and the position of Yugoslav workers in the Community contributed to the overall uncertainty. Therefore, this chapter will cover a period of great confusion. In fact, the more the Europeans discovered about the Yugoslavs, the more confused their relationship became. While it can be argued that, for the European Community, the end of the decade was a period of further progress and integration, for the Yugoslav federation it was a period of instability with a questionable future.

Introducing New Debates and Greater Concerns

The previous chapter demonstrated how the Yugoslav authorities were determined to secure additional assistance in the West. In this respect, they negotiated support with the European Economic Community whenever that seemed possible. This dependency became even more obvious in the 1980s. If analysed from the present perspective, the Community's perception of Yugoslavia remained confusing: notwithstanding the generally adopted standpoint that the only long-term solution at the time was to place Yugoslavia among its prospective members – Greece, Spain and Portugal – the Community never considered this option seriously. One may find different explanations for that European decision: for example, in his study, Denitch ignores the Community's perception and approach towards the Yugoslav federation and concludes that if Tito had developed strong links with the EEC, it 'would have permitted Yugoslavia to get into the European Community at the same time as Spain, Portugal and Greece did'.[4] Apart from the fact that these three countries did not join the Community at the same time (Greece in 1981, Spain and Portugal in 1986), Denitch's one-sided perspective should be approached cautiously, for various reasons.

First, the exclusive decision of the European Community to approach possible Member States was primarily determined by their economic potential. The existence of criticism of over-emphasis on economic performance and not enough emphasis on political aspects can be seen in one of the sessions of the EP in 1977 when one of its members, Viscount De Clercq, described the Community's approach as inappropriate and instead called the Community to take political responsibilities when confronting the Yugoslav problem since '[t]he final objective of the European Community is political in nature'.[5] This meant that the Community was there to encourage democratic societies while realizing that young democracies can easily turn into dictatorships if not dealt with properly. Second, although stressing Yugoslavia's strategic importance, primarily for trade, the Community still feared that the Belgrade leadership might have opted for even greater cooperation with the Eastern bloc, thus ignoring the Community and the growing deficit of payments towards it. According to Lionello Levi Sandri, European commissioner, the reason for such a deficit was mostly due to the existing imbalance between the two economies: in contrast to the Community, the Yugoslav economy was a developing one.[6] Third, the Yugoslav non-alignment policy represented a certain conundrum for the Community. What being non-aligned for Yugoslavia meant was a topic, in Sandri's terms 'to be left to historians to discuss', whereas inside the Community, non-alignment was understood as both prestigious among Third World countries and necessary for European equilibrium and the maintenance of peace.[7] In the end, the Community had every reason to be suspicious of Yugoslavia's future orientation. Due to its internal structure and diversity, it was not clear whether Belgrade was going to direct its path towards the Community, becoming pro-Western, or towards the Eastern bloc, usually meaning anti-Western.

No matter what, financial assistance continued to dominate relations between the Community and Yugoslavia. Negotiations about further financial cooperation, as Community officials preferred to call it, implied endless communication before concluding the following: 'Please note that on account of the political importance which it attaches to strengthening cooperation with Yugoslavia, the Council agreed that, under a Financial Protocol of five years' duration, Yugoslavia should have access to European Investment Bank loans to carry out investment projects to be financed in the common interest'.[8] This letter turned into breaking news for the Yugoslavs as the agreement was an opportunity to postpone necessary reforms at home.

However, from the very start, there were various problems accompanying the EEC–SFRY Cooperation Agreement. First, the agreement was delayed. The Council explained that the delay in concluding the Agreement was due to the new negotiating Directives,[9] but confirmed 'that for political reasons, the Council agreed that ... Yugoslavia should have access to European Investment Bank loans'.[10] More importantly, the agreement did not satisfy both sides. The Community decided to modify some clauses in order to protect its market properly. Once presented to the Yugoslavs, the EEC offer was sharply criticized as insufficient, and this was the moment when a certain tension between the two parties was accentuated. As a result, the text of the agreement had to go through a new set of modifications until 'both Delegations stated their positions and views and the Yugoslav Delegation officially confirmed its acceptance of the overall approach proposed by the Community to the agreement'.[11]

Unexpectedly, the agreement was delayed again and this was an additional aspect contributing to the already existing tensions between the Community and the Yugoslav leadership. Justification for the second delay came from the EEC officials who maintained that after the recovery program (which the Community had adopted in 1973 due to the oil crisis, and which was about to expire in 1978),[12] starting a new financial agreement aimed at supporting Yugoslavia and its worsening economic situation represented an unnecessary cost. Moreover, the Community was dedicated to its forthcoming enlargement occasioned by Greece entering as a new Member State.[13] Finally, in May 1979, the Board of Governors of the European Investment Bank (EIB) announced its decision to finance operations in Yugoslavia from the bank's own resources. Although this seemed rather positive news, the board underlined that the loan was going to be granted 'on the assumption that Member States will give the Bank the opportunity to approach their capital markets in order to raise the necessary funds'.[14] Having stipulated this, the Community considered it necessary to assure its Member States that support to Yugoslavia would not affect them negatively. The intergovernmental approach to the Yugoslav federation was not a new phenomenon: as shown in Chapter Two, this approach had already dominated some of the discussions and later, during the 1980s, it continued to condition the decisions made between the Community and outsiders. More obviously, the intergovernmental approach gained full relevance with the problem of the Yugoslav guest-workers. Finally, its triumph came with the outbreak of the Yugoslav crisis.

The 1980s: New Agreement and New Challenges

Eventually signed in April and May 1980, in Belgrade and Brussels respectively, the Economic and Financial Cooperation Agreement seemed to be an important document for a number of reasons. Its preamble defined Yugoslavia as 'a non-aligned, European, Mediterranean State and a member of the Group of 77 developing countries'.[15] Being the longest document ever signed between the two parties, the agreement offered significant observations and suggestions regarding economic, social and, to a lesser extent, political cooperation. Therefore, all these aspects are worthy of separate examination as they certainly affected developments, and contextualized some of the most alarming discussions within Yugoslavia as well as within the Community about the future of the Yugoslav federation towards the end of the 1980s.

First, the Community acknowledged its concern 'at the unsatisfactory development of exports from Yugoslavia to the Community and at the steadily mounting deficit of Yugoslavia's balance of trade' – two arguments which represented a prerequisite for a closer economic relationship between the two sides.[16] In fact, both parties agreed that it was impossible for Yugoslavia to 'make any substantial progress in its economic development unless this deficit is substantially reduced' and, at this point, the Community expressed its hope that the 1980 agreement was going to help overcome such problems by introducing 'realistic and effective cooperation schemes ... with a view to contributing to the rapid development of the Yugoslav economy'.[17] Having stressed this, the Community realized how discriminating its regime towards the SFRY had been before the agreement and how some of the reservation clauses it had adopted actually threatened the future EEC–SFRY relationship. Accordingly, the Community agreed upon 'the removal of tariff barriers as a primary means of providing the stimulus to the Yugoslav economy'.[18] Thus, for the sake of cooperation, the Community decided to amend some of the previously adopted policies concerning economic exchange.

The second aspect of the 1980 agreement regarded the social aspects of cooperation. Here, the Community spoke on behalf of its Member States as being ready 'to hold discussions with the Yugoslav authorities on the position of the Yugoslav workforce employed in the Community, with particular reference to socio-cultural problems'.[19] This argument was not a new feature. In fact, as we will see in a separate section on this matter later, the position of the Yugoslav workforce residing in the Community was often discussed. Usually, the Community relied on statistics from 1973 by which time more than a million Yugoslav workers had moved to the Community, ignoring the post-1974 reality when some 300,000 immigrants had returned to Yugoslavia.[20]

Finally, the Community tried to address the political aspects of cooperation. Here, the EP and the Yugoslav Federal Assembly were encouraged to develop stronger links that would foster further political cooperation. A joint parliamentary committee was proposed, to become an arena for political dialogue about different needs and advancements surrounding the 1980 agreement.[21] As argued elsewhere, for a long time political cooperation per se between the EEC and SFRY was almost non-existent, and this was a problem. Although it had existed on paper since the 1968 launch of diplomatic relations between the Community and Yugoslavia, political cooperation was still conducted primarily at Member State–SFRY level. As soon as it had been acknowledged as a valid component capable of connecting the two sides, political cooperation was conditioned by reasonable, if not successful, economic and social cooperation.

Although the *Fourteenth General Report* optimistically established that the 1980 agreement 'represents a new departure in the Community's relations with Yugoslavia', and second, it 'provides for information exchanges and joint analysis in a number of factors' with available financial support for 'investment projects of mutual interest under a five-year Financial Protocol', both the Community and Yugoslav representatives' acknowledgement that the economic, financial, social and institutional cooperation 'implies a reciprocal commitment, depending on the state of development of their respective economies, to promote wherever possible favourable consideration of their mutual interests',[22] was significantly weaker in practice than on paper. In order to show the instant problem linked to the implementation of the agreement, one can turn to the correspondence between the EP and the Council of Ministers when the EP noted that 'the terms of the agreement have not been adequately implemented, so that the hopes raised have been disappointed', and thus requested the Council 'to find a solution that takes due account of the real needs and possibilities of Yugoslav exports to the EEC'.[23]

In his analysis of post-Tito Yugoslavia, Richard Pomfret observes that, although the Yugoslav leadership had signed a trade agreement with the European Community in 1980, it was the economic crisis affecting the 1980s and emerging secessionist trends that 'distracted the government from consideration of trade relationships'.[24] Both of these issues were strong enough to affect the EEC–SFRY relationship. With regard to the economic crisis, there are two relevant aspects to be distinguished: first, the foreign debt, devaluation of the Yugoslav currency and the unemployment rate created a matter of serious concern within the EEC and, second, the restrictive measures the Yugoslav authorities had decided to adopt (the new devaluation of the dinar by 20 per cent, measures including a price freeze, income policy, restrictions on the outflow of currency and measures to promote export) ended up 'having direct effects on the economy of the regions of the Community bordering on Yugoslavia, such as Friuli-Venezia Giulia'.[25] In addition, the implementation of the agreement was delayed as a result of the delays in ratifying it. Again here, the intergovernmental approach enjoyed priority as some of the Member States had second thoughts about the agreement. For example, Germany and Italy, Yugoslavia's biggest trading partners in the Community, feared that the new agreement might compromise their own expectations and might eventually affect them negatively.

Here, the political dimension was highly relevant as the political cooperation had been almost ignored when the 1980 agreement was drafted. In response to possible secessionist trends, the European Parliament, in its 1981 motion for resolution, while characterizing the autonomous province of Kosovo as 'the poorest region in Yugoslavia', noted: 'Serious riots recently broke out in Kosovo, ... the army was reportedly brought in to quell the demonstrations, resulting in the deaths of between 11 and 350 people depending on the sources, and ... between 22 and 3,500 people are reported to have been imprisoned'.[26] This immediate switch of attention from the economic to the political

s a natural reaction within the EP due to the 'reports
cted against students and academics', as well as 'the
e strong demand for independence [of Kosovo] within
public of Yugoslavia'.²⁷ Accordingly, the Community
called on the Yugoslav government to re-examine the position of the
Albanian population in Kosovo, and if they were not doing so already,
to 'guarantee equal opportunities for development in the economic,
social, cultural and structural spheres'.²⁸

The 1981 enlargement of the European Economic Community represented a significant test for the Community itself: the EP advocated that political cooperation with Yugoslavia be prioritized, while economic cooperation and trade expansion, with all its mutual benefits, would inevitably continue to develop.²⁹ Moreover, when the enlargement took place the Community stipulated that 'an important feature of EEC–Yugoslavia relations was the work on the adaptation of the Cooperation and Interim Agreements signed in 1980 to take into account the accession of Greece'.³⁰ The accession of Greece affected Yugoslavia in two ways: first, exports of baby beef faced difficulties as the conditions regulating this product had changed as a result of enlargement, thus affecting a traditional trade flow,³¹ and second, lack of sufficient road transport through the Yugoslav federation seemed to affect the connection between the Community and the new Member State.³²

In order to lessen the impact of Greek accession on the Community, the EEC Political Affairs Committee, while 'stressing the geographical importance which Yugoslavia holds for the Community both as a land-link with Greece and as a pivot in relations with Eastern Europe', called both on the Commission and the Council to make the agreement operational as soon as possible and on the Foreign Ministers of the EEC Member States to work towards political cooperation with Yugoslavia and to 'use their influence to assist the country, which has a balancing effect on the non-aligned countries and plays a decisive role in furthering peace, particularly within the framework of the Conference on Security and Cooperation in Europe'.³³ To summarize the relations between the two, the Committee reported: 'There is no doubt that advocates of a pro-Western policy in Yugoslavia encounter difficulties at the moment, but majority opinion remains in favour of a policy of collaboration with the EEC, since it is clear that the Community does not intend to interfere in Yugoslavia's internal affairs and that it is entirely in its interests to assist the stabilization of the country'.[34]

'A Slight Cooling in EEC-Yugoslavia Relations'[35]

The 1980 agreement was not powerful enough to ensure any instant cooperation between the European Community and Yugoslavia. Once the gravity of the economic crisis was fully acknowledged, the Community questioned Yugoslavia's general commitment to the West. The Political Affairs Committee suspiciously noted that 'Yugoslavia's trade with the Eastern European countries is better developed than it is with the Community' and 'Yugoslavia's dependence on the COMECON countries as a market for its exports is becoming alarming' – a scenario which the EEC understood as an urgent matter to create a new set of policies that would regulate how to re-establish a more acceptable balance among the three export sectors: Eastern Europe, the Third World countries and the Community.[36]

At this point, the European Community, in order to avoid further cooling in relations with the Yugoslavs, decided to put the accent on political cooperation. Aware of its internal, rather slow, capacity for political cooperation, the EEC declared itself ready to understand and support 'a neighbor in difficulty, beginning with immediate and full recourse to the means available in the Cooperation treaty'.[37] Political cooperation implied two important matters: first, an increase in contacts between the Yugoslav Federal Assembly and the EP, and second, greater information exchange due to the Community's perception of Belgrade as 'a unique forum for East–West and North–South contacts, particularly as regards the Middle East'.[38] More importantly, as suggested in the conclusion of the report, the Cooperation Council 'should adopt its own approach interpreting the political will of the Community to support Yugoslavia economically in order to preserve the political balance of the whole of the Balkan region'.[39]

The Joint Committee meeting held in Brussels in 1982 was aimed at examining the function of the Interim Trade Agreement and Financial Protocol, both being prerequisites for the entry into force of the Cooperation Agreement. Consequently, the European Commission organized a business week in Belgrade with the purpose of bringing 'together businessmen from the Member States and Yugoslavia to enable them to make contacts in the context of economic cooperation'.[40] On the same occasion, it is important to note that the EIB decided to give Yugoslavia a ECU 67 million loan.[41] This involvement demonstrates a certain commitment between the two parties. Moreover, trade between the European Community and Yugoslavia 'progressed satisfactorily'.[42] At an official level, according to the documents available, Milka Planinc, the President of Yugoslavia's Federal Executive Council, exchanged her views with Members of the Commission with both sides expressing willingness to see an increase in bilateral agreements.[43]

Contrary to the statements and expectations with regard to the political dimension of cooperation, the mid 1980s were again almost exclusively marked by economic cooperation. Two important pillars defined the EEC–SFRY relationship: first, implementation of provisions with regard to economic, industrial, agricultural, scientific and technical cooperation, and second, preoccupation over Yugoslavia's disastrous, debt-ridden economy. Apart from the ECU 67 million loan, Yugoslavia decided to make use of the rest of the ECU 200 million from the EIB's own resources secured in the First Financial Protocol of 1980.[44] In addition, the Community approved an additional ECU 60 million loan to Yugoslavia for the trans-Yugoslav highway.[45] Since the First Protocol was due to expire in 1985, exploratory talks took place in Belgrade in October 1984 in order to discuss the Second Financial Protocol and a proposal to provide two different types of loan, the first from the EIB amounting to ECU 400 million, and the second from the Community budget amounting to ECU 80 million.[46] This period of cooperation is best understood as a one-sided benefit, demonstrating that Yugoslavia was in need of the Community's aid. Without proper support, Yugoslavia's further progress seemed questionable. Indeed, the EEC Economic and Social Committee members visited several Yugoslav republics and provinces and, while identifying growing inflation, low purchasing power and unemployment as the most alarming aspects, concluded that Yugoslavia was facing serious economic problems which 'threatened to aggravate social tensions and upset the internal equilibrium'. Apart from economic problems, Community officials insisted on the political context: 'The political context meant that the solution to the problems must go beyond a purely sectoral view of interests'. However, it is worthy of mention that at this point the Community actually marvelled at the SFRY being 'a multi-national country where political and institutional integration was very far advanced, and where the political model provided an interesting alternative to Soviet communism, namely self-management'.[47]

Still, financial support was seen as an opportunity for Yugoslav authorities to link themselves to the leaders in the West European states. In her study, Ellen Comisso notes that having international support was beneficial for two reasons: first, 'such support proved extremely helpful when it came to drawing on the financial reserves of the IMF and Western banks to help mitigate the impact of higher energy costs on the domestic economy', and second, 'pluralizing elites could hold out the promise of membership of the EEC to constituencies anxious to join for political and economic reasons'.[48] Thus, the Community's readiness to assist Yugoslavia was confirmed by the adoption of the second Financial Protocol to run from 1985 to 1990. To express its optimism, the Council 'endorsed directives enabling the Commission to open negotiations to renew and adapt the trade clauses of the Agreement to provide for relations in the period after [a new] enlargement'.[49]

However, during the first two negotiating meetings held in 1986, no agreement was reached. According to the official documents, concerned with the Chernobyl nuclear catastrophe of the same year, the Community decided 'to suspend imports of various agricultural products from certain countries, including Yugoslavia'.[50] This suspension, applicable to all non-member countries and extended to February 1987, provoked a certain discord between the Community and Yugoslavia: while the Community showed that non-member status meant being easily marginalized, the Yugoslav government expressed its concern with regard to future perspectives. For Raif Dizdarević, Minister of Foreign Affairs of Yugoslavia, the restrictions his country was subject to were 'unjustifiable measures of discrimination' deriving from a prejudice, both economic and political, harboured by the Community in relation to Yugoslavia.[51]

According to the Cooperation Council, acknowledging possible problems with regard to the relations between the two parties might help prevent future problems. During its July 1986 meeting, the Cooperation Council 'expressed satisfaction with the general development of trade up to 1984 but concern at the worsening situation in 1985'.[52] In order to fix the situation, the Council, while stressing the importance of financial cooperation, expressed its readiness to conclude the Second Financial Protocol after the positive effects of the First Financial Protocol had been acknowledged.[53] Indeed, as assessed by Oskar Kovač, member of the Yugoslav Federal Executive Council, in his introductory statement: 'The establishment of this cooperation contributed to the identification of Yugoslavia's position as a transit country, as a European, Mediterranean and developing country. The achieved level of financial cooperation to date gives special meaning to our mutual relations and represents a warrant of the further expansion of relations in this field and in general'.[54] Despite its rather optimistic echo, Kovač's convincing speech reflected the situation characterizing a very short period of time. More importantly, there was an absolute necessity to persuade Community authorities to proceed with a new financial protocol. Therefore, Kovač insisted: 'Yugoslavia attaches great significance to the structural adjustment of its economy. In that respect, exceptional efforts have been exerted to bring about changes in the economic system and in development'.[55]

The Community accepted Yugoslavia's presentation. Even questions about political cooperation, which Kovač successfully avoided, were clarified some days later. The Community heard those elements deemed most suitable by Yugoslavia: stories about their thirst for greater political dialogue and readiness to develop stronger links with the Community and its Member States.[56] Nevertheless, this was not entirely true. The Community's position was to ignore Yugoslav domestic problems. While the Cooperation Council was noting 'with interest the statement by the Yugoslav delegation on Yugoslavia's economic and financial situation and in particular the Yugoslav stabilization plan',[57] the country was entering a period of destabilization. More precisely, while Community policy towards Yugoslavia was driven by the idea that Yugoslavia had to contribute only what the EEC leadership was ready to take and at the same time be ready to accept everything the Community itself recommended, more relevant aspects were ignored. Accordingly, as advocated by both Dizdarević and Kovač, the end of the 1980s represented a crucial point in Community–Yugoslav relations: while seriously affected by Greek accession to the Community, both officials expressed Yugoslav concerns with regard to long-term economic and political stability across the Yugoslav federation.[58]

The End of the 1980s

Further enlargement of the European Economic Community, when Spain and Portugal became official members, did not affect the Yugoslav federation negatively. In fact, the SFRY benefited from their accession due to the improved concessions the Community granted to the Yugoslav federation.[59] In addition, the Second Financial Protocol provided a considerable increase in EIB loans, from ECU 200 million under the First Protocol to ECU 550 million under the new one.[60]

In order to discuss economic and technical cooperation, statistics and agriculture, advancements in the fields of the environment, energy and tourism, Jacques Delors, the President of the European Commission, visited Belgrade and his visit, according to the *General Report*, 'provided an opportunity to reaffirm the importance which the Community attaches to its relations with Yugoslavia'.[61] Indeed, the importance of this meeting was confirmed in various statements. First, the Commission provided the Council with a recommendation for a decision with regard to the opening of negotiations aimed at the improvement of trade arrangements, after the expiry of the initial arrangements specified in the Agreement between EEC Member States and Yugoslavia.[62] Second, the EP reported on Yugoslavia's role as a go-between within the Community and Mediterranean region and the need to encourage political dialogue. Accordingly, political-level meetings were given greater relevance, as one of the working parties on EEC–Yugoslavia cooperation defined cooperation guidelines.[63]

There is no doubt that the Yugoslav federation was going through a difficult period: a deteriorating economic situation followed by alarming inflation, social tensions and growing divergences among its constituent republics all threatened the political stability of the country.[64] At European level, the EP was the first institution to acknowledge these aspects. While perceiving Yugoslavia simultaneously as a Mediterranean country, thus an active party in agreements related to this particular region, a developing country in Europe and moreover, a non-aligned country, the EP insisted on the assumption that the Community might have been responsible for most of the Yugoslav problems. Recalling the three major objectives stipulated in the 1980 Agreement,[65] the EP called on the Community to react by requiring the Yugoslav authorities to commence a new process of economic reforms necessary for the restructuring of the Yugoslav economy.[66]

To clarify the argument about the relations between the Community and Yugoslavia towards the end of the decade, I draw attention to two visits which clearly demonstrate significant misinterpretation between the parties. In his longest statement ever, Budimir Lončar, Minister of Foreign Affairs of Yugoslavia, addressed the Community officials:

> Viewed in a longer historical perspective, we are, in my opinion, faced with a crucial and, in a way, similar problem: the European Community with the problem of how to avoid turning into a fortress encircled by thick walls and being transformed, whether we want it or not, from a nucleus of a broader integration in Europe, into a factor of some kind of economic and technological disintegration of Europe, and Yugoslavia, with the problem of how to avoid being pushed to the margins of European economic, technological and integration processes and, consequently, doomed to irreparable lagging behind in its overall development.[67]

Lončar's words were sound. His speech tackled something the Community itself was afraid of — becoming a fortress which would surely compromise the initial ideals of European integration. In a similar fashion, Lončar continued: 'We believe that the strengthening of the European identity by breaking down the existing economic, political, ideological and other barriers in Europe would be in the interest of all Europeans'.[68] For him, the two possessed a common interest in being open to each other. In his concluding remarks, Lončar said:

> In all the discussion and dilemmas in Yugoslavia today, there exists full consensus, both among responsible political leaders and in the general public, that Yugoslavia needs to integrate itself more widely and more fully into Europe ... This is a long-term strategic orientation imposed by the vital national interests of our country. Needless to say, Yugoslavia and Europe have never been separated whether from the historical, geopolitical or broadest civilizational point of view. Now, it is only a question of political and human wisdom to find effective and adequate modalities for identifying common interests at a time when divisions are giving way to dialogue and tolerance.[69]

However, in his statement, Lončar completely avoided the gravity of the Yugoslav domestic situation. A brief mention of constitutional, economic and political reforms that had already taken place served to convince the Europeans that the Yugoslav federation was ready to change and improve. Therefore, Lončar underlined that Yugoslavia was a country with lower levels of development, an important claim which was not intended to undermine the existing concepts surrounding the unity of Europe or intra-European interdependence, but which instead served as an open invitation for further assistance.[70]

Another meeting, this time between Lončar and Delors only, in April 1989, was dedicated to the situation in Yugoslavia.[71] Once again, it proved obvious that Yugoslavia was in a difficult position, both economically because of a debt-ridden economy and politically due to internal disputes over which direction to pursue. The Community's attempt to comprehend the situation in Yugoslavia resulted in its diplomatic engagement: 'The Community said that once the negotiations had been concluded with the IMF on the improvement of Yugoslavia's economic and financial situation it would be prepared to examine the additional measures to support reforms being carried out there and to strengthen its cooperation with Yugoslavia'.[72] In addition, the two parties discussed the possibility of Yugoslavia's participation in different Community programmes.

It was only during the 1989 Paris Summit that the equal relevance of both economic and political cooperation was recognized and seen as an absolute prerequisite for tackling growing problems in Eastern Europe. As summarized by the *EC Bulletin*, the summit 'marked an important step in the development of the Community since the [1986] Single Act', when the G7 demanded that the European Commission coordinate the necessary support for economic and political reforms in Eastern Europe.[73] On this occasion, the Twelve demonstrated 'the will to back up and encourage democratic change, the wish to confirm the stability of existing alliances and borders and the desire to respond to non-member countries' concern that the Community's market should be opened up to them'.[74] Accordingly, the programme's extension was strictly conditioned on the fulfilment of various requirements: the organization of free elections, the introduction of a multi-party system and market economy, and protection of human rights. Considering that the requirements were the same for all countries and each country was a case per se, the application of the programme differed from one state to another.[75]

In the case of the Yugoslav federation, frequent Yugoslav contacts and visits to Brussels in the late 1980s meant that something was happening, though it was impossible to predict how positive or negative the outcome might have been. Here, the *Memorandum on Yugoslav economic reforms* served as a driving document behind the intensified EEC–SFRY contacts. According to Ante Marković, Prime Minister of Yugoslavia and the author of the memorandum, the position of his country was as follows:

> The opening of Yugoslavia to the world, Europe in particular, is the cornerstone of the changes and reforms being undertaken.

Creation of a common European house is an irreversible historical trend. The pursuance of these reform objectives aimed at turning our country into a nation with market-economy, political pluralism and democracy is perceived by us in Yugoslavia as our contribution to, and role in, this historic challenge of today.[76]

Marković, at least in his 13-page official statement, believed that the SFRY was able to catch up with the West. His optimism was conditioned by numerous sectors the Yugoslav federation had to improve, but which were still achievable. Economic measures, together with a new financial arrangement with the IMF, were discussed as top prerequisites for further recovery.[77]

During his late November 1989 visit to the European Community, Lončar expanded some of Marković's optimistic ideas outlining 'the essence of the Yugoslav reforms under way, the main purpose of which is to improve overall economic efficiency and to strengthen political democracy in the country'.[78] While explaining that the Yugoslav programme was based on four key components – flexibility of economic structure, mobility of capital (both domestic and foreign), an open economy strategy and on a modern state of federal principles with clearly defined economic functions – Lončar argued the promotion of cooperation and relations with the EC to be 'an essential precondition for the success of Yugoslav reform. More substantial financial support ... has to come from EC Member States within the framework of both international financial and monetary institutions, primarily of the IMF [and] from Governments of Member States in the negotiations on rescheduling Yugoslavia's debt and their direct engagement in facilitating the implementation of measures presented in the Memorandum'.[79]

Such a demand meant that the Yugoslav authorities had understood that their next step had to be a change of system – a difficult step to take without appropriate assistance. The Yugoslav authorities called the Europeans to review the relations between them which, as stipulated, in the light of the developments across the federation and in Eastern Europe more generally, needed redefining.[80] In Lončar's words, 'the time has come to mutually find new forms of cooperation and a more adequate institutional framework that would enable further incorporation of Yugoslavia into integration processes in Europe'.[81] Indeed, the official talks between the two delegations, both in March and April of 1990, resulted in the Commission producing a document addressed to the Council about relations between the Community and Yugoslavia, allowing the opening of negotiations for a third financial protocol.[82] According to the *General Report* 'the 1990 cooperation initiatives matched in number and scope those undertaken in 1989, with a specific bias, however, towards activities aimed at bringing Yugoslavia's rules closer to those of the Community, in particular as regards standards'.[83]

In the international system, one state usually examines its relations with another for two main reasons: first, to realize what benefits the relationship generates, and second, to understand what might present itself as a problem or threat and thus undermine their future cooperation. Driven by such ideas, the Community and Yugoslavia had been examining their common positions since the 1980s. Although it could be argued that this seemed to be the right point to review the existing state of affairs and hopefully find new ways of cooperation, the Community and Yugoslavia arrived at the end of the decade confronted by two significantly different realities: the former was marching towards more profound and comprehensive integration, whereas the latter was facing more difficulties and frustration.

The Community's engagement with Central and Eastern European countries was taking a new direction: it opened negotiations with some of these countries aimed at concluding a Stabilization and Association Agreement (SAA) with each state. Thus, the EC map was heading towards a new architectural format in the future, and the Yugoslav federation seemed to be an integral part of that change: 'The EC future relations with Yugoslavia are characterized by an SAA'.[84] The Council, somehow, noted the positive results characterizing the EC–SFRY cooperation that had been obtained so far, which represented a stable basis necessary for the establishment of institutions that were a fundamental prerequisite for successful reforms in Yugoslavia. It enthusiastically reported that 'the transformation of Yugoslav political and economic systems had already commenced' and that significant progress in the field of democratic development with regard to human rights had been made – altogether valid motives to support territorial integrity of the country.[85]

Europe's lack of a proper picture of the situation across the SFRY was solely due to the Yugoslav federal authorities' readiness to support multi-party elections in the constituent republics – in Lončar's terms 'an absolute imperative to overcome the problems Yugoslavia faced'.[86] According to Comisso, 'it was very much in their political interest to choose economic policies, adjustment strategies, and foreign political alignments that would facilitate EEC entrance, even when such choices meant imposing sacrifices on parts of their constituencies'.[87] Thus, considering Lončar's proposal to 'reinforce efforts necessary for a progressive passage on a new phase, from cooperation to integration',[88] it can be concluded that according to federal authorities, Yugoslavia did start to pay considerable attention to its future as an EC Member State. But, how realistic was all this?

The outbreak of violence changed the communication between the European Community and the Yugoslav authorities. Thus, for understandable reasons, the 1991 *General Report* dedicated much more space to Yugoslavia than ever before. It stipulated: 'The Community and its Member States followed with the greatest concern the situation in Yugoslavia'.[89] As discussed elsewhere in official statements and later in academic scholarship, the European Community expressed its concerns and encouraged peaceful dialogue as soon as the collapse of the Yugoslav federation became a serious matter of discussion. While it opposed the use of force, the EC was extremely puzzled. It did not know what to propose as an instrument to approach the constitutional crisis. The *General Report* stressed:

> Relations with Yugoslavia have been severely affected by the serious crisis there. Owing to the uncertainty surrounding the future of the Yugoslav federation following the declarations of independence by Slovenia and Croatia, the third financial protocol, which was signed in Brussels on 24 June, has not been sent to Parliament and the procedure for concluding the agreement has been suspended, as have cooperation under the second financial protocol and technical assistance schemes provided for under Phare.[90]

The alarming situation with regard to the relations between the Community and Yugoslavia due to 'the worsening political and institutional crisis in Yugoslavia [and] the continuing civil war' affected trade and economy both among the Yugoslav republics and with the Community.[91] In addition, diplomatic action consisted of issuing joint statements and in the period July – September ten statements were issued,[92] which could hardly have prevented the spread of conflict and, in fact, only served to encourage it.

Yugoslavs in the European Community

The presence of Yugoslavs in the Community during the 1980s represented a serious challenge to the relationship between their homeland and the host countries within the EC. Neither the Community nor its Member States had a clearly defined policy as to how to address the presence of the Yugoslav workforce. Although seriously acknowledged as a growing concern in 1978, when the Serbian delegation paid a visit to Germany,[93] it was only later when the EP commenced discussions about the guest-workers that greater attention was paid to them. In fact, during one of its sessions, Mario Zagari called the Community to show greater understanding towards the Yugoslav guest-workers: 'It is worth keeping in mind that there are a million Yugoslav guest-workers in the Community that are supposed to be offered an indefinite leave to remain, social protection and legal status'.[94] These concerns were also evident in another document which shows to what extent the Community insisted on the problem concerning guest-workers; in its subject the Council noted: 'It is most desirable that the Commission, in its negotiations with Yugoslavia, should be able to discuss problems concerning the migration of Yugoslav workers'.[95] It would be only later in 1983 that the Community granted the Yugoslav guest-workers and their family members living in the Community an opportunity to benefit from the social security system of the country they lived in, regardless of their nationality.[96]

Thus, both Zagari's advocacy and the Community's decision indicated that the EEC took the rights of Yugoslav immigrants seriously. The Community noted 'with satisfactions the provision in the [1980]

Agreement that Yugoslav workers employed in the territory of the Member States shall be free from any discrimination as regards working conditions or pay'.[97] Although often claiming that after economic progress, social problems needed to be addressed, the Community's statement was rather weak. Even some time after, the Economic and Social Committee had to 'regret that the social provisions contained in the appendices to the 1980 agreement had not yet been implemented apart from a brief reference during the June 1984 meeting of the Cooperation Council'.[98]

A deeper insight into documents discussing Yugoslav workers within the Community clearly shows that the EEC lacked mechanisms to address the issue: despite the Community's wish to see them return to their homeland, especially after the 1970s oil crises, the majority decided to stay. The ones who stayed in the Community used and, if possible, abused the system. Still, the Yugoslav authorities perceived their compatriots in the Community as suffering hard times. In order to illustrate this misunderstanding, I rely on the Mission Statement of the SFRY, directed to the European Communities, the first note of its kind since the establishment of official relations between the two parties. The five-page document stipulated that the promises in the field of labour under the 1980 agreement were not respected in practice: 'Cooperation in this field was even discontinued after the ratification of the Agreement, when the Joint Working Group on Social Issues stopped working, which had during the preparations for concluding the Agreement on several occasions discussed all the major issues related to the employment, work, stay and return of Yugoslav nationals from work in the Community'.[99] Of course, such lack of cooperation was serious enough to undermine relations between the EEC and SFRY. However, the protest that the Yugoslav authorities expressed was a result of the ever growing uncertainty regarding Yugoslav workers in the Community, a matter which was already supposed to be regulated. Thus, while not being a recent phenomenon, the authorities feared that at some point the Community would abandon 'the formally guaranteed right of Yugoslav nationals to equal treatment' and refuse to renew their work and residence permits.[100] The statement read: 'The number of unemployed Yugoslav citizens is increasing, and their return to their homeland appears as the only solution, rather than the expression of their free choice once their motives for seeking employment abroad have been fulfilled'.[101]

The note ended by calling the Community representatives to organize an urgent meeting and address uncertainties about the Yugoslavs in the EC, the risk that a new enlargement of the Community was going to affect them negatively, and the possibility of regulating their status through agreement with clear conditions and modalities of cooperation.[102] This meeting, however, never took place, and the Community never addressed the above-mentioned concerns seriously. First, in one of the statements that followed, it focused on Yugoslavia's concerns regarding both its citizens residing in the Community and the country's position after the accession of Spain and Portugal. While completely ignoring the issues about the Yugoslav workforce, the Community discussed the new enlargement and weakly concluded: 'The EEC only hoped that the SFRY was going to continue to benefit from its Cooperation Agreement with the Community'.[103] Second, the Yugoslav workforce in the EC was mentioned during another meeting, but without any solution being proposed.[104] Finally, the forthcoming official statements hardly talked at all about the Yugoslav guest-workers, but rather about energy planning, information seminars, research projects, tourism, etc.[105]

Very soon, it became obvious that ignoring the issues surrounding the Yugoslavs in the Community had turned into a regular practice. In fact, both sides bore responsibility for this approach. On the one hand, the Yugoslav leadership was determined to secure another, even higher than initially imagined, financial protocol, and therefore, pressing the Community for a more favourable policy towards the Yugoslav workforce was not a good idea. On the other hand, the Community was happy not to address concerns over the immigrants as it did not know which policy to adopt. More often than not, it maintained that bearing in mind the economic situation in their homeland at the time, the Yugoslav immigrants had to accept the treatment they received, as long as they were permitted to reside in the Community. In order to avoid further lack of policy, the EC representatives agreed that it was not for the Community to deal with the Yugoslavs, but for the

Member States.[106] This sudden decision to transfer responsibility empowered various EC Member States to start developing their own policies and deciding upon the Yugoslavs inhabiting their territories. As the Cooperation Council put it: 'The appropriate Member States could then outline their individual views on socio-cultural problems and in particular on measures which have been or might be taken'.[107] Towards the end of the 1980s the Community talked about 800,000 Yugoslavs residing in its Member States, many of whom enjoyed the same social benefits as their own citizens – a treatment not valid during difficult times when the Community's citizens would be given priority over the Yugoslavs.[108] Among all Member States, Germany used this opportunity to criticize the Yugoslav workforce most. For the Germans, while the Yugoslavs were unwilling to integrate fully, the best scenario would have been for a specific category (the ones without permanent residence status) to leave.[109]

Conclusion

The 1980s were supposed to represent a period of communication and cooperation in many different fields. However, as demonstrated throughout the chapter, communication (as well as cooperation) between the European Community and the Yugoslav federation encountered numerous obstacles. In both the dominant area of economic cooperation, and the less prevalent activities of political dialogue and social inclusion, the two parties failed to develop a strong relationship. The outbreak of violence compounded the existence of such a failure. In a joint statement dated 5 October 1991 the Community and its Member States emphasized their inability to come up with an immediate solution to the Yugoslav crisis.[110] While the fighting continued, the Community together with the Member States, the United States of America and the Soviet Union expressed their concerns as the agreements reached in The Hague on 4 October were not respected. Once the city of Dubrovnik became a target of the Federal Army, the Community supported by its Member States concluded that 'five republics had reiterated their readiness to cooperate on the basis of the draft arrangements submitted by Lord Carrington and the Presidency and that one republic continued to reserve its position'.[111] As a measure of response to the crisis, the Council, supported by the representatives from the Member States, decided 'to suspend the application of EEC and ECSC agreements with Yugoslavia with immediate effect'.[112] Interestingly, the Community did not want its decision to affect 'those republics which had cooperated in seeking a political solution during the Hague Conference on Yugoslavia'.[113] Thus, a set of corrective positive measures was adopted privileging Slovenia, Croatia, Bosnia-Herzegovina, and Macedonia over Serbia and Montenegro.[114] Such a reaction encourages the questioning of the criteria for how and what kind of political solution those republics adopted.

The Community's admission of its unpreparedness to tackle the Yugoslav problem, and further divisions among its Member States as to how to address an increasing crisis within a country they apparently never abandoned, through good times or bad, provided a vacuum which was soon filled by other actors who felt free to wield power and speed up the outcome of the crisis. Within this atmosphere, non-state actors, including some of the most powerful in international politics, took advantage of the Community's confusion. In particular, diaspora groups, the media and the Catholic Church stuck to their common objectives and influenced policy-making in Brussels. Accordingly, the following three chapters of the book will show how those non-state actors rekindled and strengthened their links in order to approach the decision-makers in the Community. The latter, in the end, agreed that the policy of recognition of independence was the right solution to the Yugoslav crisis.

PART TWO

THE ROLE OF NON-STATE ACTORS

CHAPTER FOUR

CALLING DIASPORA AND DIASPORA CALLING

Impact of Diasporas on European Community Policy

This chapter analyses diaspora activism during the Yugoslav crisis by focusing on the role played primarily by the Slovenian and, to a lesser extent, Croatian diaspora communities. This primacy is justified by the fact that the Slovenian diaspora lobbied for the recognition of both Slovenian and Croatian independence by the European Community. Here, diasporas are understood as 'social groups that (i) settle and establish themselves in another country and (ii) are internationally heterogeneous ... Diasporas are rarely constituted by a single factor other than the broadest of connections to a specific homeland. Diasporas intervene in conflict because they can. Diasporas without access to power of some sort, whether direct or surrogate, do not intervene in conflict'.[1]

Thus, while representing an influential 'type of consciousness' permitted to make decisions, take actions and develop links with one or more societies simultaneously, diaspora populations are capable of penetrating developments of both international and domestic politics.[2] In his analysis, Zlatko Skrbiš marvels at diaspora members who 'engage in constant negotiation of identities between different, but as far as they are concerned, equally significant aspects of lives, determined by homelands, cultures, identities and – not seldom – citizenships'.[3] With regard to diaspora groups' involvement in politics, they are free to develop particular policies independently of their representative authorities. One study summarizes their freedom of choice: 'They may support or oppose the government of their home country, morally, financially, and as suppliers of weapons and even personnel to the faction they favour. They may support their homeland government when it is engaged in warfare and boycott the products of its enemies'.[4] This statement is a clear indication of how serious diaspora activism can be: it is their position, between homelands and adopted countries, which provides them with noticeable power with regard to decision-making. Moreover, this long-distance ability of migrants is often characterized by sets of irresponsible actions – a circumstance where none of the 'shrewd political manipulators' is likely to bear responsibility for the actions undertaken.[5]

If one examines the historical dimension of diaspora politics, it can be argued that the end of World War II, and in particular the post-Cold War period, signalled an increasing presence of diaspora groups in host-land and homeland affairs. For example, Skrbiš distinguishes two main reasons behind the growing involvement of diasporas: 'global restructuring and the realignment of ethno-national units in the post-Cold War era, and the increased capacity of individual actors and social groups to respond rapidly, and effectively, to homeland crises on a transnational scale'.[6] Indeed, as argued in this book, while the bureaucrats representing the European Community were trying to find a solution for the Yugoslav drama, diaspora groups had already established and worked on their objectives. Accordingly, this chapter will show that their activism contributed to overall EC policy and its final decision vis-à-vis the future of the Yugoslav state. Despite their common objective, for the clarity of the arguments presented here, parts of the chapter examine Slovenian and Croatian diaspora groups separately. However, more often, and as will be particularly obvious in the section discussing diaspora activism and its power at the EC level, the two are presented as a unitary actor.

Slovenian Activism

Slovenian diaspora groups before, during, and immediately after the Second World War, rarely considered independence as the final outcome for their homeland. For example, Louis Adamič, frequently viewed as a 'spokesman' for interwar Slovenia abroad, dedicated three volumes to the position of his beloved republic within the Yugoslav federation, not as an independent state.[7] However, Adamič's work did not have much impact on later generations. The Slovenian post-WWII political émigrés developed a different point of view, inspired by the fact that Slovenian autonomy with regard to economic, social and cultural policies (established by the Slovene National Liberation Movement during the Second World War and confirmed by the 1946 Yugoslav constitution) was almost non-existent in comparison to ever increasing Yugoslav centralism.[8] Accordingly, they formed two separate groups: *Slovenski narodni odbor* and the Action Committee for a United and Sovereign Slovene State.

The first circle, led by Miha Krek, an émigré with a Christian Democratic orientation and president of the Slovenian People's Party, focused on the prospects of Slovenian independence within a united Europe.[9] The party enjoyed a good reputation within the Union of National European Commissions in London, Paris and Strasbourg – an aspect that was to become fully relevant during the late 1980s. Furthermore, the party's programme was fully supported by the Christian Democratic Union of Central Europe (CDUCE),[10] previously established in the Slovenian Hall in New York, in 1950. Thus, it is not difficult to conclude that the beginning of the 1950s marked the greater involvement of Slovenian émigrés. The 1953 international congress of CDUCE served to examine Slovenian perception of Slovenia's own position within Yugoslavia. In this respect, Slovenian representatives demanded the following: 'A plan projecting a realistic and attractive future for Central European peoples liberated from Soviet domination, a plan assuring self-determination to great and small nations, a plan enabling them to form closer or looser regional ties through which they may enter the prospective United States of Europe'.[11] This way Slovenia openly demanded support for its ambitions. Thus, while relying on the ideas about some sort of a united Europe, the Slovenes sought to deepen their connections with Christian Democrats elsewhere. Apart from official gatherings, diaspora groups abroad 'published one weekly newspaper, six monthly journals, and one yearly almanac in the Slovene language. In addition, the Slovene national minorities in Italy and Austria had two Christian Democratic weeklies and two publishing houses'.[12]

The second circle, led by Cyril Žebot, a professor of economics, also advocated independence for Slovenia. Although comparatively small when compared to Krek's group, Žebot's committee was well-known for two reasons: it published the paper *Slovenska država/ Slovenian State* and, more importantly, it was based in Rome with direct access to the Vatican. Although most of the documents from the immediate post-World War II period have been lost or remain unavailable for research, in the 1960s the two circles developed closer ties and decided to work together in order to inform the world about Slovenian problems. By the late 1970s, there were already 75,000 Slovenes in Western Europe, including political émigrés. At home, however, they were perceived in a different light. Here, I identify one document which explicitly shows the attitude of the Slovenian Communists towards the political émigrés. During its fourteenth meeting in January 1979, the Presidency of the Slovenian Communist Party for the first time noted that the Slovenian 'fascist political emigration' was posing a serious threat to the future of the republic as Slovenian political émigrés were advocating national separatism, thus independence.[13]

On the other hand, the diaspora members understood the eventual end of the communist era 'as an opportunity to materialize their political agenda and it positively encouraged the diaspora to imagine itself as a coherent and legitimate symbolic space'.[14] In order to succeed, the émigrés began establishing new diaspora organizations and contacts within internationally recognized institutions. This activism excluded any contacts with members from other Yugoslav diasporas. Affiliation to one group or another was not considered important and neither was the question as to whether Krek or Žebot was the more committed to independence as, in the end, the diaspora members gathered around the same idea. The question was rather posed the other way round, in other words, with members asking themselves what they could contribute to the fight for independence.

As already mentioned in the academic literature, Slovenia felt frustrated within the Yugoslav federation. Its growing nationalism was a result of the economic hardship and political divisions the Yugoslav federation faced in the mid-1980s.[15] However, in order to summarize reasons behind Slovenian frustration, one scholar describes them as: 'Being deprived of their enjoyment by "Southerners" (Serbians, Bosnians) because of their proverbial laziness, Balkan corruption, dirty and noisy enjoyment, and because they demand bottomless economic support, stealing from Slovenes their precious accumulation by means of which Slovenia could already have caught up with Western Europe'.[16] The discourse about Slovenian economic advancement was easily complemented with political and ideological dimensions which, together, made the quest for independence even stronger. The process of political liberalization 'was based on the idea of global Slovenian solidarity that aimed to transcend historically conditioned political divisions among Slovenians'.[17] In his writings, Skrbiš goes even further by assessing Slovenian activism during the Yugoslav crisis:

> The processes which led to the proclamation of Slovene independence from Yugoslavia in 1991 were based on the idea of global Slovene solidarity, aimed at transcendence of historically conditioned political particularisms. This idea of solidarity conditioned the establishment of the Slovene World Congress, an institution designed to foster a sense of an overarching commitment to fostering a Slovene national community as a transnational project.[18]

In fact, the Congress represented a direct link between the homeland and diaspora. It represented Slovenian interests around the world, thus aimed at collecting greater support for independence. Still, more relevant for this study is the fact that it managed to give the Slovenian voice importance among European Community leaders.

Croatian Activism

The Croatian diaspora was the most controversial diaspora the SFRY had ever produced. While being a time-tested phenomenon, emigration from Croatia intensified on two occasions: first, before the Second World War, due to economic hardship, and second, after the war when the political conditions of the new socialist Yugoslavia caused many to leave.[19] The immediate post-WWII wave consisted of manual workers and craftsmen who fled to European markets. They were followed by middle-class emigrants 'whose primary goal was democratic and economic reform of Croatia. They considered an independent Croatia unrealizable, and in practice did not even think on those lines'.[20] In this period the process of emigration was not a smooth one: the Yugoslav communist regime kept the Yugoslav borders closed until the early 1960s and therefore emigration was considered illegal.[21] As soon as it was legalized, economic emigration intensified. Political emigration exploded after the suppression of the 1971 Croatian spring (a political movement advocating greater rights for Croatia and the Croats) by Tito's leadership, during which numerous intellectuals decided to support and join nationalist movements within the Croatian diaspora.[22] However, later, in the 1980s, the Croatian diaspora attracted more 'professionals and academics in search of a higher living standard and better chances of promotion', and these new, mostly young, people developed political convictions with regard to their homeland that were significantly different from the ones adopted by their predecessors.[23] For them Croatia was better off as an independent state.

In his analysis, Paul Hockenos sees Croatian émigré communities as 'thoroughly infiltrated by informers from a variety of national security services' and he observes 'that any contact with them was guaranteed to catch the eye of the Yugoslav authorities. For decades, Yugoslav propaganda had singled out the Croat diaspora as the incarnation of evil, as being comprised of fanatic fascist terrorists bent on destroying the socialist state'.[24] Accordingly, it is this political aspect that will re-emerge as the main reason for Croatian diaspora behaviour. For example, the *Fraternalist*, the official journal of the Croatian Fraternal Union in North America, published a letter written by N. Bilandzich:

> Those elements in Yugoslavia which are at present in control must understand that the Croatian people will never give up their rights to liberty, justice and self-determination. We want freedom and independence, and for this we do not owe an apology to anyone. In today's Croatia, foreign elements can sing and hoist their flags, but if the Croatian people do the same, they are declared an enemy of the state and placed in jail. Mr. Editor, we Croatians are slaves in our own homeland. If you examine our historical past, I am sure that you will be able to conclude that we Croatians have done so much to advance the cause of Slavism and Yugoslavism, which has brought us nothing more than oppression and misery. For this reason, I am and always will be for Croatian independence and liberty.[25]

This letter indicated many conceptions held by the Croatian diaspora about their homeland. Above all, the emphasis was on Croatian readiness to assist the situation in the homeland, an idea which never really came into being. Once that readiness proved to be an illusion, the diaspora members turned to being 'constituted as pro independence, which also implied an anti-Yugoslavist and anti-communist platform'.[26]

However, it can be argued that for a long time before the actual conflict in the Yugoslav federation, the Croatian diaspora was present in homeland affairs as the source of ideological, financial and political support. In this respect, Daphne Winland writes about the commitment diaspora Croats had vis-à-vis the homeland: '[They] have always responded to changes in Croatia ... For example, while the vast majority of Croatian diaspora efforts over the years have been devoted to lobbying host governments and raising awareness through protest and publications, some have garnered a great deal of international media and host government attention through acts of protest and even violence'.[27] Therefore, the Yugoslav crisis confirmed the power of the Croatian diaspora. Greater than ever before, its involvement became apparent through its ability to present the suffering of the Croats to the extent that such images contributed to the determination of Yugoslavia's future. Here, Winland continues by saying that

> Mutual aid organizations, clubs, parishes, and businesses provided the foundation for the proliferation of political groups committed to the establishment of an independent Croatian state ... For example, the National Federation of Croatian Americans (NFCA) and the Croatian American Congress (CAC) – the latter a part of the international Croatian World Congress – both work[ed] on representing and coordinating the activities of numerous Croatian American organizations.[28]

During the 'escalatory stage' of the Yugoslav state crisis (1987–1991), the Croatian diaspora relied on ethnic tensions in their homeland and the politics of Yugoslav 'brotherhood and unity' to advocate a greater need for democratic pluralism and political reform.[29] In this period, one individual who played a catalytic role was the historian Franjo Tudjman. He understood the link between diaspora and homeland as a prerequisite for pursuing his policies. As one diaspora expert noted, Tudjman always considered the Croatian diaspora as possessing an important voice both at home and abroad and, therefore, obtaining a 'yes' from the diaspora members facilitated his ambitions at home.[30] For example, at home, two areas were of serious relevance: first, Tudjman's narrative was aimed at minimizing the Ustasha atrocities and the numbers of their victims during the Second World War and, second, he was determined to bring Croat communists and Croat nationalists closer.[31] While the second area occupied a central position within Tudjman's political agenda, he advocated overcoming historical differences and insisted on cooperation and a joint struggle for an independent state of Croatia.

Tudjman's first visit to the Croatian diaspora in North America occurred in 1987. This visit was beneficial for three reasons. First, it established a strong bond between the pro-independence movement in Croatia and the diaspora. While lecturing at the Ontario Institute for Studies in Education at the University of Toronto, Tudjman singled out the importance of self-determination of nations:

> The whole of human history has concerned itself with the formation and self-determination of national societies and the creation

of states ... The self-determination of nations, their freedom from external influences and foreign domination, their sovereignty of state, and at the same time the desire for equality and ascendancy in the international arena, have been and remain the main characteristics of contemporary historical fluctuation.[32]

By saying this, Tudjman quite obviously envisaged the direction the situation was to take in the homeland. He was convinced of his argument as to self-determination as the one and only solution for the republic of Croatia. On the other hand, the exiles, although not entirely convinced about some of Tudjman's approaches,[33] were impressed by 'his potential to take charge and lead the nation toward its rightful destiny'.[34]

The second dimension of Tudjman's visit concerned financial support for his campaign back home. Although considered less relevant for the main issue of this chapter, it is worth mentioning that the relationship between the Croatian diaspora and the homeland was often characterized by strong financial support. The majority of my respondents acknowledged the existence of fund-raising as an act of goodwill on the part of diaspora members, both as individuals and communities. A minority argued that financial support did not exist or that, even if it did, its relevance for the achievement of an independent Croatian state was marginal. While remaining a debatable issue, Tudjman's visit was however accompanied by talks about financial influence in homeland politics. The émigrés themselves acknowledged that good service was possible only if provided with sufficient funding.[35] According to some observers, this acknowledgement led to the establishment of the Croatian National Fund and a Swiss bank account was set up under the name of 'Aid for the Economic Renewal and Sovereignty of the Republic of Croatia'.[36] The discourse about financial support was further emphasized by the journalists from *Mladina*, a Slovenian pro-independence magazine, who revealed that the Croatian Democratic Union (HDZ) received as much as US$8.2 million from diaspora organizations.[37] In fact, the involvement of the Croatian diaspora, through financial and political means, was of decisive relevance in Tudjman's electoral success in 1991. Having won the elections, the primary focus of financial support from the diaspora switched towards the acquisition of weapons.[38]

Finally, Tudjman built a co-dependent relationship between the diaspora and the homeland. Even though his own convictions with regard to Yugoslav tensions and possible solutions sometimes differed from the ones presented by diaspora organizations, his visit was nevertheless a success. According to Skrbiš, Tudjman's presence convinced the members of the Croatian diaspora that 'the changes in the homeland were rapid and real. At the same time, it allowed the diaspora to enter into a dialogue with a representative of the opposition in the homeland'.[39] As a result, within a year, the co-dependent relationship came into being and the Croatian diaspora groups were mobilized to the extent that their voice was properly heard. In his discussion of diaspora Croats, Benedict Anderson suggests: 'Consider the malign role of the Croats not only in Germany but also in Australia and North America in financing and arming Tudjman's breakaway state and pushing Germany and Austria into a fateful, premature recognition'.[40]

In 1988 and 1989 Tudjman returned to North America. This time meeting the diaspora members was supposed to be a step further than the simple confirmation of the previously established co-dependent relationship. And indeed, now '[t]he thoughts he had been pondering had coalesced into an ideological vision'.[41] For émigrés he was a hero and for him the émigrés represented primary backing for his policies. The increasing size of diaspora audiences meant approval for Tudjman's strategy. However, the academic literature suggests that the power of the Croatian diaspora was officially demonstrated during the HDZ meeting on 24 February 1990, in Zagreb. After the launch of the HDZ as a political party and soon after it had turned into a movement, Tudjman managed to gather diaspora representatives with the aim of proving his party's credentials as the optimum ones for the Croatian people. Hockenos describes the atmosphere of the event:

> Zagreb airport was witness to joyous scenes of family reunions abounding in billowing red-and-white checkerboards and previously outlawed folk songs. The comparatively wealthy, ostensibly worldly émigrés basked in the limelight, relishing a status they

could never have imagined during their days of 'exile' in the West. In coffee bars and on television, the returnees shattered four decades of taboo, unabashedly championing the virtues of an independent Croatia.[42]

While properly accommodated, the émigrés criticized the functioning of the Yugoslav federation. In their view, the Serbs represented their 'arch enemies: We were oppressed by Serbs, by the Yugoslav army, by Yugoslav diplomacy, Yugoslav trade, Yugoslav commerce, the Yugoslav banking system, Yugoslav organizations, Yugoslav domination'.[43] In addition, the idea of creating Greater Serbia was a matter of concern both among the émigrés and the homeland political elite. Accordingly, an intentional tackling of this issue within diaspora groups encouraged further objection to the idea of Yugoslav unity.

As already pointed out, the meeting identified diaspora representatives whose ideas coincided completely with what Tudjman was advocating for Croatia: independence. As a gesture of approval, Croatian representatives from Germany, coordinating twenty-five HDZ branches in their host-country, gave their support for independence. In return, they wanted the right to vote in Croatian elections, either in Germany or Croatia, and this they obtained.[44] For ethnic Croats, independent Croatia was a better option than the maintenance of a united Yugoslavia. However, restricting this understanding to within diaspora groups alone did not guarantee the desired outcome. Instead, members of the diaspora were confronted with further steps before reaching and convincing the decision-makers that international recognition of independence was the only solution to the Yugoslav crisis. By opting for this scenario, the émigrés indirectly took part in the war, whereas European diplomacy attempted to understand what was actually happening and what policy to adopt vis-à-vis the Yugoslav federation.

Diaspora Strategies within the European Community

The European Community was largely uninformed about the outbreak and rapid development of the Yugoslav state crisis. Often, this ignorance was justified by the assumptions that the Europeans were busy with their own integrationist project which marginalized the situation in Yugoslavia. Even after the outbreak of the hostilities, as noted by Warren Zimmermann, 'the Europeans couldn't believe that Yugoslavia was in serious trouble ... [T]heir approach to Yugoslavia was without any of the urgency with which they acted fourteen months later, when the breakup they said couldn't happen was upon them'.[45] In fact, it was the United States Mission to the European Communities that kept the Europeans informed of what was happening in Europe.[46] The official documents show that daily correspondence between the USA and the EU was often unilateral. This kind of communication – which frequently resembled more a brief course on current affairs rather than an exchange of positions about the Yugoslav crisis – created a state of uncertainty. In this situation, informed by a lack of engagement and thoughtful policy, diaspora groups took advantage. For them, approaching the Washington or Brussels administration, or both, signified approaching and influencing decision-makers.

The scholarship on the European response to the Yugoslav crisis offers different points of view on diaspora activism. In her study, Beverly Crawford examines the situation in Germany, and while acknowledging the existence of various lobbying attempts, she concludes that diasporas did not exert any significant societal pressure that could have led to the policy of recognition.[47] Such a conclusion is dictated by the author's decision to limit her account to the Croatian diaspora only and, more specifically, to the Croatians residing in Germany, a country where great confusion about the future of Croatia dominated public debates (primarily due to numerous mixed marriages between Croats and Serbs). By contrast, other authors agree upon the diaspora's capacity to raise awareness of the situation in the homeland, push for a rapid resolution and, indeed, affect policies. For example, Sean Carter analyses the Croatian diaspora and identifies three main areas of diaspora activism which made a difference: fundraising, political protest and public-relations campaigning.[48] In fact, while many accounts of the Croatian diaspora suggest that the Croats were very active abroad, although less successful across the EC than in

North America, Slovenian activism abroad has rarely benefited from any deep analysis.

Slovenian groups gathered around the Slovenian World Congress, a global society including organizations and conferences from all over the world.[49] Even though the Congress was active in different fields,[50] during the Yugoslav crisis, the common objective of securing international recognition of independence was given priority. In her study, Brigitta Busch assesses the link between the diaspora and the Congress: 'The Slovenian World Congress was founded and Slovenian politicians repeatedly claimed that the minorities in neighboring countries and the Slovene Diaspora should play a role as "ambassadors" of the new Slovenian state'.[51] As explained earlier, this ambassadorial tactic was not something completely new for the diaspora Slovenes: it had already been embraced in the course of the previous two decades. The crisis in the homeland served as an additional motive to adjust their strategy and this time to go a step further than in the recent past.

In 2002, the Slovenian authorities decided to commence publishing archive materials covering the period of the Yugoslav crisis. Unlike other republics that still prefer to have most of their official materials remain well-protected and almost unavailable for research, Slovenia has offered up various collections of documents that facilitate our understanding and encourage further interest in the field. For example, the fourth volume of the *Viri o demokratizaciji in osamosvojitvi Slovenije* offers various transcripts which clearly reveal how the Slovenian leadership communicated with the diaspora and how diaspora groups engaged with the crisis. Here, among the wealth of material, I draw attention to one letter in particular, drafted by Milan Kučan, the Slovenian leader. While addressing 'fellow cousins' in the diaspora, Kučan, the first democratically elected President of the Republic of Slovenia, expressed his gratitude for their commitment in the struggle for independence:

> Our main objective is to achieve independence of the Slovenian state, freely decide upon our future and we ask for nothing more ... Recently, I have received numerous friendly and encouraging messages. It is not easy to observe what Slovenia is going through at the moment and succeed in our common objective.

It is worth mentioning that our independence will be rather a weak one, if we do not reach economic stability. Therefore, I ask the diaspora to contribute with its knowledge and assistance. I am aware of the fact that most of you would like to see Slovenia not only as an independent state, but also as a democratic and stable country. I am fully aware that in order to reach our objectives, you will continue to support us, like you did before.[52]

Kučan's letter, written soon after the Ten-Day War in Slovenia in July 1991, found instant approval among diaspora members. The nature of the letter was both informative, as it described the situation in the homeland, and indicative, as it underlined the policy that the Slovenian leadership considered appropriate to pursue. Kučan pointed out that the Slovenian objectives should be focused on the present and future status of the country, whereas diaspora groups should take an active part in the process.[53] For many diaspora members, the letter represented a necessary guideline as many of them had almost no idea of the situation in the homeland or the Yugoslav federation as a whole. However, as a consequence, the diaspora began to coalesce even more. In addition, this was the case especially after the United States administration changed its initial position with regard to the Yugoslav crisis.[54]

In Europe, translated versions of Kučan's letter, according to one Slovenian official, reached European Community officials through the Slovenian diaspora: 'For Slovenian people, the lack of a clear policy on behalf of the European Union was an opportunity to try and approach decision-makers whose voice was of particular weight. The diaspora did not hesitate, it just continued fighting for something that seemed to be the Slovenian objective since the Second World War'.[55] Indeed, this comment very much complements the idea *Slovenska izseljenska matica* expressed about diaspora activism. The society demanded that diaspora groups inform host governments 'about the critical situation' in their homeland and urge them 'to help preserve peace in the world'.[56]

In order to illustrate the growing Slovenian drive for independence, I identify various aspects that became even more apparent after the Ten-Day War. First, the Slovenian leadership needed to convince the Europeans that its ambition was justified. As noted in a letter addressed to the international cultural and scientific audience: 'All the Slovenian attempts to establish in all of the Yugoslav territory, criteria of European democracy and culture have been without success. The unity of Yugoslavia, so much spoken about these days by the diplomatic representatives of your countries, in our historical experience and particularly in the light of recent events, seems possible only as a dictatorship'.[57] By doing so, the Slovenes aimed to convince the Europeans that there was something wrong with the principles the Yugoslav federation was based upon and that they were the ones trying to spread Western European values within the country. However, in their view, only after it had proved that Yugoslav unity was not achievable in conformity with European standards, they decided to go for a different strategy. This standpoint complemented what the Slovenian diaspora had already adopted as its official policy before the actual crisis: indeed, the émigrés did not focus on unity at all, but rather the prospect of Slovenian self-determination.

Second, by stressing that the Yugoslav People's Army which attacked Slovenia 'understood the viewpoint of the European and the United States government as an excuse as well as encouragement to try to re-establish a centralist dictatorship and to violently nullify the will of the Slovenian nation for self-determination expressed through free elections', the Slovenian leadership tried to show that the Yugoslavs were undermining Europeans and Americans.[58] This argument, stronger than the previous one, blamed the West for their lack of policy and at the same time forced the West to view itself as naïve. In this respect, both Slovenian and Croatian diaspora groups found themselves in an excellent position: criticizing the West for its non-response allowed them to achieve support in the West for their own already established policy.[59] Although Slovenia and Croatia continuously criticized the Community for being late to deliver a clear policy over the situation in Yugoslavia, Europe's late response was nevertheless beneficial for both republics.

Third, the Slovenian authorities insisted that they had satisfied the essential criteria to become an independent state. Accordingly, the republic was 'ready, through negotiations and assumptions of state functions, to commit itself to reliable and stable partnerships with all other nations and authorities of the international community'.[60] This part of the Slovenian strategy focused on delivering a clear message about Slovenia's capacity to fulfil conditions for independence. In addition, it was stipulated that Slovenia was going to work towards a greater stability 'in a complex region of Europe', whereas its independence was not going to be 'at the expense of the region, but as a positive step forward for the whole region and its constituent partners'.[61] The point here was clear as it argued that independence was not to affect the region negatively, but rather contribute to further progress. Controversial as it was, this strategy did not prevent the spread of violence. As Zimmermann, while examining Slovenian behaviour within the Yugoslav federation and before the crisis, notes: 'In their drive to separate from Yugoslavia [the Slovenes] simply ignored the twenty-two million Yugoslavs who were not Slovenes. They bear considerable responsibility for the bloodbath that followed their secession'.[62]

Finally, both the Slovenian leadership and diaspora members relied on emotional appeals in their communication with the Europeans. For example, they asked the Community's governments 'in the spirit of humanism and love of freedom, to help [them] in making the truth known – that today in Slovenia, we are defending the foundations of European culture, human rights and self-determination of nations'.[63] The sufferings that post-Second World War Europe had faced served to inspire the Slovenian leadership to advocate the avoidance of similar disasters in the future. The memories of divisions caused by the Cold War were still fresh and most of those directly involved in its dismantlement were facing consequences. The emotional dimension was further stressed by statements such as: 'By supporting the right of Slovenia to live a free, independent, cultural and democratic life in its own state, you will support the spirit [of humanism and love], which is our common home'.[64]

Diasporas and Individual European States

The Austrian government demonstrated significant sympathy for their Slovenian diaspora. Although Austria was not an official member state of the European Community at the time of the Yugoslav state crisis, its close links with the Community and its Member States – due to the already advanced negotiations of Austrian EC membership – meant that the Austrian standpoint on the situation in neighbouring Yugoslavia was given significant attention by the Brussels administration. As an example, Matjaž Klemenčič discusses a meeting dated 9 July 1991, when Franz Vranitzky, the Austrian socialist chancellor, gathered leaders of Western social-democratic parties in Vienna 'to exchange views on the Yugoslav crisis'.[65]

With regard to the Slovenes in Austria, one scholar showed that although they faced serious mistreatment during and after the Second World War, when the Slovenian population in the country was decimated from 80,000 to 16,000, the Yugoslav crisis showed that the Austrians had since completely reversed their approach towards the Slovenian diaspora members.[66] In addition, towards the end of the 1980s, both Slovenia and Croatia worked towards securing a stronger link with Austria and Italy through their joint involvement in a regional organization named Alps-Adriatic Working Community, with special focus on economic and political cooperation. In her analysis, Woodward acknowledges the relevance of this venture and stresses that the policies of the organization additionally encouraged the Slovenian and Croatian drive for independence.[67] Such a climate provided a favourable environment for diaspora activism. With regard to this, the Carinthian Slovenes played an instrumental role in spreading information about both the Slovenian and the Croatian situation at home and, accordingly, their ambitions abroad.[68]

Due to the geographical, historical and trade proximity, the Slovenian leadership considered Carinthia, a state of Austria, to be the most relevant starting point. One of my respondents acknowledged that communication between them intensified on two occasions: first, in the late 1980s when the Slovenian economy became affected by the economic problems that the Yugoslav federation as a whole was facing, and second, during the Slovenian struggle for independence. Although, according to the source, 'Slovenian complaints in the very beginning focused on blaming the Yugoslav leadership for domestic mismanagement, rather than asking for support in their fight for independence', it soon became obvious that 'all communication was about Slovenian independence and nothing more'.[69] The Carinthian Slovenes responded by providing Slovenian democratic forces with financial aid[70] and by organizing a protest on 27 June 1991 in front of the Yugoslav consulate in Klagenfurt, the capital of Carinthia.[71] This protest, which took place immediately after the outbreak of the Ten-Day War, presented self-determination as the only solution for both Slovenia and Croatia.

The initial Austrian position expressed by Vranitzky, who visited Belgrade before the 1990 elections in Slovenia and openly supported Yugoslav unity, provoked some concerns among the Slovenes. As a reaction, Dimitrij Rupel, first Foreign Minister of Slovenia, immediately criticized the Austrians' perceived intention of shaping and dominating Slovenia.[72] Indeed, the Austrian establishment faced a clash among different political parties in Austria over the Slovenian question. In his attempt to defend the Slovenes and undermine Vranitzky's words, Andreas Khol, a member of the Austrian People's Party, stipulated that 'the statement of the socialist chancellor was a stab in the back for Slovenia' and openly supported democratic forces which wanted to reconsider Slovenia's position within Yugoslavia.[73] This approach, which dominated political debate in Austria, was further criticized by Alois Mock, Austria's Minister of Foreign Affairs and another representative of the Christian Democrats, who explicitly supported the principles of self-determination and democratization. As he put it: 'Slovenia's future is in the hands of the Slovenes, our good neighbors ... If the outcome implies attainment of independence, Austria will react in accordance with newly displayed circumstances'.[74] For the Slovenes, this statement meant full support from Austrian diplomacy and accordingly Minister Mock was appreciated as one of the most prominent Slovenian spokespersons abroad. Having his approval meant securing the Slovenian voice within the European Community in 1991. Abroad, Mock talked about his country's appreciation for the Slovenian diaspora, Slovenes and Croats, in general, and independence as the only solution for them. In his analysis, Klaus Zeitler summarizes his intentions: 'Alois Mock was the main advocate of recognition of both Slovenia and Croatia. He tried to convince the international community to intervene militarily ... He tried to convince the Austrian government to support Slovenia logistically and in other ways. Austria even gave Slovenia loans in order to continue its import and export activities in June and July 1991'.[75]

While most of my respondents wished to remain anonymous and avoid naming individuals they viewed as being in charge of various aspects of the Slovenian diaspora policy, some directly-involved actors have offered insightful accounts and talked about individual contributions that supported the Slovenes. For example, Janez Stergar, president of the Carinthian Slovenes' Club in Ljubljana, points out that Karel Smolle, representing the Austrian Green Alternative Party, Reginald Vospernik, spokesperson for the National Council of Carinthian Slovenes, and Janko Zerzer, head of the Christian Cultural Association, together worked on the Slovenian project by fostering Slovenian diplomatic efforts vis-à-vis European leaders.[76] For all of them, the target consisted in approaching the officials in Brussels. While criticizing the European Community for being in 'a profound dream', Smolle insisted on a rapid resolution.

Karel Smolle's standpoint was of crucial relevance for both Austrian and European Community authorities. The Austrian leadership, while seeing its political involvement in line with its ethnic background, thus in favour of the Slovenian diaspora and independence of Slovenia, preferred to avoid any sort of confrontation with diaspora representatives that could have frustrated them and led to sabotage of Austria's membership of the Community.[77] In Brussels, in order to make Europeans comprehend the actual gravity of the situation, Smolle repeatedly compared the situation in Slovenia to the one in Kosovo during the 1980s. As pointed out in Chapter Three, the developments in Kosovo marked an additional cause for concern for the increasingly unpredictable relationship between the European Community and the Yugoslav federation. At the time, the Community strongly objected to the Serbian policy in Kosovo, which now seemed to be repeating itself in Slovenia. Thus, having numerous unresolved problems that extended over the whole decade, Smolle described the Yugoslav leadership as in need of expressing its frustration somehow and somewhere; accordingly, it decided to attack Slovenia.[78]

As noted in an interview with one Austrian diplomat serving in Paris at the time, daily statements drafted by diaspora organizations and press significantly shaped the overall perception of the developments of the crisis and ensured that decision-makers within the Community remained updated. The relevance of the diaspora voice is further understood if Meier's criticism of the Western diplomatic corps and their misunderstanding of the reality of Yugoslavia is taken into consideration: 'I must admit that the views which I heard from the circle of Western diplomats at this time made an almost traumatic impression'.[79] Thus, within an absence of clear policy on behalf of the official representatives, diaspora representatives were assigned an influential role.

In the interplay between diasporas, homeland and host-land leaderships and decision-makers, it was the National Council of Carinthian Slovenes which repeatedly called upon the Austrian government to recognize the independence of the Slovenian and Croatian republics. On various occasions, the Council insisted on 'urgent recognition' of the republics as a necessary step forward after they had declared their desire to leave Yugoslavia.[80] In his statement, Marijan Pipp, General Secretary of the Council, criticized the fact that the Austrian leadership paid too much attention to the information coming from Belgrade, thus ignoring the real situation across the Yugoslav federation. Based on this, the Council invited the Austrian leadership 'to take a clear standpoint in that respect and strengthen its economic relations with Slovenia and Croatia and that way help less developed regions of Carinthia and Styria'.[81]

The Slovenes insisted on their regional engagement within the remaining parts of the Yugoslav federation as well as within Austria's less-developed regions. Finally, the Council approached Minister Mock:

> The National Council of Carinthian Slovenes ... is calling the Austrian government to exploit all diplomatic means in order to prevent the bloodshed in Slovenia and Croatia ... , to consult with the United States and member states of the European Community and that way make them change their policy towards Slovenia and Croatia. Furthermore, the US and EC states should be aware of their responsibility for the situation that has

developed so far – a situation they helped develop by their ignoring policy towards Slovenia and Croatia.[82]

The majority of the documents that are available for research were drafted in the summer of 1991 and they all focus on the suffering caused by the Ten-Day War and further advocacy of international recognition of Slovenian and Croatian independence. Again here, the trend to speak in both republics' names continued: both the Slovenes in Austria, and the Austrian representatives abroad, perceived an independent Croatia as a buffer zone between Slovenia and the problematic Balkans. In their resolution, major Slovenian organizations in Austria insisted on recognition: 'We expect the governments that have already been informed about the situation in Slovenia and Croatia to recognize our independence. In addition, we expect recognition from stubborn governments who insist on Yugoslav unity at any cost, thus against the will of people who participated in its establishment ... Here, we think of the US and Member States of the European Community'.[83]

Having argued that the United States of America and, more importantly for this book, the European Community, lacked a clear and coherent standpoint on the question of Yugoslavia's unity, the Slovenian diaspora triggered doubt among European leaders. It continuously criticized their lack of attentiveness. In Brussels, EC officials knew that something was going on in Yugoslavia, but not many of them knew exactly what. Slovenian insistence on a clear EC policy meant that the officials had to sit down and study the situation in the republic and reconsider contrasting standpoints some of the Member States had already developed.[84] By doing so, the Slovenian leadership used diaspora organizations to push for additional attention at a European level.

As a result of the outbreak and outcome of the Ten-Day War, diaspora groups openly challenged both the understanding of democracy in Europe and the aim of European integration if the Yugoslav People's Army was, in their view, permitted to intervene and thus become an army of occupation.[85] Accordingly, Andrej Wakounig, president of the Unity List, a Carinthia-based party which replaced the Club of Slovenian Local Councillors, while stipulating that the attack of the

Yugoslav army 'humiliated the Slovenian nation and its young democracy', accused both the USA and the EC of 'uncivilized and malicious reservedness', implying that they had indirectly stimulated the attack through their inadequate approach towards the Yugoslav crisis.[86] The Unity List maintained that Americans and Europeans were responsible for the conflict in the homeland. This pressure for resolution was further justified due to the persistent support the Unity List had shown for Austrian membership of the European Community which at this particular point appeared to be compromised. The List questioned the point of joining the Community, an organization which does not care about its citizens: 'We do not want to join a group of states which, for their own selfish reasons, allow aggression as a response to Slovenian democratic decisions'.[87]

Other than Austria, another European state where Slovenian diaspora groups tried to contribute and speed up the process of recognition was Italy. With regard to the Italians, the resolution drafted by Slovenian organizations in Austria, despite being conceived in Carinthia, was simultaneously published in Trieste. In fact, there is nothing strange about this as the Slovenes and their diaspora representatives actually called on both Austria and Italy to recognize the independence of both Slovenia and Croatia. The Slovenian diaspora in Trieste published a newspaper article entitled 'Occupied Slovenia' in which Marij Čuk reported the attack of the Yugoslav army.[88] Consequently, the members of the Local Council referred to it as an 'unacceptable attack', and called on the international community to step in and help both Slovenian and Croatian republics in their attainment of independence.

Aware of the risk that an immediate Italian decision to recognize the two republics might encourage the further spread of conflict, the members of the Council called on the European Community to prevent military attacks and only then, once military conflict seemed impossible, they also asked the Community to support the independence of the two republics.[89] In Brussels this strategy was perceived as a direct provocation for two reasons. First, expecting a prompt response was impossible due to internal disagreements regarding the Yugoslav crisis. As already noted elsewhere, policies varied significantly among the

Member States and, in fact, most EC ambassadors expressed reluctance towards the idea of Slovenian and Croatian independence as a necessary precondition for resolution of the crisis. Second, the Community had no power to prevent military attacks; even if it had opted to rely on its Member States to step in, it would have eroded the situation both in Yugoslavia and Brussels.

However, for the Slovenian diaspora community in Italy it was important to target the Italian political elite (which held the presidency of the European Community at the time).[90] This way the Slovenes in Italy achieved a direct connection with Brussels which facilitated further communication. According to one representative of the Community, Italians tried to coordinate as many sources as possible in order to understand who was trying to obtain what and propose a solution, rather than thinking about a definitive solution for the Yugoslav federation. In this situation, diaspora groups were well aware of their own contribution. For example, most Slovenes in Italy were part of one of two main groups: the *Krizni štab Slovencev v Italiji* and the *Svet slovenskih organizacij*, both acting as intermediaries between the homeland, diaspora and decision-makers.

Although information about the activism of the first group has remained rather limited, Marko Kosin, head of the Slovenian Bureau in Rome, pointed out that its role was twofold: first, to spread the Slovenian voice on the route from Ljubljana to Brussels via Rome, and second, to collect financial aid for what was already known to be 'a new state'.[91] Indeed, communication with Rome and Brussels was smooth. In their letter addressed simultaneously to Giulio Andreotti, Prime Minister of Italy, Gianni de Michelis, Italian Foreign Minister, and Jacques Poos, European Community representative, a group of major Slovenian organizations,[92] while expressing deep concern over the unexpected hostilities in the homeland, demanded that both Italian and EC officials take an active role in resolving the Yugoslav crisis, precisely to recognize Slovenian and Croatian independence and *conditio sine qua non* for further talks and crisis resolution within the federation.[93] Here, in addition, the Slovenes insisted that the presence of the Yugoslav army in Slovenia represented an indirect threat for Italy.[94] This suggestion, which was confirmed in Trieste during demonstrations on 30

June 1991, aimed to bring about the following: an immediate end to fighting, new talks based on respect for Slovenian and Croatian independence, understanding and support from the international community, Italian and European recognition, and finally, full respect of the Osimo Agreements.[95]

The *Svet slovenskih organizacij* acted as a direct external supporter of the Slovenian government. In her letter to the homeland, Maria Ferletič, president of the organization, expressed both sorrow for the violence in the streets of Ljubljana and happiness that the same violence ended quickly and allowed the Slovenes to continue working towards their European goal.[96] In other words, the homeland was obtaining moral support for adhering to its initial policy, which was complemented by financial assistance. Here, the diaspora thought that the homeland had more chance in the fight for independence if provided with adequate financial contributions – an understanding based on the assumption that financial aid was necessary to secure additional arms if necessary, to cover unexpected official trips and to sponsor various publishing materials about the reality of the Slovenian situation.

Although predominantly active in North America, the activism of the Slovenian World Congress followed the demonstrations in Trieste and offered its full support to the diaspora members within Europe. It proclaimed the week of 8–12 July 1991 to be the week of solidarity during which different Slovenian associations would intensively lobby for their homeland. The Congress advocated that, in different ways, the Slovenes had to try to influence public opinion to recognize the independence of Slovenia. In order to succeed in this, it stipulated: 'We should get the best experts with contacts in different ministries and institutions'.[97]

Indeed, if analysed together, the *Krizni štab Slovencev v Italiji*, the *Svet slovenskih organizacij* and the Slovenian World Congress shared a common objective: an independent homeland. However, as maintained by the Slovenian minorities in Austria, Italy and Hungary, who were desperately hoping for and looking forward to the independence of their homeland as 'the best guarantee to avoid new attacks against Slovenia', continuation of good relations with all neighbouring countries was crucial.[98] Regardless of the general strategy adopted by the

Slovenes – to fight for both their statehood and that of Croatia – commitment to the surrounding countries always appeared to dominate diaspora discourse, as it was believed that advocacy of strong ties with them would contribute to the European policy that would soon after be formulated.

Conclusion

As demonstrated throughout the chapter, diaspora discourse is very much about communication. With regard to the Yugoslav state crisis, successful activism required a well developed strategy aimed at approaching targeted groups and trying to contribute to policy-making. Across the European Community, Slovenian diaspora groups played a far more important role than any other republic's diaspora members. While this may seem strange, especially if we think of the size of the Croatian diaspora, the Slovenian vision of the future of the wealthiest Yugoslav republic as an independent state was more established and better conceptualized than that shaped by the Croats. While for the Slovenian diaspora, self-determination of their homeland appeared to be the only acceptable outcome, the Croatian diaspora occasionally appeared divided as their homeland often included a significant Serbian component – obvious both at home and abroad where numerous marriages uniting Serbs and Croats offered different positions vis-à-vis the future of the Yugoslav federation. However, this did not prevent the Slovenian diaspora from advocating international recognition of both Slovenia and Croatia.

In Europe, the Slovenes relied on direct support from the Carinthian Slovenes who had strengthened their political relevance within the host-land while acting as advocates of independence. Therefore, Austria's initial and short advocacy of Yugoslav unity, vehemently criticized by the Slovenes who believed that immediate support for independence might help avoid further conflict, had nothing to do with diaspora activism. Regardless of the Austrian official standpoint, initial, intermediate or final, the diaspora members worked towards the achievement of their objective. Their work was acknowledged by Janez Dular, the Minister of Slovenian Diaspora, who expressed thanks to the Carinthian Slovenes for 'spreading information among the Austrian public and government'.[99] Once the Austrians said 'yes' to Slovenian and Croatian demands, activism spread outside Austria. Therefore, unsurprisingly, it took less time for the Italians than for the Austrians to establish a clear position on the Yugoslav crisis. Thus, this was a byproduct of diaspora activism which had already shaped public opinion in Austria; and based on its success in Carinthia, Italy was a more straightforward target. On two occasions, the Italian government demonstrated sympathy and its intention to recognize Slovenia and Croatia as independent states: first, in July 1991, during a parliamentary debate,[100] and second, in September 1991, when the Slovenian diaspora arranged for 20,000 postcards exclaiming 'Yes to Slovenian and Croatian Independence!' to reach Andreotti's cabinet.[101]

The Austrian government was the first government to openly recognize Slovenia and Croatia as independent states. The Austrians played a significant role as they encouraged other Member States of the European Community to take the situation seriously within the two republics, and in Yugoslavia in general. As observed by Vranitzky after the EC Ministerial meeting on 16 December 1991, 'in reality, the EC Foreign Ministers decided to do what we had decided two-and-a-half months ago on principle, namely to recognize Slovenia and Croatia'.[102]

In the struggle surrounding the international recognition of Slovenia and Croatia, the diaspora voice alongside its two strongest allies – media and churches – meant that decision-makers could not turn a blind eye to what prominent representatives living abroad, but fighting for their homeland, had to say and indeed demanded. The following chapter will complement the debate about the role of non-state actors during the Yugoslav crisis by looking at the media and their capacity to affect the EC policy-making processes.

CHAPTER FIVE

MEDIA POWER

Media Influence on European Community Policy

The presence of media is constant at every turn: at home while watching or listening to the morning news, at underground stations where picking up a copy of a free daily newspaper has become an almost automatic action, at work while occasionally checking the breaking news on the Internet, etc. These examples demonstrate an inevitable contact with the media that understandably encourages discourse about media power. During conflicts, propaganda-focused reporting gains significant power as it manages to shape public opinion by selecting which stories to disseminate.

Both Yugoslav and European media accompanied the outbreak of the Yugoslav crisis from its very beginning. For example, one scholar noted the controversial role of the mass media: 'The media discourse was both an indicator of and a contributor to the crisis, highlighting deep divisions that began to open up, while at the same time helping redraw boundaries between ethnic groups in conflict and establishing legitimacy for the actions of their respective political leadership'.[1] Later, the outbreak of the war in Yugoslavia simply reconfirmed the powerful activism of the media, which very soon confronted the public with the so-called media war in which opposing media representatives fought to promote their stories as the dominant ones. Therefore, as observed by Vojin Dimitrijević, the media acted as 'a transmission belt in the partitioning' of Yugoslavia as 'they served to complete its bursting along national and nationalistic seams, and they did it with unbelievable ease, without responsibility, without conscience'.[2]

The media war approached the public through sensational news or brief commentary, and often inventing enemies and victims proved to be effective strategies for polarization. Indeed, the parties in the conflict aimed at attracting the attention of the media in order to present only their own sufferings. It is 'through routine representations of reality' that 'the media can persuade, change and mobilize ... public understanding of the world, and in indirect and contingent ways, public attitudes and behaviour'.[3] In Yugoslavia it was the media that dominated public perception by presenting Serbs, Croats and Slovenes respectively as victims of the other side. The media abroad followed this pattern and reported on the Yugoslav drama by presenting the stories which had already prevailed within some of the constituent republics of the federation.

In the European Community, where decisions about the Yugoslav crisis were still pending, media coverage secured relevance. As this chapter will show, EC authorities relied on specific media reporting and accordingly produced their official statements. In his account, Tarik Jusić correctly warns: 'Since any political process is subject to interpretation, journalists' norms and routines will have a significant impact on which interpretations enter the discourses, thus contributing to the overall political atmosphere surrounding the conflict'.[4] In decision-making processes, this means that any information the media disseminate will certainly be taken into consideration: 'While rhetoric is intended to manipulate the audience, it may "strike back" and influence the thinking and actions of the speakers themselves. Politicians may become prisoners of the images and perceptions they have conjured up, both directly, as these images influence their own way of thinking, and indirectly, since politicians need the support of their followers'.[5]

The account offered here, as well as demonstrating the situation with regard to media activism in Slovenia and Croatia, will show that the Western media favoured the two republics' positions and, accordingly, those positions gained relevance for the decision-makers in Brussels. In order to develop their policies vis-à-vis the SFRY, European officials often relied on the media as a useful source of information in order to shape their own policies and, finally, the future of the Yugoslav state.

Yugoslav Media and the Public

Communist Yugoslavia was characterized by a decentralized media system. Each of the constituent republics had its own communication system which was largely independent of central government. In his study, Spyros Sofos analyses the situation prior to the 1974 constitution and notes that this system was 'segmented along republic borders ... Yugoslavia's artificial and arbitrary internal, administrative borders were progressively "upgraded" to national or "civilizational" fault-lines and increasingly became communications barriers'.[6] This segmentation, whether due to economic, political, geographical or cultural reasons, existed between Slovenian and Macedonian, Croatian and Serbian, or Serbian and Kosovo Albanian public information spheres. However, once it became obvious that Tito's era was drawing to a close, the media were presented with an opportunity to modify their activism. In short, as soon as the republican Communist leaders became increasingly critical of each other and of the federal structure of the state, the media also became critical as 'astute journalists were able to create space for genuinely independent work by exploiting new divisions among the authorities'.[7] This new atmosphere encouraged fresh concern regarding control over the media. Sofos demonstrates that as the political leadership understood the chance of benefiting from their linkage with nationalist frictions, battles over the media arose 'between those who chose nationalism as their preferred political idiom and those who, for reasons varying from an adherence to Yugoslavia and its civic connotations to retaining political control, elected to follow the increasingly unpopular route of resistance to nationalism'.[8]

In Serbia and Croatia, the media were concerned with their new leaders: the Serbian media glorified Milošević as the 'new Tito', while the Croatian media presented Tudjman as the 'father of the nation' – the switch which easily replaced the common message about Yugoslav brotherhood and unity with a negative message about the neighbours, and which invited 'propagandistic enforcement' of hatred.[9] In fact, as one author points out, '"patriotic journalism" in Serbia under Milošević and in Croatia under Tudjman operated on the same simple formula: Yugoslav patriotism was replaced with Serb or Croat patriotism, Communist ideology with nationalist ideology, the old ruling party's dictates with the new ruling party's dictates'.[10] By contrast, the Slovenian media focused on the Yugoslav system as unworkable and collapsing. Accordingly, the main change characterizing the Slovenian media which in the late 1980s experienced 'a golden age of freedom and expression', was due to the intensification of tensions developing between the statesmen of Yugoslavia's constituent republics in the 1980s: 'In particular, the leadership in Slovenia developed economic and political criticisms of the way the government in Belgrade was running the country ... As part of their campaign against Belgrade, they began to allow, if not encourage, criticisms from below. All sorts of people, including journalists, now found that they had new freedoms to express their views of society'.[11]

This new situation allowed the public to approach the media and encouraged debate over the nature of the federation and its future. The most commonly debated issue was the extent to which the population across Yugoslavia felt victimized. In the literature, victimization is generally perceived as 'the most frequently used discourse strategy ... by nationalists of different ideological orientations, from orthodoxy-inspired conservatives to left-wing critics of imperialism'.[12] In 1987, soon after Milošević's visit to Kosovo, the Serbian media produced material which talked about 'the victimization of Serbs in Yugoslavia and the danger faced by the Serbian nation if the Federation continued to ignore its plight'.[13] Therefore, the Serbian public living outside Serbia, while feeling discriminated against and threatened by local regimes and people, favoured the idea of strengthening links with Serbia. The ambition of identity construction implies even greater marginalization and exclusion between 'us' and 'them' – a relational connection between two or more opposing sides. In this regard, identification of numerous enemies of the Serbian nation – Croats, Albanians and Muslims – was expected to help construct a solid Serbian identity.

In Croatia, victimization was understood in a different way: the Croats saw themselves as victims of the Serbian enemy, but in their own country. The confrontation between the two intensified after Milošević's victory in the Serbian elections, in December 1990, which practically encouraged the Serbian Democratic Party in Croatia (SDS) to react against the Croatian police. In his study, Valere Gagnon talks about these 'purposefully provoked conflicts' which in Belgrade's view necessitated the involvement of the Yugoslav army in order to 'separate the feuding ethnic groups' and avoid 'the Croatian regime's intentions to rid itself of its Serb population' – a significant controversy as in February 1991 the Serb-populated region of Krajina proclaimed its independence from Croatia.[14] Thus, when the conflict in Croatia turned into war, it became even easier for the media to file reports of the Croatian republic as a victim due to the existence of real evidence – a number of locations where Serbian aggression was taking place.

Finally, in Slovenia, the media had the clearest vision both vis-à-vis the Yugoslav federation and the Slovenian republic on its own: the federation was no longer serving the Slovenes. In its legendary 1987 issue, the Slovenian cultural magazine *Nova Revija* published a collection of sixteen articles entitled 'Contributions to the Slovene National Program' and talked about Slovenian nationhood and need for independence.[15] This programme, which was an absolute shock for the Slovenian Communist Party, examined all sorts of opportune aspects to justify the need for independence. Within a year, the Slovenian media adopted an approach which focused exclusively on the Slovenian republic, the republican government and the Slovenes. As some authors put it: 'The belief in the inevitability of secession was so strong that announcers and journalists regularly treated Slovenia's statehood as a *fait accompli*, even before the actual proclamation of independence ... Deictic expressions signaling attachment to a wider Yugoslav "we", still so unambiguously present in 1988, had by this time almost disappeared'.[16]

No matter how significant the above-mentioned issues were, the European Community did not have any awareness of them. It is worth recalling that although from 1973 on, the Community maintained two press and information centres in Yugoslavia, one in Belgrade and one in Zagreb, their responsibilities were limited: they mainly monitored economic and, when present, political cooperation between the two sides,[17] rather than what the media and public had to say about their homeland, inter-republican relations, future aspirations, etc. Later, with the outbreak of the Yugoslav crisis, the EC, however, paid attention primarily to the American media and their reporting of the drama.[18] This American voice reached the Europeans in Brussels as a result of daily correspondence between the US and EC diplomatic missions. Still, what becomes obvious when looking at various EC documents is that media coverage of the period preceding the state crisis did not enjoy much attention from the Brussels administration. Actually, full attention to the media about the situation in Yugoslavia began specifically with the Ten-Day War in Slovenia. For the Slovenes and Croats this proved to be an opportunity for securing Western attention and receiving media support for their stories, of a kind that ensured that international recognition of their independence seemed to be the only rational solution.

Awakening of the Western Media

As already indicated, in 1988, Slovenian dissatisfaction with the SFRY was heading towards a critical level. While openly acknowledging this within its own territory and to a lesser extent across the federation, not much attention was attributed to the Slovenian situation in Western media. Thus, instead of expecting the West to become interested in Slovenian affairs, the Slovenian media and public decided to approach the Europeans, a strategy characterized by glorification of Western European values that, in their view, were continuously undermined by the Yugoslav leadership.[19] Furthermore, the media and public used the outbreak of war in Slovenia to underline that the European Community was an ideal capable of accommodating their demands: 'The Slovenes are in favour of European space ... this commitment is reflected through cultural, economic, political and other linkages with European states ... Entering European space appears essential for the nation's survival and development'.[20] Strongly supporting the West, this argument faced no obstacles from the Western media. In fact, the Western media decided to place their journalists in Slovenia in order to get a clearer picture of the conflict.[21] For example, one foreign reporter commented: 'The Slovenian Information Ministry organized a media center in a modern underground conference hall in Ljubljana. Here troops of young multilingual Slovenes constantly churned out reams of war bulletins ... We were supplied with excruciatingly detailed accounts of battles too far away to check personally before deadline. Often we learned the next day that the battles had never taken place'.[22]

As a result, some EC Member States reported Slovenia as pro-European and willing to strengthen its links with the Community in general. For *Der Standard*, while the Yugoslav crisis was threatening European stability, Slovenia was portrayed as the only republic whose standards went hand in hand with the European ones.[23] In Italy, the *Corriere della Sera* talked about links between the two neighbours – the Italian community in Slovenia and the Slovenian community in Italy – and frequently discussed Slovenia's capacity to comply with Western values and its unwillingness to be a victim of Milošević's dictatorship.[24] Being characterized as an emerging state between Europe and the Balkans, Slovenia enjoyed considerable support from the Italian media. Another newspaper reported the meeting held in the Italian Ministry of Foreign Affairs where the authorities expressed different standpoints about Yugoslavia: while the minority favoured a united SFRY, the majority respected the objectives of the Slovenian and Croatian leaderships and insisted on the right to self-determination in case of a military attack against Slovenia and Croatia – a scenario which in de Michelis' terms meant that 'Italy would support independence over unity'.[25]

Finally, the German media expressed open appreciation for the republics of Slovenia and Croatia. One scholar analysed the situation in Germany and concluded that the German media were decidedly in favour of the two seceding republics.[26] For *Die Zeit*, the Yugoslav project was over even before the outbreak of war in Slovenia. While reporting about Slovenia's aspirations to become a member of the European Community and the risk and potential gravity of civil war in Croatia, the paper portrayed the Serbs as a threat to the stability of the region.[27] This is what I identify to be the dominant coverage among Western media at the time. With regard to Slovenia and Croatia alone, although the *Süddeutsche Zeitung* initially questioned their independence, very soon its reporting changed and complemented the *Frankfurter Allgemeine Zeitung*'s (FAZ) perception of the two republics. In fact, Diana Johnstone notes how Johann Georg Reismüller, the FAZ editor, supported Slovenian and Croatian independence which would bring them closer to Europe while the Serbs were portrayed as 'militarist Bolsheviks' who had 'no place in the European Community'.[28]

In Croatia, by contrast, the media and public did not talk about European Community membership as their final objective. Indeed, the complexity of the situation did not allow any discourse that went this far. For example, some authors examine Croatian and Serbian reporting about elections in Croatia and the Serb and Croat referendums and conclude that 'the ethnic sentiments of the electorate were extensively manipulated and exploited by the parties that competed for the status' within the Croatian republic and, accordingly, dominant etiquettes characterizing the two sides usually distinguished between 'good us' and 'bad them', and referred to the national question, etc.[29] Still, as soon as the war was at Croatia's doorstep, *Die Zeit* decided to maintain certain reservations: 'It would be insane to intervene militarily of one's own free will in the Balkan chaos ... However, if they are determined to give vent to their Serbo-Croatian hatred, then one should leave them to it'.[30] In reaction, the Croatian media and public began accusing the Europeans of a lack of action.

Thus, in order to approach the West and gain attention, the Croatian strategy consisted of accusing both the Serbs of aggression and the West of being too lazy to prevent it, and then postponing any significant steps to stop it. In her reporting, Branka Magaš warned: 'The longer the war continues, the more bitter Croat-Serb relations will become and the more difficult it will be to envisage a peaceful future for this part of the Balkans. This is why it is imperative that the European Community and the nations comprising the ECSC intervene to put an end to the aggression of Serbia and its allies against Croatia, before the war spills across Yugoslavia and over its international borders'.[31] By calling on the West to intervene in the conflict, the Croatian media gained relevant attention among the media abroad. As assessed by one diplomat: 'Western media, while largely remaining short of information about the Serbs, Macedonians or Albanians, talked about Slovenian and Croatian suffering. Not surprisingly, reporting usually talked about independence as the best solution for the two republics which, in the end, the Western public unconsciously adopted'.[32] Indeed, a day-by-day development of the hostilities in Yugoslavia implied a growing interest in the media and their stories about the conflict and war. Thus, before the EC even managed to crystallize its own standpoint vis-à-vis the SFRY, the Western media had used their power to contribute to the final policy.

In addition, the whole discourse about the support from the Western media was further strengthened when Croatian intellectuals became involved in order to convince the Europeans that assisting the Croats would not have negative consequences: 'There is no objective danger that Europe would allow itself to become Balkanized ... Europe is mature enough, strong and wise and can no more be stopped on its way to welfare and progress'.[33] In his account, Boris Buden argues that the Croatian situation was gradually gaining attention within the European Community: 'In the civilized zones of Europe interest has been awoken in what is going on in this zoo. It means two things: either they are fed up with this dark pan-Slavic howling, or they are already seized by a panic that the widely-known Balkan-Byzantine-Bolshevist fairness could also infect their own people'.[34] However, on closer inspection of Buden's arguments, their relevance is highly questionable as the Europeans and, more relevantly, European policy-makers were already aware of the probability that the Community was going to enlarge and grant membership to some Slavic countries and that therefore the idea of a pan-Slavic threat was non-existent.

At this point, the above arguments surely raise the question of the position of the Serbian side. The Serbian media and public were not successful in building strong links across the European Community, mainly because the Serbian authorities were not even interested in securing Western media support. In his account, Gagnon shows that for them it was important to convince the Serbian audience, both in Serbia and elsewhere in the federation, that their policies were the right ones.[35] Therefore, the media had to be active at home and focus on developments across the federation rather than trying to influence EC officials and secure support for any later manoeuvres. By looking inwards rather than outwards, the Serbian media minimized their relevance and remained almost unheard abroad. They reported news of the SFRY and how to defend its unity. They accused Slovenian and Croatian leaders of 'political maneuvering' and questioning Yugoslavia's future.[36] However, Serbia's decision to ignore the idea of seeking approval among the Western media for its leadership's policies contributed to what some termed as the 'demonization of Serbs' – a situation in which Western media undermined the Serbs in every sense due to a complete lack of balanced information about the wars.[37]

European Community Reactions

The European Community lacked mechanisms to develop a clear standpoint and publish precise reports about what was happening in Yugoslavia and suggest necessary steps. As one article noted, '[s]everal months before the war in Slovenia, Austrian politicians talked about the danger of war in a very serious and reasonable manner, but the EC did not listen to them'.[38] When the war broke out, the article continued, 'no-one in West European ministries of foreign affairs knew any Serbian politicians or generals to approach and discuss the termination of conflict'.[39] This being the case, Western media houses decided to step in on their own and discuss the Yugoslav situation. Accordingly, their reports were rather pessimistic. For example, they communicated that Tito's dream of brotherhood and unity was over and that future developments in the SFRY were a matter of prediction, as the Serbian leadership rejected the idea of a confederation proposed by the Slovenes and Croats.[40] On various occasions, the Western media did express interest in taking EC diplomatic sources into consideration, but the incoherent nature of these sources meant that sticking to their previous model of reporting, which ignored EC official press material, was far more efficient. Therefore, the conflict in Yugoslavia allowed the Western media to benefit from the circumstances by developing a clear, recognizable and influential narrative. In fact, the full relevance of the media became apparent as soon as the Community commenced to shape its own press releases and indicate further policies based exactly on the media reporting.

With regard to the Community, within the initial months of the crisis, it managed to deliver press communications which varied significantly. In order to illustrate this, I identify three of the Community's official press releases. For example, in March 1991, the Community followed 'with the greatest concern the situation in Yugoslavia' and maintained the belief that 'the process of moving Yugoslav society in the direction of democratic reforms satisfactory to all Yugoslavia should be based on the results of a political dialogue between all parties concerned'.[41] By encouraging dialogue that in the Community's understanding might have been beneficial for all the federation, the Europeans justified their initial approach towards the SFRY – unity. This process, as stipulated in the press report, 'will enable the full development of the cooperation which already exists between the Community and the Federal authorities. In the view of the Twelve, a united and democratic Yugoslavia stands the best chance to integrate itself in the new Europe'.[42] This rather optimistic statement was an inadequate response to the events tormenting Yugoslavia at the time. The Community's immunity to the media at this stage is best explained by looking at the very last sentence of the press release in which the EC saw the SFRY within the new Europe – a concept that had already been abandoned in Slovenia where the media talked about the Slovenes as the only ones seeking and deserving a place within the new Europe, rather than the whole federation.

In May, the Community's voice lost a degree of the previous optimism and called on 'all those in charge of the institutions, bodies and constituted authorities of the country to act in accordance with the rule of law and to ensure their normal functioning'.[43] This was just another broad concept that Western diplomats considered sufficient to mitigate the crisis. Contrary to the previous statement, there was no mention of the SFRY joining the new Europe, but clear opposition to the use of force and loss of human lives. However, at this stage, the Brussels administration expressed some interest in the media. In his account, Andreas Kintis criticizes the EC Member States' lack of will which consequently resulted in 'the inevitable rendering [of the Yugoslav conflict] on the media' which 'led to widespread public disenchantment' across the Community.[44] Thus, the EC's schizophrenic approach towards the Yugoslav federation required an immediate revision and the media became a reliable source of information.

Subsequently, European confusion continued, as the June 1991 statement seemed to be in favour of the developments in the federation. The EC was optimistic again: 'The Community and its Member States have noted with satisfaction the outcome of the meeting of the six Presidents of the Republics, held on June 6 in Sarajevo ... The Community and its Member States express the hope that their future meetings will lead to further progress'.[45] Indeed, it soon proved that this was just a short-lived hope as the meeting in Sarajevo did not produce any durable results. The Community argued that normalization of the situation in Yugoslavia 'will permit a new dimension to the relations between the Community and Yugoslavia in accordance with the traditional ties that unite them'.[46] Apart from its erroneous reporting about normalization of the crisis, the Community mentioned something that requires further clarification – traditional ties. Here, the EC statement presented traditional ties as a positive link between the two parties, although they certainly did not exist. As demonstrated in Chapters Two and Three, from the moment of the official establishment of EEC–SFRY relations in 1968, traditional ties that developed implied discord, uncertainty and reconsideration of the existing agreements.

The Ten-Day War dictated a reconsideration of the above-mentioned scenarios. First, it annulled the idea of the SFRY and a new Europe. Second, it showed that diplomatic efforts were insufficient, but they still represented the option of choice due to the lack of an alternative approach. Third, the Community published erroneous facts about its relation with Yugoslavia – if it had been more positive, then the crisis could have been dealt with differently or even avoided. Fourth, and more importantly for our discussion here, the Community's approach provided a space for the media to start shaping EC policy. In their joint statement, Hans Van den Broek and James Baker, representing the European Community and the United States of America respectively, acknowledged the worsening dimension of the situation in Yugoslavia. The two officials advocated a cooling-off period which was expected to allow negotiations between the conflicting parties: 'We urge all leaders in Yugoslavia to exert maximum influence on armed forces of any kind throughout Yugoslavia and to refrain from the use of force or from provocative acts'.[47]

With regard to the situation in Yugoslavia at the time, media activism might have contributed to provocative acts, as the media on each side of the opposing republics got involved in propagandistic reporting aimed at undermining the opponent. With regard to the situation in Brussels, Michael Libal, a German diplomat, later recalled in his memoirs, that by the beginning of July 1991, 'criticism of EC policies by German politicians and the media had reached a crescendo ... the then secretary-general of the Christian Democratic Union [CDU], Volker Rühe, asked the EC to open the prospect of recognition to Slovenia and Croatia, in order to demonstrate political and moral support for these two parties. The former head of the Social Democrats, Hans-Jochen Vogel, joined in this demand'.[48] In addition, Sir Harry Hinsley, an English historian, commented for *The Times* that 'the [EC] Commission is best fitted for dealing with soap, apples and herrings, but not good at dealing with Serbs. It is composed of busybodies with not enough to do'.[49] Thus, both Libal's and Hinsley's words confirm the (direct or indirect) presence of the media and their readiness to criticize the European Community and its lack of policy.

I identify three European Community documents that took the Western media seriously: *Declaration on the situation in Yugoslavia* of 5 July 1991 and two *Declarations on Yugoslavia*, one announced on 6 August and the other on 20 August 1991, all of them drafted in The Hague where the extraordinary ministerial meetings regularly took place. The first document complemented the stories focusing on independence, already spread by Slovenian and Croatian media. This was obvious in two instances: first, the declaration stressed that 'it is only for the peoples of Yugoslavia themselves to decide on the country's future', and second, it called for a dialogue 'without preconditions between all parties on the principles enshrined in the Helsinki Final Act and the Paris Charter for a New Europe, in particular respect for human rights, including rights of minorities and the right of peoples to self-determination'.[50] With these words, the declaration openly envisaged the possibility of Slovenian and Croatian independence and thus Yugoslavia's disintegration. Nevertheless, the Community's standpoint was not fully clear, a fact obvious from the declaration's concluding remarks: 'The Community and its Member States will have to consider again their position in the event of any further breach of the cease-fire; in particular should unilateral military action be taken'.[51] By offering such a vague approach, the Community demonstrated that any sort of policy on how to deal with the Yugoslav crisis was yet to come.

The two subsequent declarations seemed to offer a clearer point of view. The first *Declaration on Yugoslavia* stressed: '[The Community and its Member States] strongly condemn the continuing use of force and attempts of any republic to impose by force solutions on other republics'.[52] Here, they indirectly objected to the Serbian attempt to keep the Yugoslav federation together at any cost. Their standpoint advocated 'a peaceful solution to Yugoslavia's problems, not only for the sake of Yugoslavia itself and its constituent peoples, but for Europe as a whole'.[53] Apart from being informed by the violence in Slovenia, this Community statement was influenced by the media as well due to their increased reporting of the Yugoslav crisis as a potential threat to European stability. While for the *Corriere della Sera*, European stability was facing different threats and the Yugoslav crisis was one of them,[54] *Le Monde Diplomatique* discussed Yugoslav liberalism and its eventual impact on European security.[55] Along the same lines, German-speaking media reported possible problems: *Der Standard* called for greater attention to be paid to the Yugoslav crisis in order to preserve European stability,[56] whereas the FAZ maintained that security and cooperation in Europe were facing a challenge and reported Germany's desire for a unified EC policy.[57]

Finally, the declaration pointed out: 'The Community and its Member States are concerned to draw to the attention of those responsible for the present deadlock the consequences, for the whole of Yugoslavia, of deterioration of the situation and of further delay in starting the negotiations of the future of the country'.[58] Thus, while much of the Community's statements only repeated what Western media had already reported, the Community abstained from naming any particular actor, or even republic, as bearing responsibility for the ongoing situation in the SFRY. As explained by one diplomat, this was often a product of the Community's indecisiveness regarding the crisis: 'Although media reporting was taken seriously among the policy-makers, none of them wanted to say that the material policies were possibly going to be inspired by what was actually taken from the media – an idea that could have discredited the seriousness of all the efforts to deal with the crisis'.[59]

The second *Declaration on Yugoslavia* went a step further. It complemented the previous one by presenting its understanding of Yugoslavia's borders: 'Any change of internal and international borders by force is not acceptable and any solution should guarantee the rights of peoples and minorities in all the Republics'.[60] Of course, if analysed word by word, this rather controversial statement indicated that peaceful changes of borders were acceptable. This Community observation was due to the already ongoing conflict in Croatia: 'The Community and its Member States cannot stand idly by as the bloodshed in Croatia increases day by day. An agreement on the monitoring of the cease-fire and its maintenance should allow the Community and its Member States to convene a peace conference and establish an arbitration procedure'.[61] However, the decision to launch a peace conference and arbitration procedure provided once again additional time for both the media and policy-makers to strengthen or shape their positions.

By the end of summer 1991, Television Ljubljana (TVL), shortly after renamed Television Slovenia (TVS), had fully embraced the idea of an independent Slovenia. Although its recognition was still pending, domestic reporting ignored the concept of Yugoslavia as a single country and discredited federal institutions, but rather talked about the Slovenian state and its future perspective within the European Community. Later, one study acknowledged: 'The gaze of TV Slovenia was directed westwards: "the West", "the world" and "Europe" now assumed the prime role of Slovenia's most significant other, one seen as mirroring the new Slovenian identity, associated with independence, democracy and Europeanization'.[62] Of course, the Ten-Day War provided the Slovenes with an additional motive to further consolidate their approach. Accordingly, the media relied constantly on the gravity of the brief war conducted in Slovenia, condemned the aggression of the Serbian leadership, while insisting that the Europeans react, or, in other words, recognize Slovenian independence as soon as possible.

Media Relevance for European Decision-Making

In his study of lobbying in the European Union, Rinus van Schendelen attributes significant importance to media power: 'The mass media need only a wisp of smoke in order to report a big fire, which may burn the officials'.[63] Here, the author refers to the existence of an inseparable relationship in which the Brussels officials 'are usually sensitive to lyric and high-grade publicity in the mass media'.[64] With regard to the Yugoslav state crisis, the Ten-Day War confirmed the link between the media and policy-makers: Slovenian and Croatian reporting, as well as the attention the Western media and public paid to the violence following the two republics' decision to leave the Yugoslav federation and declare independence, raised concerns among European officials. Most of the media supported what Noel Malcolm described as the only way forward:

> The only way to recover anything resembling stability now is for the West to recognize Croatia and Slovenia as quickly as possible, and to encourage them to complete on generous terms the unfinished negotiations over their exit from Yugoslavia. The European Community and the United States still have an enormous moral authority over the Slovenes and Croats who desperately think of themselves as fully Western. But if we continue to reject their claims to independence, we shall only weaken the Western-looking aspect of their nationalism, thereby helping to turn them into the very kind of resentful vendetta-obsessed isolationists that Western policy-makers should most fear.[65]

Although the media and public in Austria supported Slovenia and Croatia, some Austrian statesmen were initially divided: while Erhard

Busek, Vice-Chancellor of Austria, urged his state to recognize the two republics even in the eventuality of the Community not doing so, Alois Mock, Foreign Minister of Austria, disputed Busek's ambitions and maintained that Austria would prefer to recognize them alongside other EC Member States.[66] While determined not to compromise Austria's membership of the European Union, Mock used his position to warn the Europeans not to explore instant recognition without taking into consideration the negative consequences that could possibly ensue, due to the uncertain situation in Croatia.[67] Accordingly, opposing standpoints existing within some European countries encouraged policy-makers to follow the media which regularly questioned external reaction to the crisis. For example, the German media, at the time, enjoyed a significant reputation in Brussels. In her study, Lucarelli examines the situation in Germany and argues that the local media shaped the government's position, which turned into the German position when negotiating at the European Community level.[68] Indeed, the best way to understand the relevance of the German media for the Community's position is to look into the EC press releases. Very often, these officially approved statements simply repeated what the German media had already discussed and suggested.

The Community's initial response to the Yugoslav crisis was characterized by an economic dimension, rather than political considerations. This corresponds to the arguments presented in chapters on relations between the Community and Yugoslavia before the actual crisis. While in the past the relationship between them was mostly cultivated because of economic interests, the EC thought of economic measures as an instrument to prevent a greater spread of violence in the SFRY.[69] Accordingly, the 1991 *General Report* talked about 'the uncertainty surrounding the future of the Yugoslav federation following the declarations of independence by Slovenia and Croatia', and the Community's decision to suspend the third financial protocol, which was signed in Brussels on 24 June 1991 and expected to cover the period from 1 July 1991 to 30 June 1996.[70] In addition to this, Yugoslavia lost its place among the beneficiary countries under the system of generalized preferences.[71] However, the immediate effect of economic measures did not help.

The media in Slovenia and Croatia objected to the Community's behaviour as it had an obvious impact on their own economic performance. It was not clear why the Community should punish the whole country instead of only Serbia. In fact, the two republics felt illtreated because they held that only the Serbian leadership was responsible for the Yugoslav crisis. The Western media served the two republics by reporting their views which attracted further attention from policy-makers.[72] As a result, the economic measures, previously acknowledged as a good tool for combating the Yugoslav conflict, faced immediate amendments. Due to growing pressure, finding a political solution for the Yugoslav problem was given greater weight than the adverse effects of economic sanctions. In this respect, the Council adopted 'corrective positive measures' which provided Slovenia, Croatia, Bosnia-Herzegovina and Macedonia with the preferential arrangements they had already enjoyed before the Community's decision to suspend them.[73] Two other institutions were to reactivate their programmes, as well: the Commission resumed technical assistance originally intended for the SFRY, but now for the four republics only, and the EIB resumed the financial cooperation established under the second EC–Yugoslavia financial protocol.[74]

In Slovenia and Croatia, the media appreciated Europe's change of strategy. In Germany, the media insisted that the two republics should not be penalized. In their attempt to persuade EC officials, the media, while reporting Europe's Balkan dilemma, insisted that 'the Europeans should be thankful to Milošević as he drew attention to their illusions' about the Yugoslav federation.[75] Apart from this, the German media advocated an ever greater role for Western moral responsibility in assisting the SFRY.[76] This newly suggested approach was embraced in Brussels and reflected in the Community's forthcoming statements. The EC released another of its numerous declarations on Yugoslavia, expressing for the first time its opinion about actors responsible for the Yugoslav crisis: 'It is a deeply misguided policy on the part of the Serbian irregulars to try to solve the problems they expect to encounter in a new constitutional order through military means. It is even more disconcerting that it can no longer be denied that elements of the Yugoslav People's Army are lending their active support to the Serbian side'.[77]

As soon as the Community had adopted a clearer standpoint towards the SFRY and identified the culpable party, the media received indirect support for their reporting and a greater opportunity of influencing the public. Indeed, some scholars point out that politics is about persuasion: 'It hinges not just on whether citizens at any one moment in time tend to favour one side of an issue over another, but on the numbers of them that can be brought, when push comes to shove, from one side to the other or, indeed, induced to leave the sidelines in order to take a side ... Persuasion is ubiquitous in the political process; it is also the central aim of political interaction'.[78] If applied to the Yugoslav crisis at the time, persuasion developed rather quickly. From the media to policy-makers and back to the media and public, the SFRY was gaining ever growing attention. As confirmed by some Community actors and respondents in my study, most of the statements the Community delivered simply followed and repeated what the media had already said and proposed as a solution for the Yugoslav case.

The media insisted on the differences existing between the Yugoslav peoples in order to push forward the idea that these peoples should be free to decide upon their future. The Community acknowledged this aspect only prior to the Peace Conference at The Hague when it stressed its willingness to 'adopt arrangements to ensure peaceful accommodation of the conflicting aspirations of the Yugoslav peoples'.[79] Although very sound, this statement was incapable of producing any substantial result for two reasons. First, the EC limited its performance to 'monitoring activities' — activities which the media described as insufficient and inadequate. Second, most of the Community's statement was inspired by the hope of conflict resolution: 'The Community and its Member States hope that a normalization of the situation will permit them to put into effect as soon as possible the financial protocols so as to contribute to the indispensable economic recovery of the country'.[80] However, only four days later, during the opening of the Conference on Yugoslavia, the Community, while advocating a lasting solution to the crisis, noted that the conference marked 'the beginning of the negotiations on the future of Yugoslavia and its people'.[81]

The relevance of this meeting can be recognized as the beginning of the end of the Yugoslav federation.

The German media pushed further and for them it was clear that any attempt to keep Yugoslavia together was pointless. More importantly, the dissatisfaction with the European Community and its performance with regard to the crisis continued. The media perceived the Community's switch from supporting Yugoslav unity to possible recognition of Slovenia and Croatia as an immature move. Indeed, as the Germans and Danes had appeared to push for a policy of recognition, the media assessed the situation: 'People make fun of the EC because it first supported Yugoslav unity and now it has turned against the Serbs'.[82] Thus, while the media stuck to their very defensible position regarding the future of the SFRY, the Community delivered another declaration in which it communicated that a new situation in Yugoslavia 'called for new relationships and structures', but stressed that the EC and its Member States 'reiterate that it is entirely up to all people living in Yugoslavia to determine their own future'.[83] In reality, this declaration meant capitulation of the Community's solo efforts as it admitted that 'the EC mission is no longer able to perform its task in full' and was therefore constrained 'to seek the support of the nations of the CSCE and, through the UN Security Council, the international community as a whole'.[84]

Thus, the role of the European Community was not impressive. In order to sum up its performance, I draw attention to four arguments in particular. First, they constantly failed to identify the major difference between the conflicts in Slovenia and Croatia. Moreover, once the conflict in Slovenia had ended and moved to neighbouring Croatia, the Community made the mistake of insisting on peace between the warring parties while ignoring the fact that the Serbs at this point were only interested in victory. Second, the discourse about minorities was largely ignored. Although mentioned in various reports, any idea of how to address them was lacking. Accordingly, many Serbs in Croatia questioned whether recognition of Croatia meant that the Croats would regard their actions as being morally justified, and whether this would lead to further discrimination against the Serbian minority. More importantly, would that discrimination become legitimized by the EC itself as it had determined Croatia's status? This having been said, the Community's moral responsibility to react was particularly difficult due to the dilemma it faced: on the one hand, it was necessary to save the Croatian republic, but on the other, it was necessary to protect the Serbs living in Croatia. Third, the Community deliberately overestimated the role of Lord Peter Carrington, the chief negotiator in the crisis, whose power was actually very limited. Finally, the Community was involved in its Common Foreign and Security Policy (CFSP) whose 'common' dimension was going to be challenged if Germany or any other EC Member State decided to recognize any Yugoslav republics unilaterally.

The number of confusing thoughts provided an opportunity for the media in secessionist republics as well as across the European Community to further condemn the European approach towards the Yugoslav crisis, and indirectly press for a more precise plan. Western media activism focused on the increasing conflict and the Community's decreasing responsiveness. Here again, *Die Zeit* reported on the EC dilemma and Yugoslav chaos while highlighting an urgent need to address the crisis.[85] The media were aware of their capacity to contribute to EC policy-making. As noted by Veran Matić, 'the Western media presented the conflict the way they understood it. No matter whether accepted or rejected by the public, day by day, their reporting was gaining relevance among political leaderships'.[86] Judging by statements of this kind, it can be argued that the media were in a privileged position over the European Community in the eyes of the public due to their precise vision of events. This was the reason why towards the end of 1991, the EC offered a clearer position vis-à-vis the SFRY. This clarification was very much based on the continuing fighting in the country. In particular, as soon as it had become obvious that the agreement concluded in The Hague on 4 October between Presidents Tudjman and Milošević and General Kadijević had failed, the Community communicated: 'Grave doubts exist as to the will of parties to settle their disputes by peaceful means … the JNA, having resorted to a disproportionate and indiscriminate use of force, has shown itself to be no longer a neutral and disciplined institution'.[87] Among others, this meeting discussed the right to self-determination, but noted that it 'cannot be exercised in isolation from the interests and rights of ethnic minorities within the individual republics'[88] – something that the media had already elaborated on.

Another Community *Declaration on Yugoslavia* assessed: 'The continuation of military activities in Croatia threatens to extend the armed confrontation to other regions of Yugoslavia'.[89] This statement reflected what at the time the media considered a leitmotif for their reporting. Of course, the spread of violence throughout the federation was a relevant topic for discussion, as for the Yugoslavs it seemed that violence would not be limited to Croatia. At this stage, it seemed more appropriate to think in terms of the next destination of the war, than to think in terms of the termination of war.[90] However, the Brussels officials often undermined the enormity of the war, whereas the media represented it as an increasing threat to the stability of both the SFRY and the EC. Here, the media had stronger arguments to offer: while the policy-makers were relying on diplomatic means usually rejected by one of the conflicting parties, the media had a clear vision of how to go further. Indeed, as the fighting intensified, so did their reporting. For example, the attacks on Dubrovnik, which 'have given the lie to the assertion that the JNA only acts to relieve besieged garrisons or to protect Serbian communities', encouraged the Community to note its readiness to pursue the policy of recognition.[91] As the EC put it, '[t]he prospect of recognition of the independence of those Republics wishing it can only be envisaged in the framework of an overall settlement that includes adequate guarantees for the protection of human rights and rights of national or ethnic groups'.[92] As any form of dialogue and negotiation among the conflicting parties did not seem to produce positive results, the media insisted on the Community's moral responsibility to react.

The Western media discussed each side's ethnic background, their exclusivity within a broader historical perspective, their willingness to adopt Western values, or even Eastern ones, their capacity to do so, etc. As Aleksa Djilas later summarized, the German media 'uncritically supported Slovenes and Croats as democratic and "Western", while condemning Serbs as defenders of communism, and describing their policies as an expression of inferior Byzantine and "Eastern" civilization'.[93] The differences between the conflicting parties were further accentuated when the Austrian public insisted that 'the EC has to punish the

Serbs harder' based on their understanding that it was unacceptable to place the blame on both sides.[94] This initially Austrian but then general Western standpoint on blame derived from the fact that the war was taking place in Croatia, and before that in Slovenia, but never in Serbia. According to the media, the tardy European response to the crisis contributed to the spread of hatred between the Croats and Serbs – hatred that turned into Croatian determination for revenge against the Serbian minority in Croatia.

The European Community acknowledged the existence of an ethnic component in the Yugoslav conflict quite late. In their joint statement, the EC and the USA finally confirmed: 'Many States of the region now face the re-emergence of inter-ethnic tensions, which can lead to ethnic intolerance and aggressive nationalism'.[95] In fact, in his analysis, Michael Brenner criticizes EC diplomacy for failing to understand 'both the intensity of the passions dividing the Yugoslav nationalities and their readiness to use violence to achieve their purposes. Both the mentality and the behaviour were wholly alien to the world of reason and reasonableness inhabited by the Community Twelve'.[96] Still, the late acknowledgement of the ethnic dimension in the war on behalf of the EC might have meant that, while being aware of the fact that recognizing Croatia was difficult due to its questionable treatment of the Serbian minority, the Community believed that more shooting in Croatia was going to guarantee recognition, thus it allowed the war to continue – an assumption which has remained undiscussed so far.

The European Community strongly condemned the tragic episode when five members of the Monitor Mission to Yugoslavia were killed.[97] This event was an additional incentive for the Western media to call on the Community to consolidate ideas surrounding a policy of recognition. More precisely, the media insisted that the EC had to make clear that the Serbs were the aggressors in the Yugoslav wars. By asking how would the Italians and French react if their fellow citizens were being killed and other Western Europeans simply decided to watch them die, the media consciously exploited the emotional aspects of the crisis.[98] As Volker Rühe, the Secretary General of the Christian Democratic Union put it: 'If we Germans think everything else in Europe can follow a *status quo* policy and do not recognize the right of self-determination in Slovenia and Croatia, then we have no moral or political credibility'.[99] In fact, the first EC victims confirmed the monstrosity of the war for all the parties involved, no matter whether they were combatants or negotiators. As commented by Hans-Dietrich Genscher, this was clear confirmation of the kind of policy the Community had to adopt.[100]

Conclusion

As soon as the world heard about the Yugoslav drama, the media were there to interpret the events. In his work on Europe, Jürgen Habermas correctly points out that '[t]he power of the media to select messages and to shape their presentation is as much an intrinsic feature of mass communication as the fact that other actors use their power to influence the agenda, content, and presentation of public issues is typical of the public sphere'.[101] By quoting these words, I argue that the Western media opted for a narrative which favoured the Slovenes and Croats, but not the Serbs: the former were often portrayed as pro-Western, willing and capable of integrating in the Community at some point in the future, whereas the latter were often discredited for their apparently pro-Eastern ideology.

When the Brussels officials realized that they were the ones expected to deliver opinions and propose policies, their role entailed seriously considering the media. In order to address this dimension of EC policy-making, which has somehow remained overlooked in the academic literature, this chapter looked at media reporting, and the EC declarations and press releases that followed. Often, these declarations did not offer anything new regarding the Yugoslav conflict, but repeated already known facts. Aware that at one point it would have to offer a clear set of policies as to how to proceed with the Yugoslav drama, the Community relied on other sources. It is equally important to note that the problem of late response allowed the same media to criticize the Community and push for resolution even more. In this debate, the German media have occupied a central position as in most debates when talking about EC policy. As soon as they had developed their vision vis-à-vis the Yugoslav crisis and Yugoslavia's future, 'Germany was constantly undermining the EC's attempts to find a solution ... It was convincing other EC Member States to recognize Slovenia and Croatia, while at the same time undermining them by saying that it would recognize them no matter what the Badinter Commission was going to come up with'.[102] This being the case, the media did what they considered to be best. Their approach insisted on the moral responsibility to react while simultaneously talking about recognition of the two republics as a logical consequence. The overall impression was that the Western media pushed forward, while the Community hesitated. However, towards the end of 1991, it became clear that pushing was going to win over hesitation. By offering repetitive declarations, the Community reflected what the media had already said and suggested. In its attempt to calm the conflicting parties, the EC counted on diplomatic means that were not sufficient to generate peace or that might keep the SFRY united. The Community simply advocated a cease-fire and peace resolution – an approach the Western media never seriously considered.

The European Community accepted media reporting as an important component of its policies. In fact, the human aspect of the crisis and moral responsibility to react were discussed by the media first, and then acknowledged by the Brussels administration. Moreover, the policy of recognition which decided Yugoslavia's future was primarily pushed forward by the media as the option for crisis settlement, and only later by the Brussels officials. Thus, no matter how difficult the acceptance of media power during the Yugoslav crisis was, their presence and relevance appear undeniable. Apart from managing to label the developments across the Yugoslav federation as breaking news, the media acted as one of the judges in a trial that handed down the death sentence to the SFRY.

Apart from the diasporas and the media, another non-state actor that contributed to European Community policy towards the Yugoslav federation was the Catholic Church. In fact, the Western media often observed and commented on the Vatican and what its officials suggested as adequate policy with regard to the future of the Yugoslav federation. Accordingly, the following chapter will conclude the debate about the involvement of non-state actors by looking at the impact of the Catholic Church on EC policy-making.

CHAPTER SIX

WITH THE BLESSING OF THE VATICAN

The Catholic Church and European Community Policy

Twentieth century history of the Balkans often saw religion and politics travelling along parallel lines: from the Balkan Wars to the two World Wars and the wars of the Yugoslav succession, including the interwar periods, the question of religious denomination appeared as an important component characterizing further developments within Yugoslav society.[1] However, academic scholarship has paid almost no attention to the link between the religious point of view regarding the Yugoslav crisis and European Community decision-making.

In his analysis of the impact of religion on politics, Jonathan Fox distinguishes between three different forms: 'First, foreign policies are influenced by the religious views and beliefs of policymakers and their constituents. Second, religion is a source of legitimacy for both supporting and criticizing government behaviour locally and internationally. Third, many local religious issues and phenomena, including religious conflicts, spread across borders or otherwise become international issues'.[2] If applied to the Yugoslav crisis, although all three aspects were present, the first modus operandi was the most prominent at European Community level, whereas the other two primarily characterized the domestic policies of the opposing parties. On this issue, Warren Zimmermann makes a valid point when he writes that '[t]he major proponents of destructive nationalism weren't driven by religious faith. Franjo Tudjman had been a communist most of his life; he converted to Catholicism when he turned to national activities. Milošević, a lifelong communist, never, as far as I know, entered a Serbian Orthodox church, except for blatant political activities'.[3]

Abroad, official and public reactions criticized the outbreak of violence. At the same time, religious differences between warring parties were not ignored. One scholar points out that religious aspects shape our perception of the other – a perception that gains full relevance when bad things happen.[4] In Yugoslavia, while, on the one hand, the Serbs counted on moral support from the Greek and Russian Orthodox Churches, on the other hand the Slovenes and Croats sought backing from the Catholic Church. With regard to the Vatican, although it had never been able to forget some of problematic periods characterizing relations with the SFRY, it initially condemned the violence and called for a peaceful solution to the Yugoslav crisis, but without specifying what exactly the solution should be. However, with the progression of the war, the Vatican strengthened its position and commenced favouring independence for Slovenia and Croatia.

This chapter will examine the religious aspect of the Yugoslav state crisis and, more importantly, the relevance of the Catholic Church for European Community policy-making. In his account, Fox notes that '[m]any policy-makers are religious and it is likely that their religious beliefs influence their actions. Whether they truly believe or not, they often find it useful to draw upon religion to justify their actions, which indicates that religion is a source of legitimacy on the international stage'.[5] I adopt this point of view and accordingly argue that as soon as the parties commenced fighting each other, both Orthodox and Catholic churches adopted clear positions that resulted in supporting one side or the other. In this religious battle of sorts, the Catholic republics of Slovenia and Croatia gained remarkable support from the Vatican which further influenced European Community officials to recognize the two republics as independent states.

Between the Yugoslav Leadership and the Vatican

In post-war Yugoslavia, the Communist Party's objections towards the Catholic Church were twofold: on the one hand, the atheist ideology underlying Communism tended to reject any religion and even promoted anti-religious policies while, on the other, and perhaps more importantly, the Catholic Church was seen as having close associations with the Croatian *Ustasha* regime appointed by Nazi Germany in April 1941 and which was responsible for the condemnation of all Serbs, Jews and Roma in the Independent State of Croatia. Understandably, the post-war Yugoslav authorities decided to minimize the voice of the Catholic Church by placing it under direct governmental control. As a result of this, some leading clergy figures were tried and jailed, church property confiscated, religious education removed from school curricula, the religious press classified as illegal, etc.[6] This somewhat intolerant approach towards the Catholic clergy culminated in the conviction of Alojzije Stepinac, Archbishop of Zagreb and direct collaborator of the *Ustasha* regime, to 16 years' hard labour in 1946. The Communist Party insisted that the Catholic Church represented a threat to the stability of the Yugoslav state. As the public prosecutor had imagined, the trial against Stepinac served 'to unmask before the world a plot by the Western imperialist powers against the new Yugoslavia' and reveal the existence of 'a concerted conspiracy'.[7]

The Yugoslav authorities continued with their anti-religious policies. The new approach consisted in the establishment of priests' associations aimed at controlling the lower Catholic clergy and, therefore, undermining the unity of the Catholic Churches across Yugoslavia in general – a policy that in the view of both Catholic bishops and the Vatican represented a direct attack against them. Moreover, the Communists proceeded with even stronger measures, with the prohibition of catechism in all public schools and the closure of religious faculties in Zagreb and Ljubljana.[8] At this point, the West did not unequivocally object to Yugoslav policies. As Miroslav Akmadža correctly points out, this was the case mostly because of the country's reputation among the Western powers due to its worsening relationship with the Soviet Union.[9] However, when the 1952 Vatican-sponsored

Bishops' Conference prohibited priests' associations and banned priests from joining them, the Communists accused the Vatican of interfering in domestic affairs. To make the situation even more dramatic, the Vatican elevated Stepinac to Cardinal.[10] This newly established atmosphere laid the ground for the culmination of enmity between the Yugoslav government and the Vatican resulting in the complete breakdown in diplomatic relations between the two.

Various sources offer an insight into the Vatican's sympathy for the Croatian Catholic clergy in the late 1950s. For example, in a telegram dated 24 June 1959, Pope John XXIII sent a letter confirming the Vatican's support for the work of Stepinac:

> Due to painful circumstances, You were, unfortunately, compelled to leave Your regular activities and spend days in solitude, separated from the Christian people whom Your love and guidance have been entrusted with. Be brave: You are not undergoing this because of Your guilt but because of Your humbleness ... In order for Your merits, which You have acquired through Your work and endurance, to be known to everyone, the predecessor of Holy Father Pius XII wanted to honor You with the rank of cardinal.[11]

Soon after, on 15 November, the Pope addressed Stepinac again: 'We deeply regret that you could not come to Rome, our dear son, at the time when we were raised to the seat of St. Peter, so that we send you a special apostolic blessing as a guarantee of heavenly comfort'.[12]

Later, following the death of Stepinac, the Yugoslav government seemed more open to cooperating with the clergy and, indeed, the 1962 Vatican Council served to bring the opponents together. As Stella Alexander puts it, 'the Vatican was now convinced that Yugoslavia was genuinely detached from the Soviet bloc'.[13] Thus, this aspect suggests that Tito's politics of religion was conditioned by both international and domestic factors. The *Protocol of Discussions between the Representatives of the Social Federal Republic of Yugoslavia and the Representatives of the Holy See* guaranteed religious freedom to the Catholic clergy. As well as being a document that touched upon many serious issues, its main relevance was that it inaugurated a new relationship between the Yugoslav authorities and the Catholic Church.[14]

Diplomatic relations reflect relations between sovereign states and, therefore, the re-established relations should have implied relations between Yugoslavia and the Vatican, rather than relations between Yugoslav Marxists and Yugoslav Catholics or the Catholic Church in general – a connection often dependent on circumstances, given the Vatican's nature. In fact, the re-established relations between the Yugoslav federation and the Vatican did not significantly improve relations among the differently positioned ideologies in Yugoslavia. Although the Protocol in theory provided bishops with greater freedom in relation to the election of clergy members, to education and church property, in reality this was not the case. For example, the Vatican claimed that the Communist leadership was not capable of understanding the meaning of free elections for bishops and thus would be ready to interfere at every opportunity.[15] In addition, many schools continued to portray Stepinac as a criminal, rather than a cardinal.[16] Thus, while Stepinac was celebrated across regions dominated by Catholicism, his work was condemned in less Catholic ones. More importantly, a growing interest in religion in Slovenia and Croatia represented an alternative to the Yugoslav regime.[17] The character of such an alternative was not shaped to become an aggressive resistance, but rather to offer respite to citizens who thought differently. Accordingly, various articles and books promoted the work of the Catholic clergy.[18]

The following decade confirmed that the relations in question were still far from stable. In his analysis, Ivo Banac describes this period as follows: 'The tense early 1970s can only be understood as a conflict over the future of Yugoslavia. The centralist and unitarist bloc held that the distinctions between the nationalities were being blurred and that Yugoslavia could be homogenized on the traditions – real or invented – of forceful Yugoslavism'.[19] Interestingly, the concept of Yugoslavism still represents a serious topic of discussion. In fact, many misunderstandings surrounding this concept are due to the time framework in which it was used: at times, it was promoted for the sake of a common identity, desired by the peoples, at others, for political reasons, championed by the Yugoslav authorities. Admittedly, the period 1961–1981 saw a general increase in self-identification for Yugoslavs.[20] With regard to the European Community, while negotiating agreements with the SFRY and being aware of the economic disparities, the Yugoslavs were often talked about as a people who shared a common identity. Thus, for the Europeans as well as for the Yugoslav authorities who were looking forward to economic assistance, Yugoslavism existed. However, at home, the constituent peoples of the SFRY often perceived the idea of Yugoslavism as an artificially encouraged identity.

In Croatia, contrary to Slovenia which was untouched by the antagonism characterizing relations between Zagreb and Belgrade,[21] the Catholic Church gained true relevance after the Croatian Spring in 1971 which left the defenders of Croatian national interests almost powerless. Indeed, during the Twenty-First Session of the Central Committee of the League of Communists of Yugoslavia, Tito accused the leadership of the League of Communists of Croatia of supporting Croatian nationalism and favouring Croatian sovereignty over Yugoslavia's overarching sovereignty. As one scholar puts it, the Croatian Spring 'gave rise in the republic to a wide sense of disillusionment with Yugoslavia and a gaining conviction that democratic change and sovereign statehood could only be achieved by secession from the common state'.[22] In this climate, the Croatian Catholic Church was the only institution capable of promoting the national feeling of Croats. It actually became 'the national embodiment of Croatianhood. Later, after the Church had stabilized its strength on this basis, it expanded its scope of activity into impressive mass meetings always connected with the national idea'.[23] Moreover, greater independence of the Catholic Church meant greater uncertainty for the Yugoslav authorities: 'Though the Catholic Church's independence can only be a source of uncertainty for Belgrade's builders of socialism, it is the Church's re-emergence as the self-appointed champion of the exclusivist interests of the Croats and Slovenes qua Croats and Slovenes which is the more disquieting to Belgrade'.[24]

The Vatican was aware of the newly created situation. In his memoirs, Agostino Casaroli, a skilled diplomat and Cardinal Secretary of the Vatican at the time, expressed his concerns about the position of

Catholics in Yugoslavia. He visited Belgrade, Zagreb and Ljubljana in 1970 and when talking to Tito noted the main difference between the two of them: while for the Yugoslav leader, relations between his state and the Vatican were fully resolved by their official re-establishment, for Casaroli this new phase in the relationship between the two sides represented an opportunity to address numerous questions about the Catholic Church in Yugoslavia.[25] Thus, if Casaroli's contribution is taken as a reliable key to understanding the Vatican's perception of the Yugoslav federation, it is obvious that the importance the two sides attached to the Catholic Church varied significantly. The Yugoslav statesmen, as Casaroli wrote, talked about 'unity as a driving force behind the Yugoslav federation where ethnic diversity and power equilibrium peacefully coexisted'.[26] This apparently being the case, Tito decided to concentrate primarily on Yugoslavia's international affairs.

In order to explain the situation in Croatia, Vjekoslav Perica examines correspondence between the Croatian Church and government and notes that in 1972, 'when the backlash against the Movement's leaders had already begun, Archbishop Franić assured representatives of the government of Croatia that the Vatican was keeping its commitment to the Church's non-interference in domestic political affairs in Yugoslavia'.[27] But the campaign against Croatian nationalism, arrests, expulsions from the party and censorship, in fact, encouraged the position of the Croatian Catholic Church in two ways: first, it witnessed a new golden age at home and,[28] second, it fostered links with the Vatican. This set of closer relations was facilitated by the prior re-establishment of official relations between the SFRY and the Vatican as well as the Vatican's disappointment with Tito, whose decision not to address religious issues instantly was interpreted as his determination to ignore the Holy See.[29]

In his numerous contributions, Hansjakob Stehle looked at Vatican policy towards the Yugoslav federation during the 1970s and, while relying on the idea that East European politics threatened values that the Catholic Church was immensely proud of, he saw the Vatican as having two options. The first concentrated on diplomatic means that could have served to foster the Vatican's position.[30] In this case, the Vatican encouraged Yugoslav Catholics to become politically active as diplomacy was seen to depend on their involvement, rather than on the diplomatic corps that worked on behalf of the Yugoslav state. The second option concentrated on the acceptance of the Communist regime as it was.[31] In this case, the Vatican relied on small steps leading to progress in relations between the Catholic and Orthodox Churches, thus without any significant interference in Yugoslavia's domestic affairs. Of the two options, the Vatican opted for the first. As Casaroli later acknowledged, Vatican officials wanted to protect Catholic clergy in East European countries as much as possible: 'We insist on having the right to prevent eradication of the Catholic Church given the political campaign against it ... The Church has to survive'.[32]

Being aware of the circumstances, the Yugoslav leadership did not want to see the Church coming close to or influencing any aspect of the policy-making processes.[33] Accordingly, a new set of laws aimed at protecting the state from the Church was passed. Here, Pedro Ramet talks about the Church's threat to the state on a threefold basis: the first threat was apparently the Yugoslav Catholic Church's ambition 'to obstruct the drawing together of national groups' and link itself to other Catholic Churches, the second threat was motivated by the idea that the Catholic Church perceived the League of Communists 'as an alternative focus of loyalty' – an idea fuelled by the 1971 attempt of some Church members to join and infiltrate the Communist Party – and, finally, the third threat derived from understanding that Catholicism threatened the Communists ideologically.[34] This last threat remained the strongest throughout the 1980s. Although its relevance was limited at the outbreak of the war in Slovenia, with the outbreak of war in Croatia, its relevance was fully accepted.

It is important to note that the threats against the Yugoslav state outlined by Ramet are primarily associated with Catholicism in Croatia, as the situation in Slovenia in the first half of the 1970s seemed to be less problematic. As a rather quiet place for the clergy, it hosted numerous meetings on relations between Orthodox Serbs and Catholic Croats and Slovenes. Indeed, the Vatican gave its blessing to the forthcoming institutional cooperation among the faculties of theology of Ljubljana-Maribor, Zagreb and Belgrade.[35] However, the second half of the decade witnessed a completely different trend:

repressive governmental standpoints on the clergy were turned into laws, which affected Slovenia significantly. In January 1979, Ivan Likar, a Slovenian Catholic priest, argued that 'atheist propaganda and indoctrination in schools are becoming more intensive from day to day. Schoolbooks describe religion, morality and the Church in such a way that the believer cannot avoid the impression that he is not even a second-class citizen, but that he is beyond any social class, an untouchable pariah'.[36] The presence of such Yugoslav behaviour towards the end of the decade irritated the Vatican and made for a rather puzzling image of the relations between the Yugoslav state and the Catholic Church. As Ramet summarizes,

> for all the vaunted liberality of the Yugoslav system, the Catholic Church enjoys a precarious position – it has greater freedom in Yugoslavia than in most communist countries, but is repeatedly vilified and/or attacked in the party press ... it is able to conduct religious instruction openly, but those attending are discriminated against ... believers are told they enjoy equal rights with non-believers, but they are excluded from the officer corps, the diplomatic service, senior posts in economic management, the upper echelons of governmental service, and, of course, membership in the party.[37]

Considering all these points, it appeared rather improbable that the Yugoslav leadership would change its policy towards the Catholic Church any time soon. As a reaction, the Vatican accepted the fact that the SFRY authorities were disrespectful towards the Church and the only way forward it saw was to try to maintain links with Catholic believers in Slovenia and Croatia through moral support only.

Religious Aspects of the Yugoslav Crisis

Following Josip Broz Tito's death, the Yugoslav federation faced growing economic, political and inter-ethnic problems. As already discussed in Chapter Three, the Yugoslav leadership negotiated new economic support from the European Community thinking that it would be sufficient to remedy the ongoing multi-level crisis. In his study, Aleksandar Pavković examines the economic situation in the 1980s and notes that the failing economy indirectly resurrected religious aspects within the Yugoslav society.[38] Indeed, as the worsening trend continued, members of various communities abandoned their appreciation for the federation and switched their allegiance to their respective republics – a development that had already obtained approval under the 1974 Constitution.[39]

The 1981 Kosovo crisis was an opportunity for the Vatican to stress its policy towards some of Yugoslavia's constituent peoples. For example, Radio Vatican, the Croatian Church press and various Catholic representatives approved of the Kosovo riots and the Albanian drive for greater autonomy in Kosovo.[40] As a matter of support against the Serbs, Radio Vatican decided to broadcast a number of programmes in Albanian and Croatian. As mentioned, the Vatican understood Yugoslavia's ethnic diversity to the fullest extent only after Casaroli had paid a visit to the Yugoslav leadership in the summer of 1985 with the aim of advocating greater religious freedom. During the meeting with Milka Planinc, the Prime Minister of Yugoslavia, he became fully aware of the existence of ambitions across the Yugoslav federation to create a Greater Croatia, Greater Serbia or Greater Macedonia.[41] Although Casaroli himself decided to elaborate on the risk of a link between nationalism and religion, he, however, denied any involvement of religion in fostering political or nationalistic sentiments. This being the case, Casaroli's standpoint is disputable for the simple reason that he tried to ignore or, more dangerously, contradict something that was already evident across the SFRY – religious denomination had already developed into a key characteristic of the appeal of politicians and, more precisely, nationalists.

In his memoirs, Casaroli personally noted how peculiar the situation in Yugoslavia was. He concluded his memoirs about Yugoslavia by saying that his heart 'was full of contrasting feelings: joy, hope, some sort of worry and real nostalgia for the country with many latent problems – a dear country and even dearer now once some of its problems have already exploded'.[42] To complement the range of Casaroli's feelings, I identify two events that fostered the religious component within Serbian society and clearly questioned future relations between the Orthodox and Catholic churches in Yugoslavia. The first event relates to the publication of the 1986 SANU *Memorandum*, a document produced by the Serbian Academy of Sciences and Arts, arguing that decentralization was threatening the unity of the Yugoslav state in which the Serbs were already discriminated.[43] Alongside the Serbian media that understandably welcomed its content, the Serbian Orthodox Church also acknowledged the relevance and accuracy of the document. In his analysis, Paul Mojzes goes even further and warns that its role was far more relevant than its content: 'It galvanized the Serbs to become militant in demands to remake Yugoslavia and frightened non-Serbs'.[44] The second event relates to the visit Slobodan Milošević paid to Kosovo in April 1987. The Serbian Orthodox Church supported Milošević's speech to Kosovo Serbs and his famous words 'No one is allowed to beat you!', aimed at protecting their position in the province.[45] The media enthusiastically reported friendship between the Church and politics. One scholar noted that there was nothing strange about this connection given that 'the Serbian Church views itself as identical with the Serbian nation since it considers that religion is the foundation of nationality'.[46] Thus, while on the one hand, Milošević needed support for his future political engagement, on the other hand, the Serbian Church, which remained deprived of its basic rights for almost half a century, felt empowered and backed Milošević's policies – an involvement of decisive relevance and measure as the Serbian Orthodox Church managed to bridge the gap between church and state.[47]

In his analysis, Perica describes this whole period as 'the catalyst of the crisis' due to the presence of various factors that contributed to and strengthened the antagonism between the opposing parties. For example, as soon as the federal government agreed upon democratization of religious affairs in 1987, Catholic Slovenia 'whose political leaders did not worry about ethnic minorities, rushed to inaugurate religious liberty without restrictions'.[48] In contrast, this scenario was not possible in ethnically and ideologically heterogeneous Croatia where the campaigning candidates were interested in securing support from different religious institutions. Nevertheless, in the winter of 1989, the Croatian

Catholic Church openly welcomed the foundation of the ethnic and nationalistic Croatian Democratic Union with Franjo Tudjman as its leader.[49] Perica also notes growing disputes in both the Catholic and Orthodox press over holy places as both parties felt entitled to religious sites that could serve as a testimony of their long presence in specific regions.[50] Indeed, to confirm this enmity, the author describes how in the summer of 1991 Serb militants destroyed numerous Catholic churches in predominantly Serbian areas of Croatia.[51]

The Croatian Catholic Church advocated independence for the republic of Croatia and the link between religion and politics was further accentuated when the Church decided to continue supporting the newly elected president, Tudjman. Mojzes examines the events surrounding the elections and concludes that the Catholic Church showed significant support to 'the new regime's superpatriotic Croatianism'.[52] In the same vein, members of the Croatian church attended the inauguration of the Parliament of Croatia and, as observed by the author, 'did not fail to use photo opportunities in order to be seen together in the media, and much was done to reinforce the notion of the church, nation, and state'.[53] As could somehow have been predicted, the Ninth Theological Congress scheduled for September 1990 in Serbia did not host any representatives from the Faculty of Theology of Zagreb. In truth, the absence of Croatian delegates was due to the growing discord between the two Churches at the time – a discord that was further fuelled by Serbian accusations that the Croatian Catholic Church was responsible for the genocide of the Serbian population during the Second World War.[54] In this climate, by 1990, conflict seemed inevitable. While the Serbian Communists advocated a largely centralized Yugoslavia, the independence-oriented Slovenian Communists urged greater autonomy. Accordingly, both Orthodox and Croatian members of the clergy decided to take advantage of the vacuum to approach respective believers and strengthen nationalistic feelings.

The Vatican was aware of all that was happening across the Yugoslav federation. Interestingly enough, much of the diplomatic correspondence between the Catholics in Yugoslavia, the Vatican diplomatic representation in Belgrade and the Holy See in Rome was channelled through the Vatican Embassy in Vienna.[55] Although it remains unclear whether this particular office played any role in keeping European Community officials informed about the Catholics across the Yugoslav federation, its relevance would appear to have been significant considering the overall Austrian policy towards the Yugoslav state crisis and Austrian involvement in the Community's affairs at the time. More importantly, the EC official documents of this period show a growing interest in Yugoslavia's religious mosaic among the Brussels administration.

From Churches to the Brussels Officials

The outbreak of war confirmed the importance of religious denomination in the Yugoslav federation. Both Orthodox and Catholic Church representatives sought to undermine the opposing side and legitimize their own actions.[56] As expected, some accounts have tried to address the extent to which the Vatican contributed to policy-making regarding the future of the Yugoslav federation. For example, Daniele Conversi limits his argument to the fact that although some Catholic churches across the European Community provided humanitarian support 'based on a Christian vocation of social solidarity with the downtrodden, who in the case of Slovenia and Croatia, happened to be fellow Catholics', the Vatican itself did not play a major role.[57] Somehow, in the author's view, the Vatican got fully involved with the war in Bosnia-Herzegovina when Muslims became the new victims, not Catholics.[58] By saying this, he denies the relevance of the religious aspect in the early stages of the Yugoslav crisis.

In contrast, other works note the importance of historical perspective, including both the situation characterizing the activism of different churches across the SFRY and the relations some of them cultivated with the Vatican. In this respect, Michael Weithmann insists that it is not possible to ignore the situation either in Tito's Yugoslavia, a state where 'many things were never clarified' and religion was often allowed to manifest itself in a 'salient form' or in Yugoslavia after Tito, where religious aspects were apparently put on hold due to ever-increasing economic and political problems.[59] In fact, this perspective helps to understand why Vatican reaction and involvement from the very beginning were inevitable. As indicated by Weithmann, the Yugoslav crisis represented an opportunity for the renaissance of religion. Therefore, both Orthodox and Catholic Churches felt empowered to get involved and act as national representatives. While the Serbian Church gave its blessing to the beginning of a 'holy war',[60] the Croatian Church, which relied on its unique and previously acknowledged position, counted on the Vatican's support.[61] Aware of the state crisis, Croatian bishops got involved by contacting other bishops around the world. In their famous February 1991 letter, they suggested that the Croatian Catholic Church 'sees a new political framework which would be based on the people getting their independence, as a possibility for acting more freely and for more peaceful coexistence in a pluralist society, including ecumenical relations'.[62]

The bishops used their position to try to influence Western perceptions about both the Yugoslav authorities and Catholic clergy. In their view, the political programme advocating the continuation of socialism was misplaced: 'The forces advocating this program are the leading Serbian politicians, army officers (mostly Serbs) and unfortunately certain leading figures in the Serbian Orthodox church. Thus, the communist ideology, greater Serbian aspirations and military force have found common goals and for this reason they are firmly opposing the western cultural tradition, and the republics with a pronounced West European tradition'.[63]

The religious dimension of the crisis, the division between 'us' and 'them' and Church advocacy of independence were further emphasized when the European Parliament decided to pass a resolution stipulating that 'the constituent Republics and autonomous provinces must have the right freely to determine their future in a peaceful and democratic manner and on the basis of recognized institutional and internal borders'.[64] This resolution was understood as an indication as well as encouragement for further steps. Accordingly, the Catholic representatives from Croatia believed that insisting on their religion-based maltreatment in the SFRY would further the goal of international recognition of independence.

The Croatian bishops discussed politics extensively. In their view, the Serbs were responsible for the 'rejection of the democratic parliamentary way of resolving open political questions' and, therefore, 'crime against mankind'.[65] More importantly, their standpoint towards the Yugoslav authorities and their destructive power culminated with the referendum in Croatia in May 1991 resulting in 'an unavoidable decision' that Yugoslavia was facing disintegration.[66] By insisting on the distinction between the two denominations, the bishops' statements gained significant attention within the European Community due to its own religious outlook. In order to secure as much support as possible, Tudjman himself visited the Vatican on 25 May 1991. This fruitful visit was complemented by a reception at the Catholic St. Jerome Institute in Rome where 'he was greeted by the head of the Institute, Monsignor Ratko Perić, who stressed that throughout its history, the Institute has always devotedly and tirelessly strived to preserve the identity of the Croatian nation and worked in favour of its territorial integrity'.[67] On his return to Croatia, Tudjman enthusiastically talked about the great support he had been promised by the Vatican. In his analysis, Milan Bulajić points out that from this moment on, the Croatian Catholic Church adopted an even stronger advocacy of independence and put even greater pressure on the international community to recognize Croatia as an independent state: 'They appealed to statesmen and international institutions in Europe and the world to urgently and actively speak out in favour of peace and a democratic resolution of the political crisis in our country'.[68]

In the European Community, religion took on a deeply politicized role. This might seem unusual considering that the founding fathers of the Community, while busy with economic, political and social aspects of European integration, never discussed the religious aspect of the Community and its relevance for politics. However, if analysed, the historical foundation of the Community had been largely Christian-Democratic. Jeffrey Checkel and Peter Katzenstein describe this confessional tendency as 'a capacious political tradition that accommodates temperate offshoots of conservative political Catholicism as well as a social Catholicism that has proven in the past to be remarkably progressive in outlook and practice'.[69] This understanding is further developed and justified by Douglas Holmes for whom the period around the 1992 Maastricht Treaty embraced Catholic social doctrine 'to guide intellectually and regulate institutionally cognitive meanings and political exigencies of a pluralist Europe'.[70] Thus, while ignored in the early stages of the European Economic Community, with evident interest in EU membership and new rounds of enlargement, the Europeans decided to pay more attention to the religious dimension of their polity. In this respect, Catholicism was tacitly given priority. According to some directly involved actors, many informal discussions in Brussels focused on Slovenia and Croatia in terms of their confessions, complementing the increasing perception of the Community as Catholic. This focus on the religious dimension was, in their terms, due to the growing presence of the Vatican and was apparent both in the media with its statements about the Yugoslav crisis, and in the official correspondence that often insisted on religious similarities between the Community and the two republics. As explained by one respondent, the Vatican maintained that EC officials were supposed to take the religious outlook of Slovenia and Croatia seriously, when developing their policies.[71]

The interpretations offered by Checkel, Katzenstein and Holmes could be justified by looking at formal actions occurring across the board. In Germany, for example, the Christian Social Union of Bavaria called the German government to recognize Slovenia and Croatia, 'partially out of solidarity with fellow Catholics and partially out of indignation at the brutal actions of the Yugoslav army which are unconstitutional and against international law'.[72] Along these lines, the Austrian People's Party, a party fully devoted to the Roman Catholic Church,[73] offered support: both Erhard Busek, the leader of the party and Vice-Chancellor of Austria, and Alois Mock, Foreign Minister of Austria, expressed their admiration for the Slovenes and Croats.[74] Finally, in Italy, first the Christian Democracy and later the Union of Christian and Centre Democrats openly praised the two Catholic republics for their religious orientation.[75]

With regard to its interest and involvement in politics, the Church gained further relevance with the visit paid by Croatian bishops to Tudjman in August 1991. This meeting was an opportunity to criticize the Yugoslav People's Army and its war against the Croatian nation, including Croatian young men, houses, churches, schools and hospitals.[76] Thus, most of the aspects covered reflected the Church's multi-faceted interest in Croatian internal affairs. In his study, Alex

Bellamy broadens the debate over the relationship between the Croatian republic, the Croatian Catholic Church and the Vatican and concludes that Tudjman perceived the Catholic Church as a Croatian Church, while the Vatican considered itself as a global Church, thus concerned with both Croats and non-Croats.[77] If analysed, these notions lead to a twofold conclusion: first, the Church was an ideological tool of Croatian nationalism and, second, the Vatican was a global power, thus probably capable of influencing the final outcome. Tudjman's idea of giving equal importance to the Catholic and Croatian Churches was a strategic move that strengthened the overall objective. Furthermore, neither the state nor the Church had a problem with being associated with the other as long as they shared a common objective. In fact, as acknowledged by Bellamy: 'The Croatian Catholic Church played a vital role in redefining Croatian national identity in the 1990s'.[78] In addition, the author clarifies that with the outbreak of war, the Vatican's role switched from global to regional and by focusing on the events in Slovenia and Croatia, the Vatican reconfirmed its historical commitment to the Catholic republics.[79]

Having been provided with detailed knowledge about the domestic situation and having decided upon the steps to be taken, the Croatian bishops approached Catholic bishops abroad. They put forward clear arguments in order to justify Croatia's desire to secede and, as a matter of support, these arguments were further publicized in sermons abroad.[80] For example, Catholic churches such as Santa Maria Maggiore in Rome, Santa Maria delle Grazie in Milan, Dom zu St. Jakob in Innsbruck, Dom zu unserer lieben Frau in Munich and Hohe Domkirche St. Peter und Maria in Cologne all prayed for the peoples of Slovenia and Croatia and urged both the national and supranational authorities to recognize them as independent states. At the same time, this sentiment was cultivated across various Pontifical universities.[81]

Therefore, based on previously discussed developments, the Slovenian and Croatian Catholic Churches could reasonably count on political engagement by the Vatican. The characterization of the Community's confessional structure supported an ideological concept about 'us' and 'them' based on denominational difference – a divide somehow similar to that between 'good us' and 'bad them' promoted by the media before and during the Yugoslav state crisis.[82] As indicated, various churches across the European Community included sermons in their celebrations that openly discussed the situation in Slovenia and Croatia and called for Vatican officials to advocate their recognition by the EC.

Apart from geographical proximity, often used as a valid reason for the European Community's support for the two Catholic republics of the SFRY, the Community's political involvement, which was shaped within the Catholic framework, deserves equal attention. In his analysis, Holmes correctly points out that '[p]olitical discourse, under the terms of Catholic social theory, operates in such a way that issues are contextualized constantly within a wider interplay of interests and remedies'.[83] In order to apply this view to the Yugoslav case, I rely on the fact that most Brussels-based officials were Catholics themselves and many debates in the EP about the Yugoslav crisis constantly insisted on the relevance of Catholic doctrine when shaping policies. For example, representatives of the Christian Social Union of Bavaria sitting in the EP openly expressed their anti-Serbian feelings and pressed for the recognition of the two Catholic republics.[84] Therefore, while being an approach aimed at achieving a common good, it is impossible to argue that the Europeans ignored the religious affiliation of the Yugoslavs. While seriously involved in the process of further European integration and enlargement, their perception of non-Catholics was very much conditioned by their own denomination. Later, in his study, Svetlozar Andreev explained this attitude and concluded:

> Catholic/Protestant countries, countries with some previous experience with democratization, countries which had begun earlier their political and economic reforms and countries in which people who had not been officially connected with the former communist/socialist regime came into power after elections in the period 1989–91 have been viewed much more favourably by both the EU decision-makers and Western public opinion as a whole.[85]

On 29 November 1991, Hans-Dietrich Genscher, German Foreign Minister, visited the Vatican and expressed his attitude regarding the future shape of the Yugoslav federation. In his memoirs, he wrote that the Vatican agreed that the Serbs represented the greatest threat to 'the peaceful coexistence of the peoples of Yugoslavia', but '[w]hen it came to recognizing Croatia and Slovenia, the Vatican displayed extreme reluctance'.[86] Although Genscher remains silent about his private conversation with the Pope, the Vatican's initial refusal to recognize the two republics appears even more surprising in view of the fact that it was among the first to recognize the two states. As well as from this observation, Mario Nobilo, the chief foreign policy advisor to President Tudjman, analyses the Vatican's behaviour and points out that it was actually the Vatican that used the Catholic Church in Germany to influence the German government to recognize Slovenia and Croatia.[87] In fact, communication between Germany and the Vatican continued, as Genscher paid another visit to the Holy See on 24 December 1991.[88] However, he does not mention this encounter in his memoirs. While elided, its content has remained open to speculation about his relationship with the Vatican and some of its representatives. Apart from being suspected of having a conspiratorial element, his visit was important as it managed to overturn what Genscher himself initially argued to be the Vatican's position vis-à-vis the Yugoslav crisis and its settlement. The day after his visit, the German government decided to recognize the two republics.

In Nobilo's view, Pope John Paul II supported the disintegration of Yugoslavia.[89] In fact, during his visit to Poland and Hungary in August 1991, he openly assured Croatian believers of the Vatican's awareness of Croatian aspirations and his intention to call the international community to assist the Croats. *Glas Koncila* headlined this visit as 'The Pope calls on the international community to help Croatia'.[90] In fact, the Pope's standpoint was nothing new, but rather the continuation of the approach adopted by the Vatican during the whole enigma surrounding the position of the Catholic clergy in Titoist Yugoslavia. Now, his willingness to encourage the end of the SFRY was appreciated among Vatican diplomatic representations around the world. As one author noted, correspondence between the Vatican and other states never ignored the fact that Slovenia and Croatia were Catholic republics in the Yugoslav federation, and thus deserved proper support.[91]

By late winter 1991, the Vatican advocated that the recognition of Slovenia and Croatia as independent states was essential.[92] The Pope, while addressing his audience in St. Peter's Square in Rome, expressed his concern for the abuse of human rights within the Yugoslav federation. In fact, human rights represented a valid component as the EC officials claimed to have taken the issue seriously when shaping their policy of recognition.[93] For example, in one of the declarations, the Community and its Member States stressed that 'protection of human rights and rights of ethnic and national groups constitute universal, objective standards, which leave no room for compromise'.[94] Thus, the discourse of human rights consolidated the pressure in Brussels even more.

As soon as the Vatican rushed to recognize Slovenia and Croatia, it sent a note to the Yugoslav authorities in Belgrade stipulating that its decision to recognize the two republics was not intended 'to have the character of a hostile act toward Yugoslavia'.[95] In response to these words, Tanjug, the Yugoslav news agency, quoted Milan Veres, Yugoslavia's Deputy Foreign Minister, saying that 'the Vatican's decision could jeopardize peace', and that Belgrade would take the 'necessary steps' against the Vatican.[96] Indeed, while the Serbian authorities focused on their next action, the Slovenian leadership optimistically thanked the Vatican for 'the efforts aimed at securing a long-lasting peace across the Yugoslav federation' and, in particular, 'support for Slovenian independence'.[97]

For anticipating the decision of the European Community to recognize Slovenia and Croatia as independent states, the Vatican was subjected to severe criticism. In his letter to the Pope, Serbian Patriarch Pavle wrote: 'You made great diplomatic and political efforts that many other European countries might do the same, immediately after you. In doing so, you employed not only the Vatican state mechanism, but also the organism, structures and institutions of the Roman Catholic Church'.[98] More specifically, the Patriarch criticized the strong link between the Catholic Church and politics:

> We do not deny Your right as a Statesman to act in the interests of Your State, but, nonetheless, we request that You perceive the use of the authority of the Church in political aims ... In the

same way, we do not contest the right of the Croat and Slovene Peoples to have their own States outside of Yugoslavia and outside of a common State with us Serbians; but we are astonished that Your Holiness does not recognize such a right for the Serbians as well.[99]

The Patriarch's letter, representing a joint sentiment existing both among the Serbian authorities and the Orthodox Church, suggests various conclusions. First, during the Yugoslav crisis, the Orthodox and Catholic Churches were clearly identified with their respective republics. In fact, both believed that this unity was beneficial for pursuing their goals. Second, the Patriarch alone represented the State and the Church and as such approached the Vatican. As noted, for him the Vatican officials equalled the Roman Catholic Church. Third, he saw the Serbs being undermined by not having a right to secede. Here, the Patriarch ignored the fact that the wars were actually taking place on Slovenian and Croatian territories, not Serbian. Finally, the letter referred to a particular moment in Yugoslavia's history while ignoring various events that had previously occurred across the federation and questioned its future.

Some of the conclusions regarding the Patriarch's letter could surely inspire further discussion. However, as suggested by the overall analysis, the full picture is possible only if the historical dimension is taken into consideration, as well. For example, Timothy Byrnes is right when insisting on the historical events which both linked and separated the Catholic and Orthodox Churches and, more importantly, the peoples represented by these churches. While warning against misinterpretations deriving from the Western media, which often saw the recognition of Slovenia and Croatia purely as Pope John Paul II's decision to support the two predominantly Catholic republics, the author underlines that the Vatican's recognition could not be separated from two important realities: 'one, Croatia and Slovenia *were* the Catholic republics of Yugoslavia; and two, the notion of Croatian independence, as such, fairly or unfairly, was likely to be linked historically with the wartime regime and with its well-documented mistreatment of non-Catholics'.[100] Given such realities, as the author concludes, it is understandable that the Vatican officials did not find it easy to convince the public that the two Catholic republics were due recognition because of their interest in democratic values and the protection of human rights rather than because of their religious composition.[101]

Conclusion

Academic writings in the field have offered a number of very limited contributions, which remain silent about the Vatican and its relevance for the Brussels officials who were assigned significant responsibilities during the Yugoslav crisis. From its very beginning, the Catholics across Europe showed sympathy for Slovenia and Croatia.[102] As noted throughout the chapter, the Pope never denied the Vatican's appreciation of, and readiness to assist, the two Catholic republics. Even when it seemed that the European Community needed more time to think about possible policies, the religious aspect of the conflict as well as the Community's religious composition gained significant relevance for policy-making.

Still, it is important to bear in mind that Vatican support for the Catholic republics of Slovenia and Croatia in their fight for independence did not come purely as a result of the political conflict and the war between the opposing parties, but as a result of an increasingly religious dimension characterizing the conflict. As Misha Glenny later summarized, 'the wars increasingly assimilated the characteristics of religious struggle, defined by three great European faiths – Roman Catholicism, Eastern Orthodoxy and Islam, the confessional detritus of the empires whose frontiers collided in Bosnia'.[103] In such a complex situation, memories of the past relations were resurrected. While the past was truly characterized by a set of problematic relations between the Vatican and the Yugoslav federation, thus between two sovereign states, relations between the Orthodox and Catholic Churches in Yugoslavia and the deteriorating situation characterizing the last stages of the SFRY provided a social vacuum which further encouraged nationalistic feelings. In this vacuum, the representatives of the two Churches did their best to develop strong links with the nationalist elites while ignoring the consequences of these alliances. At the same time, some of them counted on support from abroad.

With the outbreak of the Yugoslav wars, the Vatican did not openly force the EC to proceed with the policy of recognition. If analysed, it did not react as strongly during the hostilities in Slovenia, when the Serbs fought against the Slovenes, thus Orthodox against Catholic, as it did during the Croatian war. In fact, the conflict in Croatia strengthened the Vatican's position, resulting in ever stronger advocacy of international recognition of independence for the two Catholic republics. In Brussels, denomination was not ignored. As noted, from the founding of the European Community to the Yugoslav crisis, the outlook of the Community reflected the doctrine of the Roman Catholic Church. For example, among others, Helmut Kohl, German Chancellor and leader of the Christian Democratic Union, a party which together with the Christian Social Union of Bavaria openly promoted the religious dimension (i.e. Catholicism) in politics, supported the two Catholic republics. Their recognition confirmed the existence of a strong link between church and state, and thus faith and politics:

> The cross of Christ stands next to the Croatian flag, Croatian bishop next to Croatian minister of state. Present at masses in churches are officers and Croatian soldiers. Guardsmen wear rosaries around their necks ... Here was not a battle for a piece of Croatian or Serbian land but a war between good and evil, Christianity and Communism, culture and barbarity, civilization and primitivism, democracy and dictatorship, love and hatred ... Thank God, it all ended well, due to the Pope and Croatian politics.[104]

CONCLUSION

> Within the Former Yugoslavia, great hopes were vested in the role of the international community. For many people, the term "Europe" had an almost mythical significance; it was considered synonymous with civilized behaviour and emblematic of an alternative "civic" outlook to which those who opposed nationalism aspired. What actually happened was deeply disappointing, giving rise to cynicism and despair.
>
> Mary Kaldor, 2006

The European Community mentioned the Socialist Federal Republic of Yugoslavia in its official annual report for the first time in 1963 when the Yugoslav authorities approached the Community to discuss trade among them.[1] However, in 1992, the *XXVIth General Report* had no section on EC relations with Yugoslavia, but rather a new one, simply entitled *Former Yugoslavia*. Understandably, the report acknowledged that the SFRY had ceased to exist. It assessed the situation across the country and concluded that the republics of Serbia and Montenegro were responsible for the wars.[2]

The outbreak of fighting in Yugoslavia, bringing with it a vortex of problems, left the Europeans bewildered. It is noteworthy that the conflict was often portrayed as a threat to European Community stability, as there was a risk of seeing Europe divided into two opposing fronts: one Western, focused on integration, and one Eastern, focused on disintegration. While insisting on this dimension, the secessionist republics expected the international community to react promptly. As some authors observed, the Community stepped into the Balkans 'not because it knew what it wanted ... but because it hoped that it would acquire the necessary security and foreign policy powers as it went along'.[3] But the Community here showed its ineffectiveness, thus calling into doubt public confidence in its capabilities.[4]

The Yugoslav drama was a European problem from the very beginning, but the main issue was that both the European Community and its Member States were unprepared to offer any sort of solution to the crisis. Their own admission of incapacity to tackle the Yugoslav drama provided a vacuum into which specific non-state actors could step. Accordingly, diaspora groups, the media and the Catholic Church developed multi-layer strategies that promoted the Slovenian and Croatian desire for independence abroad. Each chapter on these non-state actors introduced them by explaining when and how their activism was developed – an important aspect revealing that, even though they existed before the Yugoslav state crisis, they achieved greater prominence in the situation of escalating violence and external attention. Indeed, a new set of circumstances represented an opportunity for the non-state actors to put pressure on Brussels officials and, in a situation when no one knew what to do, to contribute to EC policy-making. Thus, they were powerful enough to attract attention amongst policy-makers and reflect the exclusive interests of the republics of Slovenia and Croatia, advocating their recognition as independent states.

On 16 December 1991, the Council of Ministers met in Brussels and agreed upon the Community's criteria for recognizing the Yugoslav republics seeking independence.[5] In fact, based on the impressions accompanying the Brioni Agreement signed in July, when some of the EC Member States reversed their initial position of support for Yugoslav unity, the establishment of the Peace Conference on Yugoslavia in September, and the EC meeting in Haarzuilens in October – when the Community agreed to support the right to independence – it became clear that the Yugoslav federation was living its last days. For example, contrary to the initial reaction of the French government, Roland Dumas, Foreign Minister of France, underlined: 'Yugoslavia no longer exists in its original form and we are forced to take a note of a *de facto* partition occurring ... The European Community should continue to act in complete solidarity and draw the logical consequences under international law from this situation'.[6] These words were fully confirmed as soon as the Badinter Commission, an arbitration body, announced on 29 November that 'the Socialist Federal Republic of Yugoslavia is in the process of dissolution'.[7] On 15 January 1992, the European Community and its Member States decided to grant independence to all the Yugoslav republics that, in their view, satisfied certain conditions. In order to fully recognize them, the decision-makers required any Yugoslav republic 'to commit itself, prior to recognition, to adopt constitutional and political guarantees ensuring that it has no territorial claims towards a neighbouring Community State and that it will conduct no hostile propaganda activities versus a neighbouring Community State, including the use of a denomination which implies territorial claims'.[8] This statement reflected the Community's desire to protect itself and its fellow citizens: the conflict in Yugoslavia seemed to turn into a conflict of territorial conquest when the ideas of Greater Croatia and Greater Serbia enjoyed support from the two opposing nationalistic communities.

All the arguments in this book are offered in the hope that they will contribute to a deeper understanding of how the European Community shaped its decisions with regard to the future of the Yugoslav federation. To this end, I have looked into relations between the Community and Yugoslavia and activism of three different groups of non-state actors that took advantage of the political vacuum at the outbreak of the Yugoslav wars. I also hope that my analysis will further scholarly debate in a number of ways. For example, apart from constant interest in specific events characterizing the past, there are numerous projects that seek to address future prospects. This is indispensable, as demonstrated by the fact that policy-making in the European Union can be conditioned by various factors and players, meaning that sometimes crucial policies are not purely based on well-reasoned arguments backed with data, but rather influenced by various forces. Some serious accounts have recently emerged discussing the role of non-state actors and their capacity to influence politics of individual EU Member States or the Brussels political complex.[9]

Furthermore, this book does not look into the outbreak of war in the republic of Bosnia-Herzegovina and how the European Union shaped its policy at that time; or how the Europeans came to the decision to support the bombing of the republic of Serbia in 1999. Both of these topics require research per se and would represent interesting accounts of EU policies towards a non-EU country. Admittedly, during the disintegration of the Yugoslav federation, the Europeans provided an open arena for substantiated critique. In his account, Michael Brenner summarizes the mistakes of the EC's approach:

> It was not preordained that EC countries be so shortsighted about the dangers of Yugoslavia's dismantlement and the ethnic passions it liberated; nor that they act fitfully and, too often, too late in trying to bring their influence to bear; nor that they cast the die for Bosnia through the ill-considered, premature recognition of Slovenia and Croatia; nor that they respond to the Bosnia catastrophe with hollow threats whose unfulfillment gave courage to the intransigent; nor that they refrain from interdiction measures to enforce the economic embargo or bring sustained pressure to bear on key European violators; ... nor that their stern demands for the closing of detention camps and cessation of the shelling of cities be left as paper declarations while the Twelve exhausted their time and energy on the Maastricht ratification crisis.[10]

While Brenner's list is primarily focused on the European Community as such, I note that relations between the Community/Union and its Member States should not be ignored. When the SFRY was falling apart, there was obvious discord between the Member States of the EC. Some of them had to change their initial views and adjust to those put forward by more influential Member States. More importantly, some Member States ignored the relevance of the Community. For example, the German proposal for an early recognition of Slovenia and Croatia, supported by the Italian and Austrian governments, was presented to EC ministers in December 1991 when Minister Genscher revealed his intention to disregard the common policy of the Community and recognize the two republics unilaterally.

In 1991 the European Community consisted of 12 Member States. To date, this number has increased to 27. This is of interest because the discord that existed between some of the members in the past is likely to become more obvious in a larger and more heterogeneous EU. The Member States differ significantly in their economic, political and social outlooks. Thus, with the present voting system, the lack of a common perspective from the Union implies even more margin for lobbying. Even if the Council of Ministers has the final say, interest groups and lobbyists will feel empowered to approach the Brussels officials who will push their interests to the highest levels. As demonstrated throughout the study, diaspora groups, the media and churches possessed remarkable power in penetrating EC policy-making and in this respect, the Yugoslav experience is a good basis for further questioning and examination of activism and power of non-state actors across the EU.

For example, in 2001, members of the EP met with international experts to address the growing role of religion in European policy. As the press release observed, this meeting took place 'at a time when religious institutions are increasingly interested in participating in policy debates within Europe even as the positions of some religious institutions are at odds with the values that form a European consensus on critical issues'.[11] During the meeting, Camillo Ruini, an Italian cardinal, criticized the EU Charter of Fundamental Rights adopted in December 2000 for not having included the 'historical and cultural roots of Europe, in particular Christianity, which represents Europe's soul and which still today can inspire Europe's mission and identity' – a criticism complementing an earlier point offered by Joseph Ratzinger, then cardinal and now head of the Catholic Church, for whom 'God and our responsibility before God' should have been 'anchored in the European constitution'.[12]

There is no need to explain here what kind of suspicion the words quoted above might provoke among non-Catholics or non-Christians. If applied to the Balkans, they could signify that Turkey, although a candidate country for EU membership, will remain a candidate country forever. If applied to the Western Balkans, then surely Bosnia-Herzegovina, Kosovo and Albania will have to overcome numerous hurdles before convincing Europeans that different religious denomination will not undermine their integrationist vision. At the same time, the EU claims to be committed to assisting the Western Balkans in every aspect possible.[13] Contrary to the disputable commitments that linked the two sides in the past, since 1999 a new set of commitments has apparently brought them closer and generated a deeper mutual understanding and stronger cooperation, but still not enough has been done to see the countries of the Western Balkans in the European Union.

NOTES

Introduction

1. Crnobrnja, Mihailo, *The Yugoslav Drama* (London, 1996), p.224.
2. Almond, Mark, *Europe's Backyard War: The War in the Balkans* (London, 1994), p.340. A similar standpoint is offered by Daianu, Daniel, 'Transition failures: How Does Southeast Europe Fit In?', in Daniel Daianu and Thanos Veremis (eds), *Balkan Reconstruction* (London and Portland, OR, 2001), p.104.
3. Relevant approaches include theories of European integration – from Ernst Haas's neo-functionalism to Stanley Hoffmann's intergovernmentalism, each helping understand the behaviour of the Community and particular Member States (Haas, Ernst B., *The Uniting of Europe: Political, Social and Economic Forces, 1950–1957*, Stanford, CA, 1968; Hoffmann, Stanley, *The European Sisyphus: Essays on Europe, 1964–1994*, Boulder, CO, 1995. For a more concise account, see Ben Rosamond, *Theories of European Integration*, Hampshire, 2000). Apart from these two, approaches regarding the activism of non-state actors and lobbying are equally considered: Bas Arts *et al.*'s understanding about the non-state actors (Arts, Bas, Math Noortmann and Bob Reinalda (eds), *Non-state Actors in International Relations*, Hampshire, 2001) and, more specifically, Rinus van Schendelen's discourse about lobbying in the EU (Van Schendelen, Rinus, *Machiavelli in Brussels: The Art of Lobbying the EU*, Amsterdam, 2005).
4. Various scholars acknowledge Yugoslavia's relevance in this period. For example, Benjamin Miller understands it as 'an important prize in the context of superpower rivalry' (Miller, Benjamin, *When Opponents Cooperate:*

Great Power Conflict and Collaboration in World Politics, Ann Arbor, MI, 2002, p.230) and Badredine Arfi talks about Yugoslavia's 'buffer role ... between the two camps of the Cold War' (Arfi, Badredine, *International Change and the Stability of Multiethnic States*, Bloomington, IN, 2005, p.114).

5. Hadžić, Miroslav, 'The controversies of Euro-Atlantic interventionism in the Balkans', in Peter Siani-Davis (ed), *International Intervention in the Balkans since 1995* (London, 2003), p.62.
6. Lane, Ann, *Yugoslavia: When Ideals Collide* (London, 2003), p.109.
7. Embassy of the SFRY, 'Diplomatic Relations between Yugoslavia and the European Communities', Brussels, 30 January 1968.
8. Commission of the European Communities, *Second General Report on the Activities of the Communities in 1968*, p.389.
9. The High Authority of the European Coal and Steel Community, *Second General Report on the Activities of the Community (April 1953 – April 1954)*, p.25.
10. Commission of the European Communities, *Fifth General Report on the Activities of the Communities in 1971*, p.313.
11. Council, 'Accordo commerciale tra la C.E.E. e la Iugoslavia – Dichiarazioni da iscrivere al processo verbale del Consiglio', 3 March 1970.
12. Meier, Viktor, *Yugoslavia: A History of its Demise* (London and New York, NY, 1999), p.216.
13. For example, in his account about Yugoslavia, John Allcock notes the relevance of history: 'History is not only written from the standpoint of the present, as the story of how we came to be where we are. It involves also a dialectical process which includes where we think we are going in the future. If we cannot think about the past without at least implicit reference to the future, it is equally true that engagement with the future cannot be undertaken without reference to the past' (Allcock John B., *Explaining Yugoslavia*, London and New York, NY, 2000, p.413).
14. Meier: *Yugoslavia*, p.217.
15. This milestone gained its full relevance with the recognition policy of the EC.
16. Cohen, Lenard J., *Broken Bonds: Yugoslavia's Disintegration and Balkan Politics in Transition* (Boulder, CO, 1995), p.229.
17. Kroeber-Riel, Werner and Jürgen Hauschildt, 'Decision making', in Jessica Cooper (ed), *Political Science and Political Theory* (London, 1987), p.47. Some of the reasons why the authors argue that collective decision making is complicated include: difficulty to define the actual goal, problems of communication, coordination efforts, power problems and negotiation difficulties (pp.47–48).

18. Sabl, Andrew, 'Governing pluralism', in Denis Saint-Martin and Fred Thompson (eds), *Public Ethics and Governance: Standards and Practices in Comparative Perspective* (Stamford, CT, 2006), p.250.
19. Winland, Daphne N., *We Are Now a Nation: Croats Between Home and Homeland* (Toronto, 2007), p.27.
20. Collier, Paul and Nicholas Sambanis, *Understanding Civil War* (Washington, DC, 2005), p.308.
21. Crawford, Beverly, 'Explaining defection from international cooperation: Germany's unilateral recognition of Croatia', *World Politics*, Vol.48, No.4 (1996), p.503.
22. Conversi, Daniele, 'German-bashing and the breakup of Yugoslavia', *Donald W. Treadgold Papers in Russian, East European and Central Asian Studies*, Vol.16 (1998), p.47.
23. Caplan, Richard, *International Governance of War-Torn Territories* (Oxford, 2005), p.133.
24. Gagnon, Valere Philip Jr., *The Myth of Ethnic War: Serbia and Croatia in the 1990s* (Ithaca, NY, 2004), pp.46–47, 96.
25. Liotta, P.H., *Dismembering the State: The Death of Yugoslavia and Why it Matters* (Lanham, MD, 2001), p.221.
26. On Serbian-Greek brotherhood, see, for example, Sabrina P. Ramet, 'The way we are – and should be again: European Orthodox Churches and the "idyllic past"', in Timothy A. Byrnes and Peter J. Katzenstein (eds), *Religion in an Expanding Europe* (Cambridge, 2006), pp.148–175.
27. Perica, Vjekoslav, *Balkan Idols: Religion and Nationalism in Yugoslav States* (USA, 2004), p.133, 187.
28. Zucconi, Mario, 'The European Union in the former Yugoslavia', in Abram Chayes and Antonia Handler (eds), *Preventing Conflict in the Post-communist World* (Washington, DC, 1996), p.241.
29. On limitations and risks of this approach, see, for example, James Tully (ed), *Meaning and Context: Quentin Skinner and his Critics* (Princeton, NJ, 1988).
30. Here, I refer primarily to the archives of the EU institutions and the Archive of Yugoslavia. It is interesting to note that following the collapse of Yugoslavia, the archival material has had to be divided among the newly created states. In his brief account, Jovan Popović, the Head of the Archive of Yugoslavia in Belgrade, claims that dividing archival material equals 'cultural genocide' and pretensions about such divisions are without any grounding in archival theory and practice. In this battle, Croatia claims to be entitled to the greatest part of the archival documents, followed by Macedonia and Slovenia (Jovan P. Popović, 'Sukcesija arhiva na prostorima bivše SFRJ', in Kosta Mihailović (ed), *Sukcesija i kontinuitet Savezne Republike*

Jugoslavije, Beograd, 2000, p.148). Moreover, some folders that might have complemented this research were destroyed during the NATO intervention against Yugoslavia in 1999. These folders are: Savezni društveni savet za medjunarodne odnose, Savezni društveni savet za pitanja društvenog uredjenja, Savezni društveni savet za privredni razvoj i ekonomsku politiku and Fond solidarnosti sa Nesvrstanim zemljama i zemljama u razvoju.

31. See Snežana Trifunovska (ed), *Former Yugoslavia through Documents: From its Dissolution to Peace Settlement* (Dordrecht, 1999); Daniel Bethlehem and Mark Weller (eds), *The Yugoslav Crisis in International Law: Part I* (Cambridge, 1997); Snežana Trifunovska (ed), *Yugoslavia through Documents: From its Creation to its Dissolution* (Dordrecht, 1994).
32. [Sources about Democratization and Attainment of Independence of Slovenia].
33. On limitations of interviews, see, for example, Martyn Hammersley, 'Ethnography: problems and prospects', *Ethnography and Education*, Vol.1, No.1 (2006), pp.3–14; Jonathan Potter and Margaret Wetherell, *Discourse and Social Psychology* (London, 1987); Paul Connolly, 'Playing if by the rules: the politics of research in "race" and education', *British Educational Research Journal*, Vol.18, No.12 (1992), pp.133–148.
34. Wengraf, Tom, *Qualitative Research Interviewing: Semi-Structured, Biographical and Narrative Methods* (London, 2001), p.5.

Chapter One   Writing the Collapse of Yugoslavia: Existing and Potential Arguments

1. Hitchcock, William I., *The Struggle for Europe: The History of the Continent since 1945* (London, 2004), p.384.
2. Lucarelli, Sonia, *Europe and the Breakup of Yugoslavia: A Political Failure in Search of a Scholarly Explanation* (Leiden, 2000), p.1.
3. Gerolymatos, André, *The Balkan Wars: Conquest, Revolution and Retribution from the Ottoman Era to the Twentieth Century and beyond* (Staplehurst, 2004), p.4.
4. This study draws on two mutually inclusive definitions of international community. For Marina Ottaway, it is 'the conglomerate of industrialized democracies and the multilateral agencies over which they have a preponderant role' (Marina Ottaway, 'Rebuilding state institutions in collapsed states', in Jennifer Milliken (ed), *State Failure, Collapse and Reconstruction*, Malden, MA, 2003, p.245). For Sonia Lucarelli, 'the nebulous term "international community" is conventionally used to refer to the states, international organizations and other international actors which, because they broadly share common values and purposes, contribute to the collective regulation of international security' (Lucarelli: *Europe*, pp.1–2).

5. Some valuable literature reviews are offered by Radmila Nakarada, *Raspad Jugoslavije: Problemi tumačenja, suočavanja i tranzicije* (Beograd, 2008), pp.13–137; Jasna Dragović-Soso, 'Why did Yugoslavia disintegrate? An overview of contending explanations', in Lenard J. Cohen and Jasna Dragović-Soso (eds), *State Collapse in South-Eastern Europe: New Perspectives on Yugoslavia's Disintegration* (West Lafayette, IN, 2007), pp.1–39; Sabrina P. Ramet, *Thinking about Yugoslavia: Scholarly Debates about the Yugoslav Breakup and the Wars in Bosnia and Kosovo* (Cambridge, 2005); Dejan Jović, 'The disintegration of Yugoslavia: a critical review of explanatory approaches', *European Journal of Social Theory*, Vol.4, No.1 (2001), pp.101–120; James Gow, 'After the flood: literature on the context, causes, and course of the Yugoslav war – reflections and refractions', *Slavonic and East European Review*, Vol.75, No.3 (1997), pp.446–484; Gale Stokes, John Lampe, Dennison Rusinow and Julie Mostov, 'Instant history: understanding the wars of Yugoslav succession', *Slavic Review*, Vol.55, No.1 (1996), pp.136–160.
6. Hayden, Robert M., *Blueprints for a House Divided: The Constitutional Logic of the Yugoslav Conflicts* (Ann Arbor, MI, 1999), p.19.
7. Ten-Day War in Slovenia or Slovenian Independence War (1991), Croatian War of Independence (1991–1995), War in Bosnia-Herzegovina or the Bosnian War (1992–1995) and the Kosovo War (1998–1999).
8. Slobodan Milošević (1941–2006) was present in politics as follows: President of the Presidency of the Central Committee of the League of Communists of Serbia (1986–1989), President of the Presidency of the Socialist Republic of Serbia (1989–1990), President of the Republic of Serbia (1990–1997) and President of the Federal Republic of Yugoslavia (1997–2000).
9. Franjo Tudjman (1922–1999) was present in politics as follows: Founder and President of the Croatian Democratic Union (1989–1999) and President of the Republic of Croatia (1990–1999).
10. Milan Kučan (1941-) was present in politics as follows: Chairman of the League of Communists of Slovenia (1986–1990) and President of Slovenia (1990–2002).
11. On literature discussing each of these, see Dejan Jović, *Yugoslavia: A State that Withered Away* (West Lafayette, IN, 2009), pp.18–25.
12. For example, Glenn Bowman argues that once in place, violence plays a constructive role in the formation of all nationalisms and contributes to a concept of a national enemy, which in the former Yugoslavia resulted in individuals seeing each other not as co-nationals, but as members of 'opposed national communities' living in 'an imposed federation' (Glenn Bowman, 'Constructive violence and the nationalist imaginary: The making of "The People" in Palestine and Former Yugoslavia', in Francisco Panizza (ed),

Populism and the Mirror of Democracy, London, 2005, p.120). Moreover, Misha Glenny discusses Tudjman's refusal to comprehend the complex situation faced by the Serbian community within Croatia – 'probably the most costly mistake he has ever made in his life' (Misha Glenny, *The Fall of Yugoslavia: The Third Balkan War*, London, 1993, p.3). From a different perspective, Andrew Wachtel examines the concept of Yugoslav culture and concludes that once the political elite had started paying greater attention to political centrism, the idea of cultural nation-building disappeared and thus allowed each of the republics to create its own television programmes and, more generally, to promote its own writers and artists, consequently ignoring other republics' representatives (Andrew Wachtel, *Making a Nation, Breaking a Nation: Literature and Cultural Politics in Yugoslavia*, Stanford, CA, 1998, pp.174–184).
13. Fukuyama, Francis, *The End of History and the Last Man* (New York, NY, 2006), p.31.
14. Owen, David, *Balkan Odyssey* (Orlando, FL, 1995), p.137.
15. Ed Villiamy, Rory Carol and Peter Beaumont, 'How I trapped the Butcher of the Balkans', *The Observer*, 1 July 2001. The media especially liked this metaphor and accordingly, Ian Traynor wrote 'No smoking gun for "Balkan Butcher"' for *The Guardian*, 28 February 2004, and the CNN reported '"Butcher of the Balkans" found dead', on 12 March 2006.
16. This school of thought is represented in the work of Christopher Bennett, Norman Cigar, Thomas Cushman, Bogdan Denitch, Reneo Lukić and Allen Lynch, Branka Magaš, Viktor Meier, Stjepan Meštrović, Sabrina P. Ramet, James J. Sadkovich, Michael Sells, Laura Silber and Allan Little.
17. Josip Broz Tito (1892–1980) was present in politics as follows: Head of the Communist Party of Yugoslavia (after 1952 LCY), the Prime Minister of Yugoslavia (1945–1953) and President of the SFRY (1953–1980).
18. Denitch, Bogdan, *Ethnic Nationalism: The Tragic Death of Yugoslavia* (Minneapolis, MN, 1996), p.58. A similar point is offered by Andrew Borowiec who criticizes Titoism as 'a system without a straightforward doctrine [which] vacillates between communism and liberalism, between the straitjacket and party interference and the comparative freedom of the "socialist market economy"' (Andrew Borowiec, *Yugoslavia After Tito*, New York, NY, 1977, p.15).
19. Pavlowitch, Stevan K., *The Improbable Survivor: Yugoslavia and its Problems, 1918–1988* (London, 1988), p.25. The creation of a Greater Serbia had been an idea and matter of concern in the Yugoslav federation. For example, in Bosnia-Herzegovina, it represented a plan of action interpreted by Norman Cigar as Milošević's ambition: to expel all non-Serbs and destroy

the cultural heritage of different religions, thus to convert a policy of ethnic cleansing into a rational policy (Norman Cigar, *Genocide in Bosnia: The Policy of "Ethnic Cleansing"*, College Station, TX, 1995, p.4). In addition, in analyzing Belgrade's aspirations, some other authors conclude: 'Had Milošević succeeded in recentralizing Yugoslavia and transformed it into a unitary authoritarian state, he would have achieved *de facto* a Greater Serbia that would have borne the name of Yugoslavia' (Reneo Lukić and Alen Lynch, *Europe from the Balkans to the Urals: The Disintegration of Yugoslavia and the Soviet Union*, Oxford, 1996, p.155). However, by November 1991, the Serbian leadership had realized that the idea of a Greater Serbia was not going to materialize and started favouring an alternative strategy (Steven L. Burg and Paul S. Shoup, *The War in Bosnia-Herzegovina: Ethnic Conflict and International Intervention*, Armonk, NY, 1999, p.89).

20. Malešević, Siniša, *Ideology, Legitimacy and the New State: Yugoslavia, Serbia and Croatia* (London, 2002), p.232. In addition, both James Sadkovich and Zdravko Tomac present Tudjman in a favourable light: Sadkovich shows appreciation for 'the lesser of two Balkan evils' and his 'respect for formal, procedural democracy' (James J. Sadkovich, 'Franjo Tudjman: A Political and Intellectual Biography', Online, pp.1–3), and Tomac justifies Tudjman's policies suggesting that Croatia would have gained more if it had formed a coalition with Izetbegović against the Serbs (Zdravko Tomac, *The Struggle for the Croatian State: Through Hell to Democracy*, Zagreb, 1993, p.253).
21. Denitch: *Ethnic Nationalism*, p.58.
22. Gow, James, *The Serbian Project and Its Adversaries: A Strategy of War Crimes* (London, 2003), p.209.
23. Zimmermann, Warren, *Origins of a Catastrophe: Yugoslavia and Its Destroyers* (New York, NY, 1996), p.71.
24. In fact, the *Nova Revija* supported Slovenian independence and while reporting that the SFRY was 'a historical accident' and 'without any idea of itself', it argued that Yugoslavia 'cannot exist' (Ilija Urbančić, 'Sedamdeset let Jugoslavije', *Nova Revija* 85/86 (1989), quoted in Dejan Jović, 'The Slovenian-Croatian confederal proposal: a tactical move or an ultimate solution?' in Lenard J. Cohen and Jasna Dragović-Soso (eds), *State Collapse in South-Eastern Europe: New Perspectives on Yugoslavia's Disintegration*, West Lafayette, IN, 2007, p.261).
25. Hayden: *Blueprints for a House Divided*, p.29.
26. Mario Nobilo, *Hrvatski Feniks*, p.40, quoted in Jović: 'The Slovenian-Croatian confederal proposal, p.251.
27. Meier, Viktor, *Yugoslavia: A History of its Demise* (London and New York, NY, 1999), p.xiv.

28. Ibid., pp.14–17.
29. See, for example, Patrick Moore, 'New Dimensions for the Alpine-Adria Project', *Radio Free Europe (Daily Report on Eastern Europe)*, 2 March 1990, pp.53–56.
30. The Brioni Agreement, formerly know as 'Common Declaration on the Peaceful Resolution of the Yugoslav Crisis', signed on 7 July 1991, ended the Slovenian war, whereas the leaders of Slovenia and Croatia agreed to freeze their independence claims for a period of three months. The agreement called for urgent negotiations while confirming that it was only to the peoples of the Yugoslav federation to decide upon their future. For a full analysis of the agreement, see Leo Tindemans *et al.*, *Unfinished Peace: Report of the International Commission on the Balkans* (Washington, DC, 1996).
31. Lucarelli: *Europe*, p.123.
32. It was believed that Yugoslavia had already depended too much on foreign assistance and therefore ignored its own economic development. On this matter, see Patrick F. R. Artisien and Stephen Holt, 'Yugoslavia and the EEC in the 1970s', *Journal of Common Market Studies*, Vol.18, No.4 (1980), pp.355–369.
33. Woodward, Susan L., *Socialist Unemployment: The Political Economy of Yugoslavia, 1945–1990* (Princeton, NJ, 1995), pp.355–364.
34. Zimmerman, William, *Open Borders, Nonalignment, and the Political Evolution of Yugoslavia* (Princeton, NJ, 1977), p.4.
35. Glenny: *The Fall of Yugoslavia*, p.63.
36. Ramet: *Thinking about Yugoslavia*, pp.55–56. For a more detailed explanation, see Sabrina P. Ramet, *Nationalism and Federalism in Yugoslavia, 1962–1991* (Bloomington, IN, 1992).
37. See, for example, Peter Jambrek, *Development and Social Change in Yugoslavia: Crises and Perspectives of Building a Nation* (Farnborough, 1975); William Zimmerman, *Open Borders, Nonalignment, and the Political Evolution of Yugoslavia* (Princeton, NJ, 1977); Bruce McFarlane, *Yugoslavia: Politics, Economics and Society* (London and New York, NY, 1988); David A. Dyker, *Yugoslavia: Socialism, Development and Debt* (London, 1990).
38. Lane, Ann, *Yugoslavia: When Ideals Collide* (London, 2003), pp.121–122.
39. Ibid., p.109.
40. The main IMF's intention was to fight inflation by introducing restrictions on credits and imports, but at the same time reducing production and labour, thus stimulating unemployment. For a detailed analysis, see Woodward: *Socialist Unemployment*, p.259.
41. Mastnak, Tomaz, 'From the new social movements to political parties', in James Simmie and Jože Dekleva (eds), *Yugoslavia in Turmoil: After*

Self-management? (London, 1991), pp.45–64. A similar point is offered by Vesna Bojičić, 'The disintegration of Yugoslavia: Causes and consequences of dynamic inefficiency in semi-command economies', in David A. Dyker and Ivan Vejvoda (eds), *Yugoslavia and After: A Study in Fragmentation, Despair and Rebirth* (London and New York, NY, 1996), pp.28–47.

42. Reuter, Jens, 'Yugoslavia's role in changing Europe', in D. Muller *et al.* (eds), *Veranderungen in Europa – Vereinigung Deutchlands: Perspektiven der 90er Jahre* (Belgrade, 1991), p.115.
43. Johnson, Ross A., 'Yugoslavia: In the twilight of Tito', *The Washington Papers*, Vol.2 (1974), p.55. The same point is made in Borowiec: *Yugoslavia After Tito*, p.7.
44. Allcock John B., *Explaining Yugoslavia* (London and New York, NY, 2000), pp.418–423.
45. Bowman: 'Constructive Violence and the Nationalist Imaginary', p.133.
46. Pleština, Dijana, *Regional Development in Communist Yugoslavia: Success, Failure, and Consequences* (Boulder, CO, 1992), pp.113–125.
47. Bookman, Milica Z., 'Economic aspects of Yugoslavia's disintegration', in Raju G. C. Thomas (ed), *Yugoslavia Unraveled: Sovereignty, Self-Determination, Intervention* (USA, 2003), p.120.
48. Caplan, Richard, *Europe and the Recognition of New States in Yugoslavia* (Cambridge, 2005), p.7.
49. The EC's five-year loan included 807 million ECU (European Currency Units). See, for example, Wolfgang Krieger, 'Toward a Gaullist Germany?', *World Policy Journal*, Vol.11 (1994), pp.1–30. Moreover, the Community was ready to offer additional aid through various programs amounting for 3.6 billion ECU (4.5 billion USD) altogether (Saadia Touval, *Mediation in the Yugoslav Wars: The Critical Years, 1990–1995*, New York, NY, 2002, p.20).
50. Touval: *Mediation in the Yugoslav Wars*, p.15.
51. Cohen, Lenard J., *Broken Bonds: Yugoslavia's Disintegration and Balkan Politics in Transition* (Boulder, CO, 1995), pp.215–216.
52. This switch was due to the American reaction to two internationally recognized events: first, with the end of the Cold War, Yugoslavia's geopolitical importance diminished and, second, the State Department agreed to focus more on human rights violations, particularly in Kosovo (Paul Shoup, 'The disintegration of Yugoslavia and Western foreign policy in the 1980s', in Lenard J. Cohen and Jasna Dragović-Soso (eds), *State Collapse in South-Eastern Europe: New Perspectives on Yugoslavia's Disintegration*, West Lafayette, IN, 2007, pp.338–339).
53. David Binder, 'Evolution in Europe; Yugoslavia Seen Breaking up Soon', *The New York Times*, 28 November 1990, p.7. In one of his speeches, Zimmermann

also noted: 'I would reassert to the Yugoslav authorities the traditional mantra of US policy toward Yugoslavia – our support for its unity, independence and territorial integrity. But I would add that we could only support the country's unity in the context of progress toward democracy; we would be strongly opposed to unity imposed or maintained by force' (Zimmermann: *Origins of a Catastrophe*, p.8).

54. Duncan, Raymond W., 'Yugoslavia's break-up', in Raymond W. Duncan and Paul G. Holman, Jr. (eds), *Ethnic Nationalism and Regional Conflict: The Former Soviet Union and Yugoslavia* (Boulder, CO, 1994), p.34.
55. Ullman, Richard H. (ed), *The World and Yugoslavia's Wars* (New York, NY, 1996), p.5.
56. For example, Branko Pribičević argues that the USA partly withdrew from the Yugoslav issue for two reasons: first, the SFRY problem was local in character and could not undermine balance of power in Europe after the collapse of the Soviet bloc and, second, the USA did not seek great involvement in European politics (Branko Pribičević, 'Relations with the Superpowers', in Sabrina P. Ramet and Ljubiša S. Adamovich (eds), *Beyond Yugoslavia: Politics, Economics, and Culture in a Shattered Community*, Boulder, CO, 1995, p.342). In addition, when James Baker, US Secretary of State, visited Yugoslavia, he assured that the USA would not recognize unilateral secession of Slovenia or support Serbian territorial pretensions, but if forced to react, it would opt for democracy over unity (James Baker, *The Politics of Diplomacy: Revolution, War and Peace, 1989–1992*, New York, NY, 1995, pp.481–482).
57. Zimmermann: *Origins of a Catastrophe*, p.65.
58. Wallace, William, 'National inputs into European Political Cooperation', in David Allen, Reinhardt Rummel and Wolfgang Wessels (eds), *European Political Cooperation: Towards a foreign policy for Western Europe* (Bonn, 1982), p.57.
59. Pavlowitch, Stevan K., 'Yugoslavia: Why did it collapse?', in Vassilis K. Fouskas (ed), *The Politics of Conflict* (London, 2007), p.151.
60. Meier: *Yugoslavia*, p.38.
61. Woodward, Susan L., *Balkan Tragedy: Chaos and Dissolution after the Cold War* (Washington, DC, 1995), pp.106–107.
62. The relationship between the EEC and Yugoslavia was institutionalized by the Joint Declaration in 1976 and codified into the Cooperation Agreement in 1980 with an expiration date on 8 November 1991.
63. Meier: *Yugoslavia*, pp.217–219.
64. Bennett, Christopher, *Yugoslavia's Bloody Collapse: Causes, Course and Consequences* (Washington Square, NY, 1995), p.244.
65. Ibid., pp.13–14.

NOTES 185

66. Radan, Peter, *The Break-up of Yugoslavia and International Law* (London, 2002), p.160.
67. Buzan, Barry and Ole Wæver, *Regions and Powers: The Structure of International Security* (Cambridge, 2003), p.387.
68. Quoted in Mark Almond, *Europe's Backyard War: The War in the Balkans* (London, 1994), p.32.
69. Buzan and Wæver: *Regions and Powers*, p.383.
70. Zimmermann: *Origins of a Catastrophe*, p.147.
71. Thomas, Raju G. C., 'Sovereignty, self-determination, and secession: principles and practice', in Raju G. C. Thomas (ed), *Yugoslavia Unraveled: Sovereignty, Self-Determination, Intervention* (USA, 2003), p.3.
72. Even Zimmermann himself admits that the policy of recognition was premature, as it excluded any compromise. For him, both the US and the EC failed in this respect: 'I was urging Washington to try to persuade the Community to defer recognition. All the EC ambassadors in Belgrade were also lobbying their governments against premature recognition ... Washington shared these concerns but didn't do enough about them' (Zimmermann: *Origins of a Catastrophe*, p.176).
73. Pocock, John Greville A., 'Deconstructing Europe', in Peter Gowan and Penny Anderson (eds), *The Question of Europe* (London, 1997), p.305.
74. Therborn, Göran, 'Europe in the twenty-first century: the world's Scandinavia?', in Peter Gowan and Penny Anderson (eds), *The Question of Europe* (London, 1997), p. 358.
75. For a detailed account, see Marc Weller, 'The international response to the dissolution of the Socialist Federal Republic of Yugoslavia', *The American Journal of International Law*, Vol.86, No.3 (1992), pp.569–607.
76. The Troika consisted of the past, present and coming EC Foreign Ministers, thus Gianni de Michelis (Italy), Jacques Poos (Luxembourg) and Hans van den Broek (the Netherlands). For a full account of the responsibilities of the Troika, see James Gow, *Triumph of the Lack of Will: International Diplomacy and the Yugoslav War* (London, 1997), pp.50–53.
77. The new setting included the EC-Troika, the five permanent members of the Security Council, the OSCE-Troika, one member of the Organization of the Islamic Countries and two representatives of neighboring states. See 'Report of the Secretary General on the International Conference of the Former Yugoslavia', UN Doc. S/24795, 11 November 1992.
78. Joint statement delivered on 28 August 1991 only pointed out that 'the relevant authorities will submit their differences' to the Commission, thus leaving the arbitration Commission to adopt its own rules and procedures. See, for example, Matthew C. R. Craven, 'The European Community

Arbitration Commission on Yugoslavia', *British Year Book of International Law*, Vol.66 (1995), pp.333–413.
79. Caplan: *Europe*, p. 25.
80. McGoldrick, Dominic, 'The tale of Yugoslavia: lessons for accommodating national identity in national and international law', in Stephen Tierney (ed), *Accommodating National Identity: New Approaches in International and Domestic Law* (Leiden, 2000), p.24.
81. Opinion No. 2 and Opinion No. 3 of the Arbitration Commission of the Peace Conference on Yugoslavia. These two opinions are discussed in detail in Radan: *The Break-up*, pp.222–224.
82. Pavković, Aleksandar and Peter Radan, *Creating New States: Theory and Practice of Secession* (Surrey, 2007), p.163.
83. Burg and Shoup: *The War in Bosnia-Herzegovina*, p.98.
84. Hoffmann, Stanley, 'Yugoslavia: implications for Europe and for European institutions', in Richard H. Ullman (ed), *The World and Yugoslavia's Wars* (New York, NY), p.111.
85. Lak, Marteen, 'The Involvement of the European Community in the Yugoslav Crisis during 1991', in Martin van den Hauvel and Jan G. Siccama (eds), *The Disintegration of Yugoslavia* (Amsterdam and Atlanta, GA, 1992), p.175.
86. Cohen: *Broken Bonds*, p.46.
87. Woodward: *Balkan Tragedy*, p.205.
88. Ibid., p.183.
89. Ibid.
90. Ibid., p.189. The author criticizes the Austrian leadership for advocating 'a purist notion of a nation-state' (p.205), Italy for its contradictory policy (pp.159–160), the Vatican for having 'openly lobbied for the independence of the two predominantly Roman Catholic republics' (p.149).
91. Crawford, Beverly, 'Explaining defection from international cooperation: Germany's unilateral recognition of Croatia', *World Politics*, Vol.48, No.4 (1996), p.483.
92. Ibid., p.516.
93. Ibid., p.521.
94. Ibid., p.497. Moreover, this well-publicized German position also emerges in Johan Galtung's understanding that the Yugoslav conflict offered a 'tremendous opportunity' for a unified Germany to turn old possibilities of 'political-economic-cultural penetration' into new ones, while the European Community 'hesitatingly' failed to stand up to the 'strongest member' and followed (Johan Galtung, 'Reflections on the peace prospects for Yugoslavia', in Tonči Kuzmanić and Arno Truger (eds), *Yugoslavia War* (Ljubljana, 1992), p.24.

NOTES

187

95. Pratt, Jeff, *Class, Nation and Identity: The Anthropology of Political Movements* (London, 2003), p.152.
96. Ibid., p.151.
97. Both, Norbert, *From Indifference to Entrapment: The Netherlands and the Yugoslav Crisis, 1990–1995* (Amsterdam, 2000), pp.90–91.
98. Both's understanding is inspired by the relations between the Netherlands and Germany that existed during German reunification which had been opposed by the Dutch (Both: *From Indifference to Entrapment*, pp.114–118).
99. Schloer, Wolfgang, 'Germany and the break-up of Yugoslavia', in Raju G. C. Thomas and Richard H. Friman (eds), *The South Slav Conflict* (New York, NY, 1996), p.315.
100. Conversi, Daniele, 'Germany and the recognition of Slovenia and Croatia', in Brad K. Blitz (ed), *War and Change in the Balkans: Nationalism, Conflict and Cooperation* (Cambridge, 2006), p.64.
101. Lukić and Lynch: *Europe from the Balkans to the Urals*, p.271.
102. Both: *From Indifference to Entrapment*, p.131.
103. Ibid., p.134.
104. Hanson, Alan, 'Croatian Independence from Yugoslavia, 1991–1992', in Melanie Greenberg, John H. Barton and Margaret E. McGuinness (eds), *Words Over War: Mediation and Arbitration to Prevent Deadly Conflict* (Lanham, MD, 2000), p.79.
105. Glenny: *The Fall of Yugoslavia*, p.101.
106. Roberts, Walter R., 'The tragedy in Yugoslavia could have been averted', in Raju G. C. Thomas and H. Richard Friman (eds), *The South Slav Conflict* (New York, NY, 1996), p.370.
107. Niemeyer, Ralph Thomas, *The Verdict: When A State Is Hijacked* (Bloomington, IN, 2003), p.31.
108. See, for example, Gabriel Sheffer, *Diapora Politics: At Home Abroad* (Cambridge, 2006).
109. Gow, James and Cathie Carmichael, *Slovenia and the Slovenes: A Small State and the New Europe* (London, 2000), p.181.
110. 'Diasporas: A World of Exiles', *The Economist*, 2 January 2003, pp.25–27.
111. Hockenos, Paul, *Homeland Calling: Exile Patriotism and the Balkan Wars* (Ithaca, NY, 2003), pp.15–102. A similar approach is adopted in Jakša Kučan, *Bitka za Novu Hrvatsku* (Rijeka: 2000) and Zlatko Skrbiš, *Long-Distance Nationalism: Diasporas, Homelands, and Identities* (Sydney, 1999).
112. Stark, Hans, 'Dissonances franco-allemandes sur fond de guerre serbo-croate', *Politique etrangere*, Vol.57, No.2 (1992), p.341.
113. Lyons, Terrence, 'Diasporas and homeland conflict', Online, p.9.

114. Mutz, Diana C., *Impersonal Influence: How Perceptions of Mass Collectives Affect Political Attitudes* (Cambridge, 1998), p.91.
115. In addition, she accuses the Serbian media of closing down the Albanian-language radio and television in Kosovo, whereas in Slovenia and Croatia the opposition had access to state-controlled media (Branka Magaš, *The Destruction of Yugoslavia: Tracking Yugoslavia's Break-up, 1980–1992*, London, 1992, p.263).
116. See, for example, Mark Thompson, *Forging War: The Media in Serbia, Croatia and Bosnia-Herzegovina* (Luton, 1999). Moreover, Christopher Bennett points out that 'the media had always played a critical role in Yugoslav society but had, hitherto, been employed to bring Yugoslavia's peoples together in the Titoist spirit of "brotherhood and unity", and to smooth over national disputes, not to create ethnic conflict' (Bennett: *Yugoslavia's Bloody Collapse*, p.10).
117. Blagojević, Marina, 'War on Kosovo: a victory for the media?', in Florian Bieber and Zidas Daskalovski (eds), *Understanding the War in Kosovo* (London and Portland, OR, 2003), p.169.
118. Conversi: 'German-bashing,' p.47.
119. Crawford: 'Explaining defection', p.503.
120. Glenny: *The Fall of Yugoslavia*, p.103.
121. For example, Stevan Pavlowitch argues that in the 1980s '[t]he Churches began to extend their social involvement. The religious press blossomed, particularly on the Catholic side. A survey undertaken in 1983 accounted for some 200 religious periodicals, with a total annual circulation of 15 million copies' (Pavlowitch: *The Improbable Survivor*, p.105).
122. Huntington, Samuel P., *The Clash of Civilizations and the Remaking of World Order* (London, 2002), p.267.
123. Ramet, Sabrina P., *Balkan Babel: The Disintegration of Yugoslavia from the Death of Tito to the Fall of Milošević* (Boulder, CO, 2002), p.95.
124. Liotta, P. H., 'Religion and war: fault lines in the Balkan enigma', in Raju G. C. Thomas (ed), *Yugoslavia Unraveled: Sovereignty, Self-Determination, Intervention* (USA, 2003), p.89.
125. Michas, Takis, *Unholy Alliance: Greece and Milosevic's Serbia* (College Station, TX, 2002), p. 29.
126. Woodward, Susan L., 'The West and the international organisations', in David A. Dyker and Ivan Vejvoda (eds), *Yugoslavia and After: A Study in Fragmentation, Despair and Rebirth* (London and New York, NY, 1996), p.163.
127. The term 'Western Balkans' was established during the Austrian presidency of the European Union in 1998 and it is used by the EU when addressing Croatia, Bosnia-Herzegovina, Serbia, Montenegro, Macedonia and Albania together (Council, 'Vienna European Council: Presidency Conclusions', 11–12 December 1998).

NOTES 189

Chapter Two The European Community and Yugoslavia from Unofficial to Official Relations

1. Watson, Adam, *Diplomacy: The Dialogue between States* (London, 1982), p.14.
2. Fabinc, Ivo, 'Federalism: the crossroads', in George Macesich (ed), *Yugoslavia in the Age of Democracy* (Westport, CT, 1992), p.92.
3. The main objective of this Soviet-style plan was to double the pre-war national income by augmenting industrial production five times. Accordingly, the plan to support Yugoslavia's economy advocated that all assistance including credits, loans and materials, would be provided by the Soviet Union. For a detailed analysis of the plan, see Dragomir Vojnić, 'Reforms in Retrospect', in George Macesich (ed), *Yugoslavia in the Age of Democracy* (Westport, CT, 1992), p.27.
4. Lane, Ann, *Yugoslavia: When Ideals Collide* (London, 2003), p.112.
5. Byrnes, Robert F., 'The Dispute: historical background', in Vaclav L. Benes, Robert F. Byrnes and Nicolas Spulber (eds), *The Second Soviet-Yugoslav Dispute* (Bloomington, IN, 1959), pp.xii-xiii.
6. Lampe, John R. *et al.*, *Yugoslav-American Relations since World War II* (Durham, NC, 1990), p.29.
7. Byrnes: 'The Dispute', p.xiii.
8. Lane: *Yugoslavia*, p.113.
9. Ibid., pp.113–114.
10. Shoup, Paul, *Communism and the Yugoslav National Question* (New York, NY, 1968), pp.184–189.
11. Marković, Ljubisav, 'Socialism: illusion and reality', in George Macesich (ed), *Yugoslavia in the Age of Democracy* (Westport, CT, 1992), p.31.
12. Cohen, Lenard J. and Paul Warwick, *Political Cohesion in a Fragile Mosaic: The Yugoslav Experience* (Boulder, CO, 1983), p.73.
13. Auty, Phyllis, *Yugoslavia* (London, 1965), p.120.
14. Pavlowitch, Stevan K., *Yugoslavia* (New York, NY, 1971), p.225.
15. Auty: *Yugoslavia*, p.112. By 'the outside world' the author intends the United Kingdom and the United States of America 'due to Yugoslav resentment at continued Allied occupation of Zone A and uncertainty about Zone B, the areas claimed by both Italy and Yugoslavia' (Ibid.).
16. European Coal and Steel Community.
17. Delors, Jacques, *Our Europe: The Community and National Development* (London, 1992), p.17.
18. The High Authority of the European Coal and Steel Community, *General Report on the Activities of the European Community (August 1952 – April 1953)*, p.25.
19. For example, Lane depicts Yugoslavia as 'ambiguous since it had interests in developing and sustaining working relationships with both East and West in the Cold War; its domestic organization was innovative, dynamic and highly experimental' (Lane: *Yugoslavia*, p.115).

20. The High Authority of the European Coal and Steel Community, *Third General Report on the Activities of the Community (April 1954 – April 1955)*, p.25.
21. McAllister, Richard, *From EC to EU: An Historical and Political Survey* (London, 1997), pp.7–8.
22. Ibid., pp.8–9.
23. The High Authority of the European Coal and Steel Community, *Second General Report on the Activities of the Community (April 1953 – April 1954)*, p.25.
24. Mates, Leo, *Međunarodni odnosi socijalističke Jugoslavije* (Beograd, 1976), p.168. The author uses the following examples to illustrate Yugoslavia's readiness to cooperate: forgiveness of reparations in regard to Bulgaria, Romania and Hungary, willingness to reach an agreement with Italy over the border dispute, and, what Mates considers of crucial importance, Yugoslavia's decision to recognize Western Germany (pp.90–92, 186).
25. Ibid., pp.169–170.
26. Rusinow, Dennison, *The Yugoslav Experiment, 1948–1974* (London, 1977), p.241.
27. Ibid., p.213.
28. This point is clearly stressed in 'Speech of J. B. Tito at Labin', *Borba*, 16 June 1958. Moreover, what appears interesting is that at the same time the Soviet reputation in Yugoslavia started to decline. In Stevan Pavlowitch's terms, 'the conflict with the USSR began to be expressed in ideological terms, and the Yugoslav Party press began to attack the Soviet system'. The core values were undermined and 'the Soviet Union was no longer the 'ultimate guarantor' of the Yugoslav Communist leaders' hold over their country; it was against them' (Pavlowitch: *Yugoslavia*, p.235).
29. Lane: *Yugoslavia*, pp.121–122.
30. Yugoslav relations with Turkey improved once Yugoslavia had agreed to pay compensation for the nationalized Turkish property, in 1951. With regard to Greece, the Macedonian question represented a serious problem requiring third-party mediation, in this case, the USA. In the case of Italy, the Trieste area was an obstacle as both Italy and Yugoslavia had territorial pretensions on the city (Auty, Phyllis, 'The post-War period', in Stephen Clissold and Henry Clifford Darby (eds), *A Short History of Yugoslavia from Early times to 1966*, Cambridge, 1968, p.260).
31. For a detailed analysis, see Dragan Bogetić, *Jugoslavija i Zapad 1952–1955: Jugoslovensko približavanje NATO-u* (Beograd, 2000).
32. Pavlowitch: *Yugoslavia*, p.245.
33. Monnet, Jean, *Memoirs* (Glasgow, 1978), p.522.
34. 'Council of Europe,' p.596.

NOTES 191

35. Mitrany, David, 'The functional approach to world organization', *International Affairs*, Vol.24, No.3 (1948), p.73.
36. *The Times*, 8 May 1953.
37. Commission of the European Economic Community, *Third General Report on the Activities of the Community (March 1959 – May 1960)*, p.250.
38. Ibid., p.251.
39. Interview with a member of the Yugoslav government. For example, lack of information and misinterpretation characterized the reporting about rapprochement between Yugoslavia and the Soviet Union, during the mid 1950s.
40. Lane: *Yugoslavia*, p.122.
41. Pavlowitch: *Yugoslavia*, p.250.
42. Quoted in 'Rapport des conseillers commerciaux des pays members de la CEE en Yougoslavie', Belgrade, 22 June 1959.
43. The program consisted of three chapters: first, entitled 'Social, economic and political relations in the contemporary world', second, 'The struggle for socialism under new conditions', and third and the most important for this study, 'International political relations and the foreign policy of socialist Yugoslavia'.
44. 'Speech of J. B. Tito at Labin', *Borba*, 16 June 1958.
45. For a full account of Yugoslavia's position, see, for example, Barry Hughes and Thomas Volgy, 'Distance in foreign policy behaviour: a comparative study of Eastern Europe', *Midwest Journal of Political Science*, Vol.14, No.3 (1970), pp.488–490.
46. Pavlowitch: *Yugoslavia*, p.266.
47. Ibid., p.264.
48. See, for example, Andrew Shonfield, *Europe: Journey to an Unknown Destination* (London, 1973).
49. Quoted in 'Rapport des conseillers commerciaux des pays members de la CEE en Yougoslavie', Belgrade, 22 June 1959.
50. In 1958, the deficit was over $65 million, while in 1959 it increased to $72 million.
51. *The Program of the League of Communists of Yugoslavia*, Chapter 3: 'International Economic Cooperation and Problems of Integration'.
52. Quoted in 'Rapport des conseillers commerciaux ...', 22 June 1959.
53. *The Program of the League of Communists of Yugoslavia*, Chapter 3.
54. Nicoll, William and Trevor C. Salmon, *Understanding the New European Community* (Hemel Hampstead, 1994), p.22.
55. Commission of the European Economic Community, *Fifth General Report on the Activities of the Community (May 1961 – April 1962)*, p.240. In addition, the European Commission enjoyed greater visibility: it 'is receiving more

and more numerous requests for information from both official and private circles, which bears witness to the growing interest of world opinion in the European Economic Community' (Ibid.).
56. Ćosić, Dobrica, *Kosovo* (Beograd, 2004), p.7.
57. McAllister: *From EC to EU*, pp.19–20. In addition, the author identifies various moments challenging the EC: France vs. the rest, the UK accession bid, the constitutional crisis of 1965–66 ending with the Luxembourg Agreement, the Merger Treaty of 1965, the second veto of the second UK membership application, etc (Ibid., pp.25–30).
58. Although free trade was permitted for almost one-third of imports, simultaneously, the administration responsible for effective distribution of resources continued to protect favoured industries.
59. Pavlowitch: *Yugoslavia*, p.284.
60. While incapable of satisfying the demand for consumer goods, thus in a position to import much faster than export, by mid 1962, the Yugoslav economy was in constant deterioration. Increasing inflation was another alarming signal. The government initially disregarded it thinking that foreign aid might be a substitute, but when the inflationary trend continued apace, the government opened discussions with the constituent republics.
61. Commission of the European Economic Community: *Fifth General Report...*, p.240.
62. Commission of the European Economic Community, *Sixth General Report on the Activities of the Community (May 1962 – March 1963)*, p.252.
63. Conseil de la Communauté économique européenne, CM 2/1962, No. 0781.
64. Lane: *Yugoslavia*, p.126.
65. Pavlowitch: *Yugoslavia*, p.287.
66. Meier, Viktor, 'Yugoslav Communism', in William E. Griffith (ed), *Communism in Europe: European Communism and Sino-Soviet Rift* (Cambridge, MA, 1964), p.65.
67. Quoted in 'Rapport des conseillers commerciaux des pays members de la CEE en Yougoslavie', Brussels, 30 July 1959.
68. Commission of the European Economic Community: *Sixth General Report...*, pp.250–251.
69. Ibid., p.251.
70. Zimmerman, William, 'Hierarchical regional systems and the politics of system boundaries', *International Organization*, Vol.26, No.1 (1972), p.30. Moreover, Romania decided to undertake the Iron Gates project with Yugoslavia under the Danube Commission, not COMECON. This was an extremely subtle ploy since after Stalin's death as 'the Danube Commission

was used as a test case for several innovations of Soviet foreign policy' including 'the attempt to appease and renew relations with Yugoslavia' (Cattell, David T., 'The politics of the Danube Commission under Soviet control', *American Slavic and East European Review*, Vol.19, No.3 (1960), pp.380–381).
71. Commission of the European Economic Community, *Eighth General Report on the Activities of the Community (April 1964 – March 1965)*, p.283.
72. As a response, the official letter written on 30 January 1968 stated: 'The Embassy of the SFRY expresses its thankfulness to the Directorate General for External Relations of the Commission of the European Communities, and the government of the SFRY is honored by the offer to enter into official relations with the Communities'.
73. Commission of the European Communities, *Second General Report on the Activities of the Communities in 1968*, p.389.
74. The High Authority of the European Coal and Steel Community, *Second General Report* ... , p.25.
75. Commission of the European Communities: *Second General Report* ..., p.390.
76. Lane: *Yugoslavia*, p.128.
77. In June 1971, the Consortium of Economic Institutes discussed the gravity of the economic situation across the SFRY and called for instant measures (Konzorcijum ekonomskih instituta, 'Svetski ciljevi i pravci razvojne politike Jugoslavije do 1985. godine').
78. Artisien, Patrick F. R. and Stephen Holt, 'Yugoslavia and the EEC in the 1970s', *Journal of Common Market Studies*, Vol.18, No.4 (1980), p.357.
79. Ibid.
80. Gavrilović, M., 'A Europe of Ten', pp.28–30, quoted in Artisien and Holt: 'Yugoslavia and the EEC', p.357.
81. Johnson, Ross A., 'Yugoslavia: in the twilight of Tito', *The Washington Papers*, Vol.2 (1974), p.41.
82. For Ross Johnson, if excluding the country's ties with Western Europe, 'the altered circumstances of the 1970s include development of Yugoslavia from the rural society of 25 years ago into a quasi-industrialized and semi-urbanized state and re-emergence of the "national question"' (Johnson: 'Yugoslavia', p.1).
83. Commission of the European Communities, COM (70) 177 final, Brussels, 24 February 1970.
84. Ibid. In addition, the Yugoslav leaders expressed their concern with regard to the increasing deficit characterizing trade exchange with the Community and demanded to be treated like the other OECD members.
85. Ibid.

86. Commission of the European Communities, *Fifth General Report on the Activities of the Communities in 1971*, p.313.
87. 'Accordo commerciale tra la C.E.E. e la Iugoslavia – Dichiarazioni da iscrivere al processo verbale del Consiglio', 3 March 1970.
88. Sednica komisije SIV za koordinaciju saradnje izmedju SFRJ i SEV, 7 February 1972.
89. Sednica komisije SIV za koordinaciju saradnje izmedju SFRJ i SEV, 5 May 1972.
90. 'Rapports des conseillers commerciaux des pays de la CEE en Yougoslavie', CM 2/1972, No. 1576.
91. Commission of the European Communities, *Sixth General Report on the Activities of the Communities in 1972*, p.265. In addition, scientific and technical cooperation continued.
92. *Journal officiel*, No. C 39, 24 April 1971.
93. Commission of the European Communities, *Seventh General Report on the Activities of the European Communities in 1973*, p.411.
94. It stipulated: 'Where one of the Member States is concerned, the safeguard clause contained in the Community/Yugoslavia trade agreement may be invoked even before the ceilings of voluntary restraint laid down in the agreement on cotton products have been attained'. See the Letter from the Commission of the European Communities to H.E. Mr Van Elslande, President of the Council of the European Communities, Brussels, 2 April 1973.
95. Confidential letter No. 2. See the Letter from the Commission of the European Communities to H.E. Mr Van Elslande, Brussels, 2 April 1973.
96. Commission of the European Communities: *Seventh General Report...*, p.411. According to Yugoslav sources, more than 1 million Yugoslavs worked abroad, almost 60% of whom worked in the Community: Federal Republic of Germany: 480,000; France: 80,000; Netherlands: 12,000; Belgium: 6,000; Luxembourg: 1,500 (*General Economic Situation in Yugoslavia*, p.2, S/58/74 (RCC 5), Brussels, 14 January 1974). The reason for this alarming number of Yugoslav guest-workers in the Community goes back to the mid 1960s, when a net decrease in manufacturing jobs was accompanied by a jump in unemployment rate. Consequently, according to Carmelo Mesa-Logo, 'the most effective, immediately successful policy ... has been emigration of the labour surplus ... A Government bill on emigrant labour was proposed in mid-1966, opening Yugoslav frontiers to all laborers who wished to work abroad. In October 1966, the Federal Assembly removed all restrictions on labour emigration to Western Europe' (Carmelo Mesa-Lago, 'Unemployment in a socialist economy: Yugoslavia', *Industrial Relations*, Vol.10, No.1 (1971), p.63).

97. This constitution was later cited on many occasions discussing the Yugoslav federation and its breakup. Above all, it advocated that '[t]he territory of a Republic cannot be changed without the consent of the Republic and the territory of an Autonomous Province not without the consent of the Autonomous Province ... [T]he border between Republics can only be changed on the basis of their agreement and, when the border of an Autonomous Province is involved, on the basis of its consent'. Thus, the 1974 constitution created republics as sovereign states and while the federation was made of peoples or nationalities, all of them had right to secede from it.
98. Commission of the European Communities, *Eighth General Report on the Activities of the European Communities in 1974*, p.243.
99. *Bulletin EC*, 4–1974, point 2324.
100. *Bulletin EC*, 10–1974, point 2329.
101. Artisien and Holt: 'Yugoslavia and the E.E.C. in the 1970s', p.359.
102. 'Foreign policy retains its independence', *Financial Times*, 19 June 1978.
103. Artisien and Holt: 'Yugoslavia and the E.E.C. in the 1970s', p.361.
104. Council, 'Rapport des Conseillers commerciaux des pays de la Communauté économique européenne en Yougoslavie (15ème rapport)', Brussels, 17 June 1974.
105. Artisien and Holt: 'Yugoslavia and the E.E.C. in the 1970s', p.367.
106. Yugoslavia was viewed as a country benefiting 'from a favourable geographical position as a transit for road and rail traffic between Western Europe and the Near and Middle East and her ports serve the Central European landlocked countries' – a perception to be reconfirmed later while negotiating the entry of Greece in the Community (Artisien and Holt: 'Yugoslavia and the E.E.C. in the 1970s', p.364).
107. Commission of the European Communities: *Eighth General Report ...* , p.250. In addition, 'both sides acknowledged the necessity to discuss possible measures to remedy the increase in Yugoslavia's trade deficit with the EEC, and the possibility of strengthening and expanding their cooperation in order to help correct the present situation' (*RFE Special*, Brussels, 16 June 1975).
108. See, for example, Council 'General economic situation in Yugoslavia', S/58/74 (RCC 5), Brussels, 14 January 1974.
109. Johnson: 'Yugoslavia: in the twilight of Tito', p.1.
110. Artisien and Holt: 'Yugoslavia and the E.E.C. in the 1970s', p.369.
111. Commission of the European Communities, 'Memorandum de la Mission de la R.S.F. de Yougoslavie, en date du 10 juin 1975, concernant les relations commerciales et economiques CEE/Yougoslavie', p.1. In addition,

two documents that offer a good insight into Yugoslavia's standpoint at the time are: Josip Broz Tito's 'Address to the Conference on European Security and Cooperation in Helsinki' (31 July 1975) and Edvard Kardelj's 'Historical Roots of Non-Alignment' (8 September 1975).
112. Ibid., p.6.
113. Commission of the European Communities, *Ninth General Report on the Activities of the European Communities in 1975*, p.259.
114. Commission of the European Communities, *Tenth General Report on the Activities of the European Communities in 1976*, p.265.
115. *Bulletin EC*, 5–1976, point 2338.
116. *Communication à la Presse*, 1414/76 (Presse 153), 3 December 1976.
117. Commission of the European Communities: *Tenth General Report ...*, p.265. For a detailed discussion in the Council, see Council, 'EEC-Yugoslavia relations', I/412/76, Brussels, 12 November 1976.
118. European Parliament, Doc. 26/77, April 1977.
119. *Bulletin EC*, 6–1977, point 2333.
120. USD 2,400 million in 1977 (Commission of the European Communities, *Twelfth General Report on the Activities of the European Communities in 1978*, p.283).
121. *Bulletin EC*, 11–1976, point 2340.
122. Artisien and Holt: 'Yugoslavia and the E.E.C. in the 1970s', p.367.
123. Commission of the European Communities: *Twelfth General Report ...*, p.283.
124. European Parliament, Doc. 370/77, November 1977.
125. *Journal officiel*, No. C 223/34, 14 November 1977.
126. *Journal officiel*, No. C 223/35, 14 November 1977.
127. European Trends, Special Report 2, 'Yugoslavia and the EEC', August 1979, p.28.

Chapter Three   The European Community and Yugoslavia from Integration to Disintegration

1. For example, in 1971, Slovenia and Croatia clearly expressed their reluctance to use international loans in order to prioritize the development of less developed regions across the SFRY (Savezno izvršno veće, 'Društveni plan Jugoslavije za period 1971–1975', Beograd, 5 November 1971). Similarly, in 1972 another meeting acknowledged that some Yugoslav republics would always be in favour of their own development while ignoring the rest of the federation – an approach labelled as 'selective politics' (SIV, 'Koordinacija saradnje izmedju SFRJ i SEV', Beograd, 19 January 1972).

2. *Journal officiel*, No. C 223/36, 14 November 1977.
3. *Journal officiel*, No. C 223/37, 38, 14 November 1977.
4. Denitch, Bogdan, *Ethnic Nationalism: The Tragic Death of Yugoslavia* (Minneapolis, MN, 1996), p.58. In addition, Yugoslavia's place in the Community 'could have mobilized European aid in the transition from authoritarianism to democracy' (Ibid.).
5. *Journal officiel*, No. C 223/39, 14 November 1977.
6. *Journal officiel*, No. C 223/40, 14 November 1977.
7. Ibid.
8. 'Letter from the President of the Council to the President of the EIB', Brussels, 6 December 1978.
9. The new directives were primarily related to commercial matters (industrial and agricultural sectors) and cooperation (manpower, transport, tourism and fisheries). See, for example, Zdenko Antić, 'New EEC position for negotiating with Yugoslavia', *Radio Free Europe* (Research), 9 February 1979.
10. Council, 'Relations with Yugoslavia: drawing up of new negotiating directives – Financial Cooperation', Brussels, 15 December 1978.
11. Commission of the European Communities, *Thirteenth General Report on the Activities of the European Communities in 1979*, pp.255–256.
12. Economic and Social Committee, 'Medium-term economic policy', Brussels, 12 December 1979.
13. On this particular issue, see Dudley Seers and Constantine Vaitsos (eds), *The Second Enlargement of the EEC. The Integration of Unequal Partners* (Basingstoke, 1986).
14. European Investment Bank, 'Bank operations in Yugoslavia', Luxembourg, 14 May 1979.
15. Cooperation Agreement between the European Economic Community and the Socialist Federal Republic of Yugoslavia: Preamble.
16. European Parliament, 'Report', 1–165/80, pp.5–6.
17. Ibid., p.6.
18. Ibid.
19. Ibid., p.14.
20. Ibid., p.10.
21. In this respect, the so-called Cooperation Council included representatives from the Community and Yugoslavia with three major responsibilities: to define cooperation and keep it on the right track, to secure the most appropriate ways of implementing cooperation and, finally, to ensure the proper functioning of the Agreement (with particular emphasis on the trade aspects).
22. Commission of the European Communities, *Fourteenth General Report on the Activities of the European Communities in 1980*, p.276.

23. European Parliament, Doc. 1–742/81, 13 November 1981.
24. Pomfret, Richard, 'The European Community's relations with the Mediterranean countries', in John Redmond (ed), *The External Relations of the European Community: The International Response to 1992* (New York, NY, 1992), p.88.
25. European Parliament, Doc. 1–893/82, 15 November 1982.
26. European Parliament, Doc. 1–337/81, 2 July 1981.
27. Ibid. The justification for such Albanian demands might have been found in the 1966 UN International Covenant on Economic, Social and Cultural Rights, with Article 1 stating: 'All peoples have the right of self-determination. By virtue of that right they freely determine political status and freely pursue their economic, social and cultural development' (Ibid.).
28. European Parliament: Doc. 1–337/81.
29. *Journal officiel*, No. C 101/63, 9 April 1981.
30. *Official Journal*, L 130, 27 May 1980.
31. Variations in the quantity of exports of baby beef depended on the Community's own needs. While during some months the need was lower, for the months from June to September, the Community market's needs increased as a result of tourism (Council, Fiche No.107, 3 February 1982). However, in Yugoslavia this was perceived as an inappropriate approach due to its relatively constant production of baby beef.
32. The Council was particularly insistent on the road transit problem and thus called the Commission 'to negotiate a joint declaration with Yugoslavia ... expressing how important the Community considers it to be that Yugoslavia should envisage, in a spirit of cooperation, an appropriate improvement of road transit facilities, particularly with regard to Greece' (Council, Fiche No.873, 5 August 1981).
33. Political Affairs Committee, 'Motion for a resolution', 3 February 1983.
34. Ibid.
35. This was the Political Affairs Committee's assessment of the relations between the EEC and SFRY after it had become obvious that Yugoslavia was not going to compromise or abandon its links with the East.
36. In addition, the EEC pointed out: 'If Yugoslavia succeeds in consolidating its economy it will be able to show greater certainty in its foreign policy whose objectives and interests correspond in large measure to those of Western Europe' (Political Affairs Committee, 'Motion for a resolution', 3 February 1983).
37. Ibid.
38. Ibid.
39. Ibid.

40. Commission of the European Communities, *Sixteenth General Report on the Activities of the European Communities in 1982*, p.255.
41. Ibid. The loan was primarily for installations necessary for more secure control and management of the electricity supply network.
42. Commission of the European Communities, *Seventeenth General Report on the Activities of the European Communities in 1983*, p.272. The report stipulated: 'The trade week held in Belgrade in March was considered by both sides to be a great success and a first step towards closer economic cooperation.' What proves interesting is the change of priority on how to spend a 67 million ECU loan: not on electricity supply network as originally agreed, but 'for the construction of the trans-Yugoslav highway totaling 38 km'. The reason for such a switch is explained by Greek accession and Community's willingness to secure a safe ground connection with its Southern Member State (Ibid).
43. *Bulletin EC*, 4–1983, point 2.2.28.
44. *Bulletin EC*, 2–1984, point 2.4.36.
45. *Bulletin EC*, 3–1984, point 2.1.174.
46. *Bulletin EC*, 12–1984.
47. Economic and Social Committee, 'Relations between the European Community and Yugoslavia', 12 March 1985.
48. Comisso, Ellen, 'State structures and political processes outside the CMEA: a comparison', *International Organization*, No.40 (1986), p.592.
49. Commission of the European Communities, *Nineteenth General Report on the Activities of the European Communities in 1985*, p.302.
50. Conseil, 'Cinquième reunion du comité de cooperation CEE-Yougoslavie', Brussels, 9 July 1986.
51. *Communication conjointe à la presse*, CEE-YU 1015/86, Brussels, 22 July 1986.
52. Commission of the European Communities, *Twentieth General Report on the Activities of the European Communities in 1986*, p.320.
53. *Communication conjointe à la presse*, CEE-YU 1015/86.
54. Council, 'Introductory statement of Dr Oskar Kovač at the opening meeting of the negotiations of the Second SFRY-EEC Financial protocol', 23 March 1987.
55. Ibid.
56. Council, 'Aide: memoire', 27 March 1987.
57. Cooperation Council, 'Note', 30 October 1987.
58. *Communication conjointe à la presse*, CEE-YU 1015/86.
59. Council, 'Council decision concerning the conclusion of an Additional Protocol to the Cooperation Agreement between the EEC and the SFRY establishing new trade arrangements', 21 December 1987.

60. Commission of the European Communities, *XXIst General Report on the Activities of the European Communities in 1987*, p.304. It is worthy of mention that the initial amount of EIB loan under the Second Financial Protocol was ECU 380 million which was soon after raised to ECU 550 million as the projects Yugoslavia was planning to pursue required greater financial investment (Council, Fiche No.713, 9 June 1987).
61. Commission of the European Communities, *XXIst General Report ...* , p.304.
62. For the initial arrangements, see *Official Journal*, L 41, 14 February 1983.
63. *Bulletin EC*, 4–1988, point 2.2.23. In addition, the Cooperation Council ministerial-level meeting on 19 December 1988 adopted Decision 1/88 on cooperation during 1989 and Resolution 1/88 aimed at strengthening cooperation links (Commission of the European Communities, *XXIInd General Report on the Activities of the European Communities in 1988*, p.366).
64. In-depth analyses of these issues are offered in John B. Allcock's *Explaining Yugoslavia*, Jens Stilhoff Sörensen's *State Collapse and Reconstruction in the Periphery: Political Economy, Ethnicity and Development in Yugoslavia, Serbia and Kosovo* and Susan L. Woodward's *Socialist Unemployment*.
65. Under the Agreement, the EEC was expected to do the following: first, to contribute to the development of Yugoslavia, second, to encourage consolidation of the relations between the two parties and, finally, to intervene by a complementary action and thus influence the Yugoslav authorities to pursue the necessary policies for further development.
66. European Parliament, 'Resolution sur les relations économiques et commerciales entre la Communauté européenne et la Yougoslavie', Doc. A2–258/87.
67. Seventh Meeting of the EEC-Yugoslavia Cooperation Council, 19 December 1988.
68. Ibid.
69. Ibid.
70. Ibid.
71. Commission of the European Communities, *XXIIIrd General Report on the Activities of the European Communities in 1989*, p.340.
72. Ibid.
73. The Council, 'Paris informal meeting', 18 November 1989, *Bulletin EC*, 11–1989, p.56. The programme launched under the name of 'Phare' and linked to the agreement with the IMF, was initially aimed at coordinating economic assistance for Poland and Hungary only, but was extended to Czechoslovakia, Bulgaria, Yugoslavia and, later, to Romania (Ibid.).
74. Ibid.

75. Maresceau, Marc, 'The European Community, Eastern Europe and the URSS', in John Redmond (ed), *The External Relations of the European Community: The Internal Response to 1992* (New York, NY, 1992), p. 97.
76. 'Memorandum on Yugoslav economic reforms sent by Ante Marković, Prime Minister of Yugoslavia, to Jacques Delors, President of the Commission of EEC', 9 November 1989.
77. Ibid.
78. *Communication à la presse*, CEE-YU 1009/89, Brussels, 28 November 1989.
79. Ibid.
80. Commission of the European Communities, *XXIVth General Report on the Activities of the European Communities in 1990*, p.287.
81. *Communication à la presse*, CEE-YU 1009/89, Brussels, 28 November 1989. Lončar 'proposed to examine establishment of EC-Yugoslavia relations on the basis of the "proximity policy" and on a status for Yugoslavia similar to that accorded to some European countries, such as EFTA and some Mediterranean non-Member States, with which the Community has an agreement on association' (Ibid.).
82. *Bulletin EC*, 5–1990, point 1.3.25.
83. Commission of the European Communities: *XXIVth General Report ...* , p.288.
84. 'Declaration du Conseil de Cooperation CEE-Yougoslavie sur l'avenir des relations entre la Communauté et la Yougoslavie', Brussels, 18 December 1990.
85. Ibid.
86. Ibid.
87. Comisso: 'State structures', p.592.
88. *Communication à la presse*, CEE-YU 1006/90, Brussels, 18 December 1990.
89. Commission of the European Communities, *XXVth General Report on the Activities of the European Communities in 1991*, p.343.
90. Ibid., p.281.
91. Ibid.
92. The statements were issued as follows: on 2 July – the EC expressed its alarm in regard to the hostilities in Slovenia; on 5 July – the EC decided to set a monitoring mission and arms embargo; on 10 July – the EC required all parties to comply with the Brioni Agreement; on 19 July – the EC asked for the withdrawal of the Yugoslav People's Army from Slovenia; on 6 August – the EC advocated a cease-fire which the troika was trying to establish; on 20 August – the EC expressed its concern about the infringements of the cease-fire and stressed that any change of borders by force is not acceptable; on 28August – the EC called the Federal Presidency to stop the illegal use of

force while calling on Serbia to let the monitoring mission pursue its activities in Croatia; on 3 September – the EC welcomed the readiness of all the Yugoslav parties to find a solution for the crisis by signing a cease-fire agreement and the Memorandum of Understanding on the extension of the EC monitoring mission; on 7 September – the EC established a Conference on Yugoslavia in the Peace Palace in The Hague and an arbitration procedure; on 19 September – the EC acknowledged Lord Carrington's contribution in bringing about a cease-fire while it regretted that the EC monitoring mission was no longer capable of doing its job. Thus, the EC called the Western European Union to step in and find a way to support the activities of the monitoring body (See, for example, *Bulletin EC*, 7/8–1991).

93. German representatives noted that they did not need foreign workforce anymore and hoped that the Yugoslavs would return to their homeland (Savezno izvršno veće, 'Izveštaj o poseti delegacije Republike Srbije Severnoj Rajni-Vestfaliji, 4–10 September 1978').
94. *Journal officiel*, No. C 223/37, 14 November 1977.
95. Council, 'Negotiations with Yugoslavia', 12 April 1978.
96. *Journal officiel*, No. L 41/12, 14 February 1983.
97. European Parliament, 'Report', 1–165/80, p.6.
98. Economic and Social Committee, 'Relations between the European Community and Yugoslavia', 12 March 1985.
99. Mission of the SFR of Yugoslavia to the European Communities, 'Verbal vote', No.185/85, Brussels, 28 May 1985.
100. Ibid.
101. Ibid.
102. Ibid.
103. Council, 'Concéquences de l'adhésion de l'Espagne et du Portugal sur les relations CEE-Yougoslavie', 10 June 1985.
104. Council, 'Cinquième réunion du comité de cooperation CEE-Yougoslavie', 9 July 1986.
105. See, for example, EEC-Yugoslavia Cooperation Council, Decision No.1/86, 22 July 1986.
106. Council, 'Note à l'attention des Membres du Groupe "Mediterranée" (Yougoslavie)', MED/28/87, 30 October 1987.
107. Council, 'Note for the *ad hoc* Working Party on Yugoslav labour', SN 2894/88, 13 July 1988.
108. Cooperation Council, 'Cooperation entre la Communauté économique européenne et la Yougoslavie', 18 November 1988.
109. Ibid.
110. *Bulletin EC*, 10–1991, point 1.4.6.

111. Commission of the European Communities: *XXVth General Report* ..., p.345.
112. Ibid., p.281. The measures Yugoslavia was subjected to can be summarized as follows: first, the trade concessions guaranteed by the agreements were suspended; second, the right to benefit under the system of generalized preferences was abolished; and finally, on 25 November the Council voted to denounce the agreements linking the Community and Yugoslavia in accordance with the procedure provided for by them (*Official Journal*, L 325, 27 November 1991).
113. Commission of the European Communities, *XXVth General Report* ..., p.281.
114. *Official Journal*, L 342, 12 December 1991; *Bulletin EC*, 12–1991. The privileged treatment consisted of continuation of technical assistance under the Phare program with these four republics, financial cooperation established under the second financial protocol and re-establishment of generalized tariff preferences for agricultural products. In addition, the Council adopted a decision to finance victims of the fighting under a European emergency aid plan.

Chapter Four   Calling Diaspora and Diaspora Calling

1. Smith, Hazel, 'Diasporas in international conflict', in Hazel Smith and Paul Stares (eds), *Diasporas in Conflict: Peace-makers or Peace-wreckers?* (Tokyo, New York and Paris, 2007), p.5. Similar accounts about diaspora groups are found in William Safran, 'Diasporas in modern societies: myths of homeland and return', *Diaspora*, Vol.1, No.1 (1991), pp.83–99; Gabriel Sheffer (ed), *Modern Diasporas in International Politics* (London and Sydney, 1986).
2. Vertovec, Steven, 'Three meanings of "Diaspora", exemplified among South Asian religions', *Diaspora*, Vol.6, No.3 (1997), p.278.
3. Skrbiš, Zlatko, 'Nationalism in a transnational context: Croatian diaspora, intimacy and nationalist imagination', *Revija za Sociologiju*, Vol.32, No.2–3 (2001), p.3.
4. Esman, Milton J., *Diasporas in the Contemporary World* (Cambridge, 2009), p.8.
5. Anderson, Benedict, *Long-Distance Nationalism: World Capitalism and the Rise of Identity Politics* (Amsterdam, 1992), p.13.
6. Skrbiš, Zlatko, 'The mobilized Croatian diaspora: its role in homeland politics and war', in Hazel Smith and Paul Stares (eds), *Diasporas in Conflict: Peace-makers or Peace-wreckers?* (Tokyo, New York and Paris, 2007), p.220.
7. Adamič, Louis, *The Native's Return. An American Immigrant Visits Yugoslavia and Discovers his Old Country* (New York, NY, 1934); Adamič, Louis, *My Native Land* (New York, NY, 1943); Adamič, Louis, *The Eagle and the Roots* (Garden

City, NY, 1952). In all of these works, the author talks about democratic Slovenia within Yugoslavia, thus about unity and cooperation, not secession.

8. Klemenčić, Matjaž, 'Slovenes as immigrants, members of autochthonous minorities in neighboring countries and members of multiethnic states (1500–1991)' in Ann Katherine Isaacs (ed), *Languages and Identities in Historical Perspective* (Pisa, 2005), p.106.

9. In 1954, the Party published its manifesto which stipulated that although '[t]he Slovenes made a free decision to enter a state union with the Croats, Serbs, and other Southern Slav nations ... [t]he precondition for their future happiness, however, is liberty'. See Article 7, 'Program Slovenske ljudske stranke', *Slovenija, priloga Ameriške domovine*, 54 (179), 20 September 1954, pp.1–3.

10. Apart from the Slovenian CD People's Party of Yugoslavia, the CDUCE included similar parties from Czechoslovakia, Hungary, Latvia, Lithuania and Poland (Papini, Roberto, *The Christian Democrat International*, Lanham, MD, 1997, pp.76–77).

11. Christian Democratic Union of Central Europe, *Freedom: Prerequisite to Lasting Peace* (New York, NY, 1957), p.14. In Yugoslavia, the idea of a United Europe was present only among Slovenian intellectuals. For them, it was necessary to secure Christian Democratic support for their fight for independence. Indeed, the second congress of the CDUCE, held in 1955, pointed out that 'the ambitious idea of a European Federation and eventually of a United Europe has its protagonists in a number of outstanding statesmen and personalities belonging to the Christian Democratic movement. It is the task of the Union to influence public opinion in Europe in this direction, to educate younger generations, including young people in exile, in the federalist spirit and to promote the idea of federalism at universities, among others at the University of Europe' (quoted in Matjaž Klemenčič, 'Slovenia as Part of a United Europe in the Political Philosophy of Slovene Migrants from Louis Adamic to Miha Krek', in Irena Gantar Godina (ed), *Intellectuals in Diaspora*, Ljubljana, 1999, p.56).

12. Klemenčič: 'Slovenia as part of a United Europe', p.52.

13. Predsedstvo CK ZSK, Document 1. X, 29 January 1979.

14. Skrbiš, Zlatko, '"The First Europeans" fantasy of Slovenian Venetologists: emotions and nationalist imaginings', in Maruška Svašek (ed), *Postsocialism: Politics and Emotions in Central and Eastern Europe* (Oxford, 2007), p.149.

15. On this particular issue, see Jasna Dragović-Soso, *Saviours of the Nation: Serbia's Intellectual Opposition and the Rise of Nationalism* (London, 2002), pp.162–205, and Dejan Jović, *Yugoslavia: A State that Withered Away* (West Lafayette, IN, 2009), pp.225–306.

16. Žižek, Slavoj, 'Eastern Europe's republics of Gilead', *New Left Review*, No.183 (1990), p.55.
17. Skrbiš: "'The First Europeans'", p.148.
18. Skrbiš, Zlatko, 'The emotional historiography of Venetologists: Slovene diaspora, memory, and nationalism', *European Journal of Anthropology*, No.39 (2002), pp.47–48.
19. See, for example, Jure Prpić, *Hrvati u Americi* (Zagreb, 1997).
20. Goldstein, Ivo, *Croatia: A History* (London, 1999), p.184.
21. See, for example, Susan L. Woodward, *Socialist Unemployment: The Political Economy of Yugoslavia 1945–1990* (Princeton, NJ, 1995).
22. On the Croatian spring, see, for example, Marcus Tanner, *Croatia: A Nation Forged in War* (New Haven, CT, 1997), pp.184–202, and Steven L. Burg, *Conflict and Cohesion in Socialist Yugoslavia: Political Decision Making Since 1966* (Princeton, NJ, 1983), pp.21–60.
23. Goldstein: *Croatia*, p.193.
24. Hockenos, Paul, *Homeland Calling: Exile Patriotism and the Balkan Wars* (Ithaca, NY, 2003), p.20.
25. 'Letter to the Editor', *Fraternalist*, 9 January 1985.
26. Skrbiš: 'The mobilized Croatian diaspora', p.225.
27. Winland, Daphne N., 'Croatian diaspora', in Marvin Ember, Carol R. Ember and Ian Skoggard (eds), *Encyclopedia of Diasporas: Immigrant and Refugee Cultures around the World* (USA, 2005), p.77.
28. Ibid., pp.80–81.
29. Skrbiš: 'The mobilized Croatian diaspora', p.226.
30. Interview with Marko Lopušina.
31. See, for example, Milan Bulajić, *Tudjman's "Jasenovac Myth": Genocide against Serbs, Jews and Gypsies* (Beograd, 1994).
32. *Otpor*, No.5, 1987, pp.24–28.
33. The émigrés were not sure about the destiny of the Yugoslav federation and, more alarming, what to do with Bosnia-Herzegovina, which both the émigrés and Tudjman perceived as an artificial creation.
34. Hockenos: *Homeland Calling*, p.44.
35. Interview with Marko Lopušina.
36. Hockenos: *Homeland Calling*, p.84.
37. Quoted in Mark Thompson, *A Paper House: The Ending of Yugoslavia* (London, 1992), p.269.
38. In his letter to the diaspora, Gojko Šušak, a distinguished émigré leader and Croatian Minister of Defense in Tudjman's government, wrote: 'You know that when democracy dawned in Croatia, the weapons that the republic had for its defense were confiscated. Now they [the Yugoslav authorities]

again want to disarm Croatia, which has gone through great pains and suffered many victims to succeed as a sovereign state and to obtain a portion of the arms it needs. It is understood that the Republic of Croatia will not permit this to happen again. It is obvious that with our young democracy in such a condition, we cannot ignore our own economic and national needs because of the needs of the others. In spite of everything, Croatia must survive and will survive. For this, Croatia is depending on your help' (*National*, 23 December 1999).
39. Skrbiš: 'The Mobilized Croatian Diaspora', p.228.
40. Anderson, Benedict, 'Exodus', *Critical Inquiry*, Vol.20, No.1 (1994), p.327.
41. Hockenos: *Homeland Calling*, p.50.
42. Ibid., p.55.
43. John (Ivica) Zdunić, head of the HDZ coordinating committee in North America, quoted in Hockenos: *Homeland Calling*, p.56.
44. The HDZ-created voting system provided for the diaspora to elect 12 representatives out of the 127-member Sabor.
45. Zimmermann, Warren, *Origins of a Catastrophe: Yugoslavia and its Destroyers* (New York, NY, 1996), p.65.
46. Interview with a former US diplomat to the European Communities.
47. Crawford, Beverly, 'Explaining Defection from International Cooperation: Germany's Unilateral Recognition of Croatia', *World Politics*, Vol.48, No.4 (1996), pp.502–503.
48. Carter, Sean, 'The geopolitics of diaspora', *Area*, Vol.37, No.1 (2005), p.57. A similar point is offered by Rey Koslowski, *Migrants and Citizens: Demographic Change in the European State System* (Ithaca, NY, 2000), p.174, and Francesco Ragazzi, 'The invention of the Croatian diaspora: unpacking the politics of "diaspora" during the war in Yugoslavia', *Working Paper No.10*, George Mason University, 2009, p.5.
49. American Slovenian Congress, Canadian Slovenian Congress, German Slovenian Congress, SKK in Italy, Austria, Australia, Argentina and Great Britain and Carinthia Conference.
50. Promoting Slovenian identity and language, securing mutual support, fostering cultural linkages, encouraging equality, promoting Slovenian national interests both at home and abroad, integrating all Slovenes, promoting tolerance and respect.
51. Busch, Brigitta, 'Shifting political and cultural borders: language and identity in the border region of Austria and Slovenia', *European Studies: An Interdisciplinary Series in European Culture, History and Politics*, Vol.19 (2003), p.137.
52. 'Milan Kučan's letter to the diaspora', 22 July 1991.

53. Similar points were made in statements originated from various ministries. For example, Jelko Kacin, Minister of Information, whose headed paper bore the logo 'Independent Slovenia 1991', stipulated that his Ministry focused on informing the international audience about the situation at home. This way, diaspora organizations had an opportunity to shape their activism (Jelko Kacin's 'Letter to the émigrés', quoted in *Viri o demokratizaciji in osamosvojitvi Slovenije*, p.25).
54. Having in mind the aim of this study, I do not question to what extent, if at all, the diaspora impacted on the new approach of the US administration, but rather argue that shifting from pro-Yugoslavia to pro-Slovenia was a further encouragement for the diaspora itself. As Matjaž Jančar, representative of Slovenia in Cleveland, addressed the Slovenian American organizations and Americans of Slovenian descent: 'Slovenia has made strides at being internationally recognized as a sovereign and independent nation. As a representative of the Republic of Slovenia, please accept my sincere thanks and appreciation for the help you have extended and we asked for your continued support until our goal of peace and the acknowledged independence of Slovenia is accomplished' (*Prosveta*, 10 July 1991, p.4). Thus, in his letter, Jančar acknowledged the existence of support by stipulating that various organizations showed their understanding by providing assistance. Moreover, while advocating what would be the best that the Americans could do – recognize Slovenian independence – Jančar underlined: 'As Americans, please confirm your commitment to the ideals of American Democracy' (Ibid). Similar points were transmitted in the letter by Lojze Peterle, leader of the Slovene Christian Democrats (*Ameriška domovina*, 24 January 1991, p.8).
55. Interview with a Slovenian liberal politician.
56. Letter from Mirko Jurak, President of the Slovene Immigrants' Society, to all Slovenes entitled 'An appeal for support', (*Ameriška domovina*, 11 July 1991).
57. 'Letter to the international cultural and scientific audience, 28 June 1991', in *Viri o demokratizaciji in osamosvojitvi Slovenije (IV del: Slovenci v zamejstvu in po svetu)*, p.32.
58. Ibid.
59. Interview with Marko Lopušina.
60. 'Letter to the Heads of State, Prime Ministers and Ministers of the Commonwealth Nations, 17 October 1991', in *Viri o demokratizaciji in osamosvojitvi Slovenije (IV del: Slovenci v zamejstvu in po svetu)*, p.34.
61. Ibid.
62. Zimmermann: *Origins of a Catastrophe*, p.71.
63. 'Letter to the Heads of State, Prime Ministers and Ministers of the Commonwealth Nations, 17 October 1991'.

64. Ibid.
65. Klemenčič, Matjaž, 'The international community and the FRY/Belligerents, 1989–1997', in Charles Ingrao and Thomas A. Emmert (eds), *Confronting the Yugoslav Controversies: A Scholars' Initiative* (West Lafayette, IN, 2009), p.158. For other examples of Austria–EC (Member States) joint efforts in regard to the Yugoslav crisis, see Daniel Bethlehem and Marc Weller (eds), *The Yugoslav Crisis in International Law* (Cambridge, 1997).
66. Cox, John K., *Slovenia: Evolving Loyalties* (London, 2005), p.169.
67. Woodward, Susan L., *Balkan Tragedy: Chaos and Dissolution after the Cold War*, (Washington, DC, 1995), p.159. Thus Woodward's understanding complements Vukadinović's discussion about Slovenia and Croatia and their intentions after the Cold War: 'These two republics, closest to the West, will make maximum efforts to join all European institutions. There will be initiatives to connect these two new states with the Alpe-Adria Community, with the European Council, the EC, the West European Union and even NATO. They are perfectly aware that only through Europe can they realize their interest' (Radovan Vukadinović, 'Yugoslavia and the East: from non-alignment to disintegration', in Martin van den Heuvel and Jan G. Siccama (eds), *The Disintegration of Yugoslavia*, Amsterdam, 1992, p.152).
68. For a full account of the Carinthian Slovenes and their activism, see, Tina Bahovec (ed), *Eliten und Nationwerdung: die Rolle der Eliten bei der Nationalisierung der Kärntner Slovenen* (Klagenfurt, 2003).
69. Interview with a Slovenian liberal politician.
70. The aid consisted of two cheques: one amounting for 870,000 schilling and the other for 470,000 schilling. See, 'Čez milijon šilingov pomoči', *Slovenski vestnik,* 25 September 1991.
71. The protest, the main objective of which was to condemn the Ten-Day War in Slovenia, gathered members of the following Slovenian organizations in Carinthia: National Council of Carinthian Slovenes, Association of Slovenian Organizations, Slovenian Unity List, Christian Cultural Association, Slovene Cultural Association, etc. The participants relied on the principle of self-determination and called on the international community to support Slovenian and Croatian bids for independence.
72. *Delo*, 6 April 1990.
73. *Delo*, 19 April 1990.
74. *Delo*, 14 March 1991.
75. Zeitler, Klaus P., *Deutschlands Rolle bei der völkerrechtlichen Anerkennung der Republik Kroatien unter besonderer Berücksichtigung des deutschen Außenministers Genscher* (Marburg, 2000), p.109.

76. Stergar, Janez, 'Delovanje Koroških Slovencev v Avstriji za neodvisno Slovenijo', in *Viri o demokratizaciji in osamosvojitvi Slovenije (IV del: Slovenci v zamejstvu in po svetu)*, p.38.
77. Klemenčič: 'The international community', p.158.
78. 'Pomoč Evrope k emancipaciji: drugačno mišljenje, ki ne bi zagotovilo prihodnosti samo Sloveniji', *Naš tednik*, 26 July 1991.
79. Meier, Viktor, *Yugoslavia: A History of Its Demise* (London and New York, 1999), p.21. The author primarily thinks of Warren Zimmermann (USA), Sergio Vento (Italy), Hansjörg von Eiff (Germany), Michel Châtelais (France) and Peter Hall (UK).
80. 'Narodni svet koroških Slovencev zahteva da Avstrija prizna samostojnost Slovenije: Tudi minister Busek podpira prizadevanje mladih demokracij', *Naš tednik*, 1 March 1991.
81. Ibid.
82. 'Letter to Dr Alois Mock on behalf of the National Council of Carinthian Slovenes, 27 June 1991'.
83. 'Resolucija udeležencev zborovanja za spoštovanje pravic narodov do samoodločbe in protest proti vojaškemu nasilju v Sloveniji i Hrvaškem', *Primorski dnevnik*, 28 June 1991.
84. Interview with HE Lidija Topić.
85. 'Izjava glavnih odborov Zveze slovenskih organizacij na Koroškem in vključenih organizacij ob državni osamosvojitvi Slovenije in vojaškem posegu jugoslovanske armade', *Slovenski vestnik*, 3 July 1991.
86. 'Zahteva Andreja Wakouniga, predsednika Enotne liste – EL, za avstrijsko priznanje državne samostojnosti Republike Slovenije', *Naš tednik*, 5 July 1991.
87. Ibid.
88. 'Slovenija okupirana', *Primorski dnevnik*, 28 June 1991.
89. In Consiglio comunale, in *Viri o demokratizaciji in osamosvojitvi Slovenije (IV del: Slovenci v zamejstvu in po svetu)*, p.66.
90. For example, James Minahan talks about 120,000 Slovenes in Italy (James Minahan, *Miniature Empires: A Historical Dictionary of the Newly Independent States*, Westport CT, 1998, p.247). Indeed, most of my respondents talked about a 100,000–160,000 Slovenian population in Italy.
91. Kosin, Marko, 'Slovenska manjšina v slovensko-italijanskih odnosih', *Razprave in gradivo*, Vol.33 (1998), p.59.
92. Slovenska kulturno-gospodarska zveza, Svet slovenskih organizacij, Organizacije videmske pokrajine, Slovenska komisija PSI, Slovenska komponenta DSL, Slovenska skupnost, Gibanje za komunistično prenovo.
93. 'Ustaviti agresijo', *Primorski dnevnik*, 29 June 1991.

94. 'Izjava Slovenske deležne komisije', *Primorski dnevnik*, 29 June 1991.
95. *Primorski dnevnik*, 1 July 1991. The 1975 Osimo Agreements settled the territorial dispute between Italy and Yugoslavia and led to greater bilateral cooperation. For a full analysis of the relevance of the agreements, see Pamela Ballinger, *History in Exile: Memory and Identity at the Borders of the Balkans* (Princeton, NJ, 2003), pp.92–96.
96. 'Pismo Sveta slovenskih organizacij predsedniku vlade Republike Slovenije Lojzetu Peterletu', *Primorski dnevnik*, 28 June 1991.
97. 'Poziv deželnega odbora Svetovnega slovenskega kongresa za Furlanijo-Julijsko krajino', *Primorski dnevnik*, 9 July 1991.
98. 'Skupna izjava treh slovenskih narodnih manjšin', *Primorski dnevnik*, 14 July 1991.
99. 'Zahvalno pismo Ministra Dr. Janeza Dularja koroškim Slovencem za dveletno pomoč v osamosvojitvenih prizadevanjih Republike Slovenije', *Naš tednik*, 24 January 1992.
100. 'Predstavniki manjšin v poslanski zbornici zahtevali priznanje neodvisnosti Slovenije', *Primorski dnevnik*, 5 July 1991.
101. 'Prva pobuda združenja Italia-Slovenia. Dvajset tisoč razglednic Andreottiju za priznanje Slovenije in Hrvaške', *Primorski dnevnik*, 29 September 1991.
102. Chancellor Vranitzky quoted in Thomas D. Grant, *Recognition of States: Law and Practice in Debate and Evolution* (Westport, CT, 1999), p.188.

Chapter Five Media Power

1. Jusić, Tarik, 'Media discourse and the politics of ethnic conflict: the case of Yugoslavia', in Pål Kolstø (ed), *Media Discourse and the Yugoslav Conflicts: Representation of Self and Other* (Burlington, 2009), p.21.
2. Quoted in Stjepan Gredelj, 'The Media's Role in Producing Conflict', in Svetlana Slapšak *et al.* (eds), *The War Started at Maksimir: Hate Speech in the Media* (Belgrade, 1997), p.203.
3. Curran, James, *Media and Power* (London, 2002), p.165.
4. Jusić: 'Media discourse', p.34.
5. Kolstø, Pål (ed), *Media Discourse and the Yugoslav Conflicts: Representation of Self and Other* (Burlington, 2009), p. 2.
6. Sofos, Spyros, 'Culture, media and the politics of disintegration and ethnic Ddivision in former Yugoslavia', in Tim Allen and Jean Seaton (eds), *The Media of Conflict: War Reporting and Representations of Ethnic Violence* (London, 1998), p.164.
7. Thompson, Mark, *Forging War: The Media in Serbia, Croatia and Bosnia-Herzegovina* (Luton, 1999), p.9.
8. Sofos: 'Culture, media and the politics', p.166.

NOTES 211

9. Kurspahić, Kemal, *Prime Time Crime: Balkan Media in War and Peace* (Washington, DC, 2003), pp.25–26.
10. Ibid, p.86.
11. Sparks, Colin, 'Media theory after the fall of European communism', in James Curran and Myung-Jin Park (eds), *De-Westernizing Media Studies* (London, 2000), p.40.
12. Bakić, Jovo and Gazela Pudar, 'The Yugoslav succession wars and the war for symbolic hegemony', in Pål Kolstø (ed), *Media Discourse and the Yugoslav Conflicts: Representation of Self and Other* (Burlington, 2009), p.109.
13. Sofos: 'Culture, media and the politics', p.168.
14. Gagnon, Valere Philip Jr., *The Myth of Ethnic War: Serbia and Croatia in the 1990s* (Ithaca, NY, 2004), p.100.
15. 'Prispevki za slovenski nacionalni program', *Nova Revija*, February 1987.
16. Mihelj, Sabrina, Veronika Bajt and Miloš Pankov, 'Reorganizing the identification matrix: televisual construction of collective identities in the early phase of Yugoslav disintegration', in Pål Kolstø (ed), *Media Discourse and the Yugoslav Conflicts: Representation of Self and Other* (Burlington, 2009), p.49.
17. Report from the Information Officers of the Countries of the European Communities in Yugoslavia (2nd report), Brussels, 17 July 1973.
18. For example, the United Press International reported: 'Slovenia and Croatia advocate for Yugoslavia to be transformed into a confederation of independent states in order to avoid the domination of Serbia, the largest republic ruled by communists. All the three republics are refusing to recognize the federal authorities' (UPI Report, 15 January 1991). This report, as noted by one senior diplomatic source, reached the Europeans as a surprise.
19. 'Dnevnik', *TVL*, 17 June 1991.
20. Toš, Niko, 'Nove vrednote v funkciji deblokade družbenega razvoja', in Niko Toš et al. (eds), *Slovenski utrip. Slovensko javno mnenje 1988–89* (Ljubljana, 1989), p.23.
21. Lampe, John R., *Yugoslavia as History: Twice there Was a Country* (Cambridge, 2000), p.370.
22. Sylvia Poggioli, 'Scouts without compasses', p.4, quoted in Tomislav Z. Longinović, 'Yugoslavism and its discontents: a cultural post-mortem', in John Burt Foster Jr. and Wayne Jeffrey Froman (eds), *Thresholds of Western Culture: Identity, Postcoloniality, Transnationalism* (London, 2002), pp.154–155.
23. 'Samostojna Slovenija – quo vadis', *Der Standard*, 1 July 1991.
24. 'La crisi jugoslava', *Corriere della Sera*, 4 July 1991.
25. *La Repubblica*, 4 July 1991.

26. Lantis, Jeffrey S., *Strategic Dilemmas and the Evolution of German Foreign Policy since Unification* (Santa Barbara, CA, 2002), p.86. In addition, the author argues that the *Bayerische Rundfunk*, a broadcasting authority from Munich, 'provided focused coverage of the situation in the former Yugoslavia that was strongly influenced by the Catholic Church' (Ibid.).
27. Hirsch, Helga, 'Titos Staat löst sich auf', *Die Zeit*, 2 November 1990.
28. Johnstone, Diana, 'Seeing Yugoslavia through a dark glass: politics, media and the ideology of globalization', *Covert Action Quarterly*, No.65 (1998), p.49.
29. Djurić, Ivana and Vladimir Zorić, 'Foreclosing the other, building the war: a comparative analysis of Croatian and Serbian press discourses during the conflict in Croatia', in Pål Kolstø (ed), *Media Discourse and the Yugoslav Conflicts: Representation of Self and Other* (Burlington, 2009), pp.64–65.
30. Leicht, Robert, 'Europas jugoslawische Zwickmühle', *Die Zeit*, 12 September 1991.
31. Magaš, Branka, *The Destruction of Yugoslavia: Tracking Yugoslavia's Break-up, 1980–1992* (London, 1992), p.316.
32. Interview with HE Mohamed Halili.
33. Buden, Boris, 'Europe is a whore', in Nena Skopljanac Brunner, Stjepan Gredelj, Alija Hodžić and Branimir Krištofić (eds), *Media & War* (Zagreb and Belgrade, 2000), p.56.
34. Ibid.
35. Gagnon: *The Myth of Ethnic War*, p.94.
36. 'Dnevnik', *TVB*, 22 June 1991.
37. Vlajki, Emil, *Demonization of Serbs: Western Imperialism and Media War Criminals* (Ottawa, 2001), pp.74–81.
38. Schmitz, Michael, 'Der Haβ wächst mit jedem Tag', *Die Zeit*, 15 November 1991.
39. Ibid.
40. Grotzky, Johannes, 'Titos Traum zerbricht', *Die Zeit*, 12 October 1990.
41. 'Declaration on Yugoslavia', *Press release 35/91*, 26 March 1991.
42. Ibid.
43. 'Statement on Yugoslavia', *Press release 42/91*, 8 May 1991.
44. Kintis, Andreas G., 'Between ambition and paralysis: the European Union's Common Foreign and Security Policy and the war in the former Yugoslavia', in Carl C. Hodge (ed), *Redefining European Security* (New York, NY, 1999), pp.281–282.
45. 'Statement on Yugoslavia', *Press release 54/91*, 8 June 1991.
46. Ibid.
47. 'Joint statement on the situation in Yugoslavia', 3 July 1991.
48. Libal, Michael, *Limits of Persuasion: Germany and the Yugoslav Crisis, 1991–1992* (Westport, CT, 1997), p.19.

Notes

49. Quoted in Jonathan Eyal, *Europe and Yugoslavia: Lessons From a Failure* (London, 1993), p.27.
50. 'Declaration on the situation in Yugoslavia', 5 July 1991.
51. Ibid.
52. 'Declaration on Yugoslavia', 6 August 1991.
53. Ibid.
54. 'La crisi jugoslava', *Corriere della Sera*, 4 July 1991.
55. Samary, Catherine, 'La Yougoslavie a l'épreuve du libéralisme', *Le Monde Diplomatique*, July 1991.
56. 'Samostojna Slovenija – quo vadis', *Der Standard*, 1 July 1991.
57. 'Genscher will einheitliche EG-Politik', *Frankfurter Allgemeine Zeitung*, 6 July 1991.
58. 'Declaration on Yugoslavia', 6 August 1991.
59. Interview with a German diplomat, policy-maker and advisor.
60. 'Declaration on Yugoslavia', 20 August 1991.
61. Ibid.
62. Mihelj, Bajt and Pankov: 'Reorganizing the identification matrix', p.50.
63. Van Schendelen, Rinus, *Machiavelli in Brussels: The Art of Lobbying the EU* (Amsterdam, 2005), p.299.
64. Ibid., p.231.
65. Malcolm, Noel, 'Yugoslavia at Breakpoint', *The National Review*, 29 July 1991.
66. Perger, Werner A., 'Wir haben recht gehabt', *Die Zeit*, 12 July 1991.
67. Ibid.
68. Lucarelli, Sonia, *Europe and the Breakup of Yugoslavia: A Political Failure in Search of a Scholarly Explanation* (Leiden, 2000), p.148.
69. European Parliament, PE 152.616/rev, 9–13 September 1991.
70. Commission of the European Communities, *XXVth General Report on the Activities of the European Communities 1991*, p. 281.
71. *Official Journal*, L 325, 27 November 1991.
72. Walsh, James, James L. Graff, William Mader and Frederick Ungeheuer, 'Yugoslavia: the flash of war', *Time*, 30 September 1991.
73. *Official Journal*, L 342, 12 December 1991.
74. Commission of the European Communities, *XXVth General Report ...*, p.281.
75. Schwelien, Michael, 'Ein Staat zerbirst', *Die Zeit*, 9 August 1991.
76. Ibid.
77. 'Declaration on Yugoslavia', 27 August 1991.
78. Mutz, Diana C., Paul M. Sniderman and Richard A. Brody, 'Political Persuasion: The Birth of a Field of Study', in Diana C Mutz, Paul M. Sniderman and Richard A. Brody (eds), *Political Persuasion and Attitude Change* (Ann Arbor, MI, 1996), p.1.

79. 'Declaration on Yugoslavia', 3 September 1991.
80. Ibid.
81. 'Declaration on the occasion of the ceremonial opening of the Conference on Yugoslavia', 7 September 1991.
82. Leicht: 'Europas jugoslawische Zwickmühle'.
83. "Declaration on Yugoslavia," 19 September 1991.
84. Ibid.
85. Dönhoff, Marion Gräfin, 'Kopflos in das Chaos?', *Die Zeit*, 19 September 1991.
86. Interview with Veran Matić.
87. 'Informal meeting of Ministers of Foreign Affairs', Haarzuilens, 6 October 1991.
88. Ibid.
89. 'Declaration on Yugoslavia', 18 October 1991.
90. Interview with Aleksandar Tijanić.
91. 'Statement on Dubrovnik', 27 October 1991.
92. 'Extraordinary EPC Ministerial meeting', Rome, 8 November 1991.
93. Djilas, Aleksa, 'Germany's policy toward the disintegration of Yugoslavia', in Stephen E. Hanson and Willfried Spohn (eds), *Can Europe Work? Germany & the Reconstruction of Post-communist Societies* (Seattle, WA, 1995), p.151.
94. Schmitz: 'Der Haß wächst mit jedem Tag'.
95. 'EC-US statement on peaceful and democratic transformation in the East', Brussels, 9 November 1991.
96. Brenner, Michael J., 'EC: confidence lost', *Foreign Policy*, No.91 (1993), p.6.
97. 'Statement on the death of five members of the European Community Monitor Mission to Yugoslavia', Brussels, 7 January 1992.
98. 'Die Pflicht der Welt', *Die Zeit*, 10 January 1992.
99. Quoted in Edward Mortimer and Lionel Barber, 'Diplomacy Tested by Territorial Integrity', *Financial Times*, 4 July 1991.
100. Zweites Deutsches Fernsehen.
101. Habermas, Jürgen, *Europe: The Faltering Project* (Cambridge, 2009), p.154.
102. 'Die Pflicht der Welt', *Die Zeit*, 10 January 1992.

Chapter Six   With the Blessing of the Vatican

1. This understanding is properly acknowledged in Stella Alexander's remarkable volume that covers the relations between the Catholic and Orthodox Churches within and with the Yugoslav state from 1945 to 1974 (Stella Alexander, *Church and State in Yugoslavia since 1945*, Cambridge, 1979). To continue with the debate, other scholars focus on the comportment of the

Churches and the Yugoslav state from the early 1970s to the moment of its disintegration. See, for example, Larry A. Dunn, 'The roles of religion in conflicts in the former Yugoslavia', *Religion in Eastern Europe*, Vol.16, No.1 (1996), pp.13–27; Paul Mojzes, *Yugoslavian Inferno: Ethnoreligious Warfare in the Balkans* (New York, 1994); Vjekoslav Perica, *Balkan Idols: Religion and Nationalism in Yugoslav States* (Oxford, 2002); Sabrina P. Ramet, *Balkan Babel: The Disintegration of Yugoslavia from the Death of Tito to the Fall of Milošević* (Boulder, CO, 2002); Pedro Ramet, 'Factionalism in Church-State interaction: the Croatian Catholic Church in the 1980s', *Slavic Review*, Vol.44, No.2 (1985), pp.298–315; Pedro Ramet, 'Catholicism and politics in socialist Yugoslavia', *Religion in Communist Lands*, Vol.10, No.3 (1982), pp.256–274.
2. Fox, Jonathan, 'Religion as an overlooked element of international relations', *International Studies Review*, Vol.3, No.3 (2001), p.59.
3. Zimmermann, Warren, *Origins of a Catastrophe: Yugoslavia and Its Destroyers* (New York, NY, 1996), p.210.
4. See Clifford Geertz, *The Interpretation of Culture* (New York, NY, 1973).
5. Fox: 'Religion as an Overlooked Element', p.72.
6. Ramet: 'Catholicism and politics', p.257; Alexander: *Church and State*, pp.57–61, 115.
7. Ibid., p.117.
8. Akmadža, Miroslav, 'Uzroci prekida diplomatskih odnosa izmedju Vatikana i Jugoslavije 1952. godine', *Croatica Christiana*, Vol.XXVII (2003), p.194.
9. Ibid., p.200.
10. Ibid., p.197.
11. Quoted in Milan Bulajić, *The Role of the Vatican in the Break-up of the Yugoslav State* (Belgrade, 1993), p.169.
12. Ibid., p.210.
13. Alexander: *Church and State*, p.245.
14. Ibid., p.247.
15. 'Ostkontakte des Vatikans', *Die Zeit*, 17 June 1966.
16. Della Rocca, Roberto M., 'La vita cristiana nella Jugoslavia communista', in Luciano Vaccaro (ed), *Storia religiosa di Croazia e Slovenia* (Gazzada, 2008), p.458. In addition, the author talks about greater participation in the seminaries in Slovenia and Croatia towards the end of the 1960s – an argument which shows that Yugoslav ideology allowed clergy recruitment (Ibid, p.460).
17. See, for example, 'Katoliška cerkev in oblast', in *Viri o demokratizaciji in osamosvojitvi Slovenije (I del: Opozicija in oblast)*, pp.146–147.
18. Šagi-Bunić, Tomislav, 'Ekumenizam bez romantike', *Glas Koncila*, No.7, 1967; 'Kršćanstvo i nacionalizam', *Glas Koncila*, No.12, 1969, pp.3–4;

'Katolička Crkva i ekumenizam', *Vjerske zajednice u Jugoslaviji* (Zagreb, 1970), pp.104–115; Janez Vodopivec, *Ekumenizam je ipak počeo* (Zagreb, 1968).
19. Banac, Ivo, 'Yugoslavia', *The American Historical Review*, Vol.97, No.4 (1992), p.1088.
20. Sekulić, Duško, Garth Massey and Randy Hodson, 'Who were the Yugoslavs? Failed sources of a common identity in the former Yugoslavia', *American Sociological Review*, Vol.59, No.1 (1994), p.84. For a more detailed account, see Steven L. Burg and Michael L. Berbaum, 'Community, integration, and stability in multinational Yugoslavia', *The American Political Science Review*, Vol.83, No.2 (1989), pp.535–554.
21. Grycz, Wolfgang, 'Katholische Kirche in Jugoslawien', *Kirche in Not*, No. 20, 1971, pp.88–89.
22. Dragović-Soso, Jasna, *Saviours of the Nation: Serbia's Intellectual Opposition and the Rise of Nationalism* (London, 2002), p.47.
23. Meier, Viktor, *Yugoslavia: A History of Its Demise* (London and New York, NY, 1999), p.19.
24. Ramet: 'Catholicism and politics', p.262.
25. Casaroli, Agostino, *Il martirio della pazienza: La Santa Sede e i paesi comunisti, 1963–89*, (Torino, 2000), p.245.
26. Ibid., p.246.
27. Perica, Vjekoslav, *Balkan Idols: Religion and Nationalism in Yugoslav States* (USA, 2004), p.58.
28. For a fuller account about inseparability of the Church from the Croatian nation and Catholicism from the Croatian national identity, see the writings of Tomislav Šagi-Bunić in the *Glas Koncila*, February-September 1972.
29. According to Casaroli, it was rather difficult to predict whether a new round of relations was going to improve the relations between the Vatican and Yugoslavia (Casaroli: *Il martirio*, p.246).
30. Stehle, Hansjakob, 'Die schwarze Mär vom roten Papst', *Die Zeit*, 22 March 1974.
31. Ibid.
32. Quoted in Hansjakob Stehle, 'Kompromiss bei bitterem Champagner', *Die Zeit*, 20 Juni 1975.
33. For example, the *Glas Koncila* and *Družina*, Croatian and Slovenian Catholic magazines, frequently reported about the discrimination of the Catholic clergy within the public sector across the Yugoslav state.
34. Ramet: 'Catholicism and politics', p.265.
35. Tenšek, Tomislav Zdenko, 'L'ecumenismo cattolico: dal "Glas Koncila" alla ricerca della riconciliazione dopo la guerra nella ex Jugoslavia', in Luciano Vaccaro (ed), *Storia religiosa di Croazia e Slovenia* (Milano, 2008), pp. 469–470.

36. Quoted in Ramet: 'Catholicism and politics', p.267.
37. Ibid., p.272.
38. Pavković, Aleksandar, *The Fragmentation of Yugoslavia: Nationalism and War in the Balkans* (London, 2000), p.79.
39. Ustav SFRJ (1974), Odnosi u federaciji i prava i dužnosti federacije, Articles 244–281. For an analysis of the 1974 Constitution, see, for example, Vojin Dimitrijević, 'The 1974 constitution and constitutional process as a factor in the collapse of Yugoslavia', in Payam Akhavan and Robert Howse (eds), *Yugoslavia, the Former and Future: Reflections by Scholars from the Region* (Washington, DC, 1995), pp.45–74.
40. Perica: *Balkan Idols*, p.145.
41. Casaroli: *Il martirio*, p.248.
42. Ibid., p.249.
43. For a detailed analysis of the SANU *Memorandum*, see Jasna Dragović-Soso, *Saviors of the Nation: Serbia's Intellectual Opposition and the Rise of Nationalism* (London, 2002), pp.177–195.
44. Mojzes: *Yugoslavian Inferno*, p.162. In addition, the author doubts that the authors of the Memorandum could have imagined its disastrous impact (Ibid.).
45. Arfi, Badredine, *International Change and the Stability of Multiethnic States* (Bloomington, IN, 2005), p.143.
46. Ramet: *Balkan Babel*, p.162.
47. Perica: *Balkan Idols*, p.138.
48. Ibid.
49. Ibid., pp.140–141.
50. Ibid., pp.152–153.
51. Ibid., p.153.
52. Mojzes: *Yugoslavian Inferno*, p.133.
53. Ibid.
54. Tenšek: 'L'ecumenismo cattolico', p.473.
55. Interview with a senior Vatican source.
56. Palmer, Peter, 'The Churches and the conflict in former Yugoslavia', in Ken R. Dark (ed), *Religion and International Relations* (New York, NY, 2000), pp.83–99.
57. Conversi, Daniele, 'Germany and the recognition of Slovenia and Croatia', in Brad K. Blitz (ed), *War and Change in the Balkans: Nationalism, Conflict and Cooperation* (Cambridge, 2006), p.65.
58. Ibid.
59. Weithmann, Michael W., 'Renaissance der Religion auf dem Balkans', *Gewerkschaftliche Monatshefte*, No.46 (1995), pp.760–761.

60. For a detailed account, see Milorad Tomanić, *Srpska crkva u ratu i ratovi u njoj* (Beograd, 2001).
61. In 1984, during a celebration of the 1300th anniversary of the Christianization of Croatia, Pope John Paul II underlined: 'God put Croatia between West and East meaning that it plays the role of a diplomat, but not a defender' (quoted in Weithmann: 'Renaissance der Religion', p.761).
62. 'Our Bishops warn the world', *Glas Koncila*, 24 March 1991, p.2.
63. Ibid.
64. European Parliament, 'Resolution on Yugoslavia', 13 March 1991.
65. Quoted in Bulajić: *The Role of the Vatican*, p.181.
66. 'An unavoidable decision', *Glas Koncila*, 26 May 1991.
67. Quoted in Bulajić: *The Role of the Vatican*, pp.177–178.
68. Ibid., p.181.
69. Checkel, Jeffrey T. and Peter J. Katzenstein, 'The politicization of European identities', in Jeffrey T. Checkel and Peter J. Katzenstein (eds), *European Identity* (Cambridge, 2009), p.14.
70. Holmes, Douglas R., 'Experimental identities (after Maastricht)', in Jeffrey T. Checkel and Peter J. Katzenstein (eds), *European Identity* (Cambridge, 2009), p.63.
71. Interview with a senior Italian official.
72. 'Possible recognition of Croatia, Slovenia urged', *Foreign Broadcast Service*, 13 July 1991.
73. Rosenberger, Sieglinde K., 'Political parties and religion', in Günter Bischof, Anton Pelinka and Hermann Denz (eds), *Religion in Austria* (New Brunswick, NJ, 2005), p.70.
74. Zucconi, Mario, 'The European Union in the former Yugoslavia', in Abram Chayes and Antonia Handler (eds), *Preventing Conflict in the Post-communist World* (Washington, DC, 1996), p.241.
75. During his visit to a religious site of Medjugorje, Giulio Andreotti, Prime Minister of Italy, expressed his sympathy for the Catholics in Yugoslavia ('Andreotti in visita a Medjugorje', *Glas Koncila*, 4 August 1991).
76. T. Vuković, 'The Astonishment of "Buffer Generals"', *Glas Koncila*, 4 August 1991.
77. Bellamy, Alex J., *The Formation of Croatian National Identity: A Centuries-old Dream?* (Manchester and New York, NY, 2003), p.159.
78. Ibid., p.163.
79. B. Sichtermann, 'Mit dem Segen der Kirche', *Die Zeit*, 17 February 1989. For a detailed account, see Hansjakob Stehle, *Eastern Politics of the Vatican, 1917–1979* (Athens, OH, 1981).
80. Palmer: 'The Churches', p.89. Similarly, Daphne Winland examines the churches in Canada and notes that Sunday sermons continuously talked

NOTES 219

about the political situation in Croatia (Daphne N. Winland, *We Are Now a Nation: Croats Between Home and Homeland*, Toronto, 2007, p.65).
81. Interview with a senior Vatican source.
82. For a fuller analysis of the 'us vs. them' debate, see, for example, Patrick H. Patterson, 'On the edge of reason: the boundaries of Balkanism in Slovenian, Austrian, and Italian discourse', *Slavic Review*, Vol.62, No.1, (2003), pp.110–141.
83. Holmes: 'Experimental identities', p.64.
84. Paterson, William, 'The German Christian Democrats', in John Gaffney (ed), *Political Parties and the European Union* (London, 1996), p.64.
85. Andreev, Svetlozar A., 'Path dependence and external shocks: the dynamics of the EU enlargement eastwards', in Finn Laaursen (ed), *Comparative Regional Integration: Theoretical Perspectives* (Hampshire, 2003), p.264.
86. Genscher, Hans-Dietrich, *Rebuilding a House Divided: A Memoir by the Architect of Germany's Reunification* (New York, NY, 1998), p.91.
87. Nobilo, Mario, *Hrvatski Feniks* (Zagreb, 2000), p.170.
88. Paul, Rachel, 'Serbian-American mobilization and lobbying: the relevance of Jasenovac and Kosovo to contemporary grassroots efforts in the United States', in Thomas Ambrosio (ed), *Ethnic Identity Groups and U.S. Foreign Policy* (Westport, CT, 2002), p.108.
89. Nobilo: *Hrvatski feniks*, p.170.
90. *Glas Koncila*, 25 August 1991.
91. Byrnes, Timothy A., *Transnational Catholicism in Postcommunist Europe* (Lanham, MD, 2001), pp.106–107. In his interview with Monsignor Celestino Migliore, undersecretary for relations with States, Byrnes noted that the Vatican considered 'normal that the Holy See would intervene in cases where the interests of Catholic states were involved' and, as admitted by Migliore, for the Holy See, 'favouring of Catholic communities is natural, normal' (Ibid.).
92. 'Holy See's position on Yugoslav states', *L'Osservatore Romano*, 1–8 January 1992.
93. Commission of the European Communities, *XXVth General Report on the Activities of the European Communities 1991*, pp.343–345.
94. 'Declaration on the situation in Yugoslavia', Brussels, 28 October 1991. Similar points are found in 'EC-US statement on peaceful and democratic transformation in the East' (Brussels, 9 November 1991) and 'Declaration on the guidelines on the recognition of new states in Eastern Europe and in the Soviet Union' (Brussels, 16 December 1991).
95. Cowell, Alan, 'Vatican formally recognizes independence of Croatia and Slovenia', *New York Times*, 14 January 1992.

96. 'Slovenia and Croatia win recognition', *Wilmington Morning Star*, 13 January 1992.
97. 'Zahvalno pismo Milana Kučana papežu Janezu Pavlu II ob mednarodnem priznanju Vatikana Slovenije', 13 January 1992.
98. 'Letter presented at the Holy Assembly of bishops of the Serbian Orthodox Church, held in Belgrade, on 17 January 1992'.
99. Ibid.
100. Byrnes: *Transnational Catholicism*, p.106.
101. Ibid.
102. Newhouse, John, 'Bonn, der Westen und die Auflösung Jugoslawiens: das Versagen der Diplomatie. Chronik eines Skandals', *Blätter für deutsche und internationale Politik*, No.10 (1992), p.1192.
103. Glenny, Misha, 'Carnage in Bosnia, for Starters', *New York Times*, 29 July 1993.
104. Beljan, Josip, 'Priznata vjernost', *Veritas*, September/October 1992, quoted in Mojzes: *Yugoslavian Inferno*, p.130.

Conclusion

1. Commission of the European Economic Community, *Sixth General Report on the Activities of the Community (May 1962 – March 1963)*, p.252.
2. The report stipulated: 'Relations with the former Yugoslavia remained very unsettled because of the continuing civil war in the area and its extension to Bosnia-Herzegovina ... As responsibility for the conflict lay mainly with Serbia and Montenegro, the Council, pursuant to UN Security Council Resolution 757, imposed a total trade embargo on the two republics' (Commission of the European Communities, *XXVIth General Report on the Activities of the European Communities 1992*, p.283). In contrast, the newly recognized Slovenia faced an establishment of direct cooperation with the Community (Bulletin EC 3–1992, point 1.3.27; Bulletin EC 7/8–1992, point 1.4.26).
3. Eyal, Jonathan, *Europe and Yugoslavia: Lessons from a Failure* (London, 1993), p.74.
4. Dinan, Desmond, *Europe Recast* (Basingstoke, 2004), p.234.
5. The twin document is known as 'Guidelines on the recognition of new states in Eastern Europe and the Soviet Union' and 'Declaration on Yugoslavia'.
6. Quoted in 'Yugoslavia no longer exists, say France', *The Times*, 10 October 1991.

7. Opinion No.1. For a full account of this and other opinions of the Badinter Commission, see Peter Radan's chapter 'The Badinter Commission: Secession, Self-determination and *Uti-possidetis*', in his *The Break-up of Yugoslavia and International Law* (London, 2002), pp.204–243, and Richard D. Caplan's chapter 'Recognition of States: Legal Thinking and Historic Practice' in his *Europe and the Recognition of New States in Yugoslavia* (Cambridge, 2005), pp.49–72.
8. 'Declaration on Yugoslavia', 16 December 1991.
9. See, for example, Anne-Marie Le Gloannec (ed), *Non-State Actors in International Relations: The Case of Germany* (Manchester: 2007) and Georg Menz, *The Political Economy of Managed Migration: Non-State Actors, Europeanization and the Politics of Designing Migration Policies* (Oxford, 2009).
10. Brenner, Michael J., 'EC: confidence lost', *Foreign Policy*, No.91 (1993), p.31.
11. 'European Parliament addresses growing role of religion in European policy; Experts cite rise of religious intolerance', 28 November 2001.
12. Ibid.
13. See, for example, European Commission, 'Communication from the Commission to the European Parliament and the Council – Western Balkans: enhancing the European perspective', COM (2008) 127 final, 5 March 2008.

BIBLIOGRAPHY

Archive Sources

European Union: Official Documents (in chronological order)

The High Authority of the European Coal and Steel Community, *General Report on the Activities of the European Community (August 1952 – April 1953)* – Relations with the other European Countries (Point 15), Publications Department of the European Community, 1009–53 H.A., 12 April 1953.

The High Authority of the European Coal and Steel Community, *Second General Report on the Activities of the Community (April 1953 – April 1954)* – Relations with Other European Countries (Point 14), Publications Department of the European Community, 1326–54 H.A., 11 April 1954

The High Authority of the European Coal and Steel Community, *Third General Report on the Activities of the Community (April 1954 – April 1955)* – External Relations of the Community (Point 16), Publications Department of the European Community, 1576-E-55 H.A., 10 April 1955

Conseil, 'Rapport des conseillers commerciaux des pays members de la CEE en Yougoslavie', 22 June 1959, Belgrade, RCC 12 f/59

Conseil, 'Rapport des conseillers commerciaux des pays members de la CEE en Yougoslavie', 30 July 1959, Brussels, RCC 12/59

Commission of the European Economic Community, *Third General Report on the Activities of the Community (March 1959 – May 1960)* – External Relations of the Community (Points 380 and 382), Publications Department of the European Communities, 4266/5/60/5, May 1960

Commission of the European Economic Community, *Fifth General Report on the Activities of the Community (May 1961 – April 1962)* – Point 210, Publishing Services of the European Communities, 1011*/5/XI/1962/5, June 1962

BIBLIOGRAPHY

Conseil de la Communauté économique européenne, CM 2/1962, No. 0781 including Extrait document R/843/62 (14 November 1962), Brussels, 28 November 1962

Commission of the European Economic Community, *Sixth General Report on the Activities of the Community (May 1962 – March 1963)* – Relations with the Eastern Bloc Countries (Point 274), Publishing Services of the European Communities, 1014*/5/VI/1963/5, June 1963

Commission of the European Economic Community, *Eighth General Report on the Activities of the Community (April 1964 – March 1965)* – Relations with State-trading Countries (Point 289), Publishing Services of the European Communities, 1022*/5/VII/1965/5, June 1965

Embassy of the SFRY, 'Diplomatic relations between Yugoslavia and the European Communities', 30 January 1968, CEAB5, No. 1484

Séance d'inauguration – 'Négociations Yougoslavie-Communauté', 15 October 1968, BAC 3/1968, No. 870/2

Commission of the European Communities, *Second General Report on the Activities of the Communities in 1968* – Commercial policy towards Eastern European countries (Point 543), Publications Department of the European Communities, 4510/5/69/1, February 1969

Commission des Communautés Européennes, Accord commercial entre la Communauté Economique Européen et la Republique Socialiste Federative de Yougoslavie – Communication de la Commission au Conseil, COM (70) 177 final, 24 February 1970

Council, 'Accordo commerciale tra la C.E.E. e la Iugoslavia – Dichiarazioni da iscrivere al processo verbale del Consiglio', 3 March 1970; R/468/70 (COMER 101)

Commission of the European Communities, *Fifth General Report on the Activities of the Communities in 1971* – The Agreement with Yugoslavia (Point 409), Office for Official Publications of the European Communities, February 1972

Conseil, 'Rapports des conseillers commerciaux des pays de la CEE en Yougoslavie', CM 2/1972, No. 1576

Commission of the European Communities, *Sixth General Report on the Activities of the Communities in 1972* – Agreements with Yugoslavia (Point 391), Office for Official Publications of the European Communities, February 1973

Letter from the Commission of the European Communities to H.E. Mr Van Elslande, President of the Council of the European Communities, I/78 e/73 (COMER 26), Brussels, 2 April 1973

Council, 'Report from the Information Officers of the Countries of the European Communities in Yugoslavia (2nd report)', S/858/73 (RCI 23), Brussels, 17 July 1973

Commission of the European Communities, *Seventh General Report on the Activities of the European Communities in 1973* – Agreements with Yugoslavia (Points 508 and 509), Office for Official Publications of the European Communities, February 1974

Council, 'General Economic Situation in Yugoslavia', S/58/74 (RCC 5), Brussels, 14 January 1974

Conseil, 'Rapport des Conseillers commerciaux des pays de la Communauté économique européenne en Yougoslavie (15ème rapport), S/702/74 (RCC 34)', 17 June 1974, Brussels

Commission of the European Communities, *Eighth General Report on the Activities of the European Communities in 1974* – Relations with Yugoslavia, Office for Official Publications of the European Communities, February 1975

Commission des Communautés Européennes, 'Memorandum de la Mission de la R.S.F. de Yougoslavie, en date du 10 juin 1975, concernant les relations commerciales et economiques CEE/Yougoslavie', SEC (75) 2369

RFE Special, Brussels, 16 June 1975

Commission of the European Communities, *Ninth General Report on the Activities of the European Communities in 1975* – Yugoslavia (Points 465 and 466), Office for Official Publications of the European Communities, February 1976

Council, 'EEC-Yugoslavia Relations', I/412/76, Brussels, 12 November 1976

Commission of the European Communities, *Tenth General Report on the Activities of the European Communities in 1976* – Yugoslavia (Point 516), Office for Official Publications of the European Communities, February 1976

European Parliament, Working Documents 1977–1978, Doc. 26/77, April 1977

European Parliament, Working Documents 1977–1978, Doc. 370/77, November 1977

Council, 'Negotiations with Yugoslavia', 12 April 1978

Letter from the President of the Council to the President of the EIB, I/346/78 (YU 7), Brussels, 6 December 1978

Council, 'Relations with Yugoslavia: drawing up of new negotiating directives – Financial Cooperation', I/369/78 (YU 9), Brussels, 15 December 1978

Commission of the European Communities, *Twelfth General Report on the Activities of the European Communities in 1978* – Yugoslavia (Point 506), Office for Official Publications of the European Communities, February 1979

European Investment Bank, 'Bank operations in Yugoslavia', Luxembourg, 14 May 1979

European Trends, Special Report 2, 'Yugoslavia and the EEC', Brussels, August 1979

Economic and Social Committee, 'Medium-term economic policy', Letter No. 4877/79, Brussels, 12 December 1979

Commission of the European Communities, *Thirteenth General Report on the Activities of the European Communities in 1979* – Yugoslavia (Point 559), Office for Official Publications of the European Communities, February 1980

Council, 'The 1980 Cooperation Agreement between the European Economic Community and the Socialist Federal Republic of Yugoslavia', 24 March 1980

European Parliament, Working Documents 1980–1981, Doc. 1–165/80, 19 May 1980

BIBLIOGRAPHY 225

Commission of the European Communities, *Fourteenth General Report on the Activities of the European Communities in 1980* – Yugoslavia (Point 656), Office for Official Publications of the European Communities, February 1981
European Parliament, Working Documents 1981–1982, Doc. 1–337/81, 2 July 1981
Council, Fiche No.873, 5 August 1981
European Parliament, Working Documents 1981–1982, Doc. 1–742/81, 13 November 1981
Council, Fiche No.107, 3 February 1982
European Parliament, Working Documents 1982–1983, Doc. 1–893/82, 15 November 1982
Commission of the European Communities, *Sixteenth General Report on the Activities of the European Communities in 1982* – Yugoslavia (Points 687 and 688), Office for Official Publications of the European Communities, February 1983
Political Affairs Committee, 'Motion for resolution', 3 February 1983
Commission of the European Communities, *Seventeenth General Report on the Activities of the European Communities in 1983* – Yugoslavia (Points 686–689), Office for Official Publications of the European Communities, February 1984
Economic and Social Committee, 'Record of the Proceedings on Relations between the European Community and Yugoslavia', 12 March 1985
Mission of the SFR of Yugoslavia to the European Communities, 'Verbal vote', No.185/85, Brussels, 28 May 1985
Conseil, 'Concéquences de l'adhésion de l'Espagne et du Portugal sur les relations CEE-Yougoslavie', CEE-YU 1004/85, 10 June 1985
Commission of the European Communities, *Nineteenth General Report on the Activities of the European Communities in 1985* – Yugoslavia (Point 844), Office for Official Publications of the European Communities, February 1986
Council, 'Cinquième réunion du comité de cooperation CEE-Yougoslavie', MED/12/86, Brussels, 9 July 1986
Cooperation Council, 'Cooperation between the EEC and Yugoslavia', Decision No. 1/86, 22 July 1986
Commission of the European Communities, *Twentieth General Report on the Activities of the European Communities in 1986* – Yugoslavia (Points 859 and 860), Office for Official Publications of the European Communities, February 1987
Council, 'Introductory statement of Dr Oskar Kovač at the opening of the negotiations of the Second SFRY-EEC Financial protocol', MED 12/87 (YU) (FIN), Brussels, 23 March 1987
Council, 'Aide: memoire', 27 March 1987
Council, Fiche No.713, 9 June 1987

Council, 'Sixth meeting of the EEC-Yugoslavia Cooperation Committee', Brussels, 30 October 1987
Council, 'Note à l'attention des Membres du Groupe "Mediterranée" (Yougoslavie)', MED/28/87, 30 October 1987
Council, 'Council decision concerning the conclusion of an Additional Protocol to the Cooperation Agreement between the EEC and the SFRY establishing new trade arrangements', 21 December 1987
European Parliament, 'Resolution sur les relations économiques et commerciales entre la Communauté européenne et la Yougoslavie', Doc. A2–258/87
Commission of the European Communities, *XXIst General Report on the Activities of the European Communities in 1987* – Yugoslavia (Point 788), Office for Official Publications of the European Communities, February 1988
Council, 'Note for the *ad hoc* Working Party on Yugoslav labour', SN 2894/88, 13 July 1988
Cooperation Council, 'Cooperation entre la Communauté économique européenne et la Yougoslavie: Compte-rendu de la reunion du Groupe de travail "Etats members/Yougolsavie" (main d'oeuvre yougoslave employee dans la Communauté)', CEE-YU 1008, Brussels, 18 November 1988
Seventh Meeting of the EEC-Yugoslavia Cooperation Council, CEE-YU 1019/88, Brussels, 19 December 1988
Commission of the European Communities, *XXIInd General Report on the Activities of the European Communities in 1988* – Yugoslavia (Points 925–927), Office for Official Publications of the European Communities, February 1989
'Memorandum on Yugoslav Economic Reforms', sent by Ante Marković, Prime Minister of Yugoslavia, to Jacques Delors, President of the Commission of EEC, 9804/89, Brussels, 9 November 1989
European Council, 'Paris Informal Meeting', 18 November 1989
Commission of the European Communities, *XXIIIrd General Report on the Activities of the European Communities in 1989* – Yugoslavia (Point 808), Office for Official Publications of the European Communities, February 1990
Council, 'Declaration du Conseil de Cooperation CEE-Yougoslavie sur l'avenir des relations entre la Communauté et la Yougoslavie', Brussels, 18 December 1990
Commission of the European Communities, *XXIVth General Report on the Activities of the European Communities in 1990* – Yugoslavia (Point 728), Office for Official Publications of the European Communities, February 1991
European Parliament, 'Resolution on Yugoslavia', 13 March 1991
'Declaration on the situation in Yugoslavia', 5 July 1991
'Declaration on Yugoslavia', 6 August 1991
'Declaration on Yugoslavia', 20 August 1991
'Declaration on Yugoslavia', 27 August 1991
'Declaration on Yugoslavia', 3 September 1991
'Declaration on the occasion of the ceremonial opening of the Conference on Yugoslavia', 7 September 1991
European Parliament, PE 152.616/rev, 9–13 September 1991

'Declaration on Yugoslavia', 19 September 1991
'Informal meeting of Ministers of Foreign Affairs', Haarzuilens, 6 October 1991
'Declaration on Yugoslavia', 18 October 1991
'Declaration on the Situation in Yugoslavia', 28 October 1991
'Extraordinary EPC Ministerial meeting', Rome, 8 November 1991
'EC-US statement on peaceful and democratic transformation in the East', Brussels, 9 November 1991
'Declaration on the Guidelines on the Recognition of New States in eastern Europe and in the Soviet Union', Brussels, 16 December 1991
Commission of the European Communities, *XXVth General Report on the Activities of the European Communities in 1991* – Yugoslavia (Point 1093), Office for Official Publications of the European Communities, February 1992
'Report of the Secretary General on the International Conference of the Former Yugoslavia', UN Doc. S/24795, 11 November 1992
Commission of the European Communities, *XXVIth General Report on the Activities of the European Communities in 1992* – Yugoslavia (Points 838–841), Office for Official Publications of the European Communities, February 1993
Council, 'Vienna European Council: Presidency Conclusions', 11–12 December 1998
'European Parliament Addresses Growing Role of Religion in European Policy; Experts Cite Rise of Religious Intolerance', 28 November 2001
European Commission, 'Communication from the Commission to the European Parliament and the Council – Western Balkans: enhancing the European perspective', COM (2008) 127 final, 5 March 2008

EU Statements in the Official Journal (Journal officiel), Bulletins and Press Releases

Journal officiel, No. C 39, 24 April 1971
Bulletin EC, 4–1974, point 2324
Bulletin EC, 10–1974, point 2329
Bulletin EC, 5–1976, point 2338
Bulletin EC, 11–1976, point 2340
Conseil, 'Communication à la Presse', 1414/76 (Presse 153), 3 December 1976
Bulletin EC, 6–1977, point 2333
Journal officiel, No. C 223/34, C 223/35, C 223/36, C 223/37, C 223/39, C 223/40, 14 November 1977
Official Journal, No. L 130, 27 May 1980
Journal officiel, 'Adaptation de l'accord de coopération avec la Yougoslavie après l'adhésion de la Grèce (débat)', No. C 101/63, 4 May 1981
Journal officiel, 'Accord de coopération entre la Communauté économique européenne et la république socialiste federative de Yougoslavie', No. L 41/12, 14 February 1983

Bulletin EC, 4–1983, point 2.2.28
Bulletin EC, 2–1984, point 2.4.36
Bulletin EC, 3–1984, point 2.1.174
Bulletin EC, 12–1984
Communication conjointe à la presse, CEE-YU 1015/86, Brussels, 22 July 1986
Bulletin EC, 4–1988, point 2.2.23
Communication à la presse, CEE-YU 1009/89, Brussels, 28 November 1989
Bulletin EC, 5–1990, point 1.3.25
Communication à la presse, CEE-YU 1006/90, Brussles, 18 December 1990
'Declaration on Yugoslavia', Press release 35/91, 26 March 1991
'Statement on Yugoslavia', Press release 42/91, 8 May 1991
'Statement on Yugoslavia', Press release 54/91, 8 June 1991
'Joint statement on the situation in Yugoslavia' Press release, 3 July 1991
Bulletin EC, 7/9–1991
Bulletin EC, 10–1991, point 1.4.6
'Statement on Dubrovnik', Press release 105/91, 27 October 1991
Official Journal, L 325, 27 November 1991
Official Journal, L 342, 12 December 1991
Bulletin EC, 12–1991.
'Statement on the death of five members of the European Community Monitor Mission to Yugoslavia', Brussels, 7 January 1992
Bulletin EC, 3–1992, point 1.3.27
Bulletin EC, 7/8–1992, point 1.4.26

Archive of Yugoslavia

'Program Komunističke partije Jugoslavije, 1958' [single stored document]
Konzorcijum ekonomskih instituta, 'Svetski ciljevi i pravci razvojne politike Jugoslavije do 1985', Beograd, 1971
Savezno izvršno veće, 'Nacrt društveni plana SFRJ: problemi zapošljavanja i mere', Beograd, 1971, Folder 130/1887
Savezno izvršno veće, 'Društveni plan Jugoslavije za period 1971–1975', Beograd, 5 November 1971
Savezno izvršno veće, 'Koordinacija saradnje izmedju SFRJ i SEV', Beograd, 19 January 1972
Sednica komisije SIV-a za koordinaciju saradnje izmedju SFRJ I SEV, 7 February 1972
Sednica komisije SIV-a za koordinaciju saradnje izmedju SFRJ I SEV, 5 May 1972
'Ustav Socijalističke Federativne Republike Jugosalvije 1974', *Službeni list SFRJ*, Vol. 30, No. 9, Belgrade, 21 February 1974
Savezno izvršno veće, 'Izveštaj o poseti delegacije Republike Srbije Severnoj Rajni-Vestfaliji', 4–10 September 1978, Folder 803/658

Archives of the Republic of Slovenia

Program Slovenske ljudske stranke, *Slovenija, priloga Ameriške domovine*, 54 (179), 20 Setember 1954
Predsedstvo CK ZSK, 29 January 1979, Document 1.X
Letter to Dr Alois Mock on behalf of the National Council of Carinthian Slovenes, 27 June 1991
Letter to the international cultural and scientific audience, 28 June 1991
Milan Kučan's letter to Diaspora, 22 July 1991
Letter to the Heads of State, Prime Ministers and Ministers of the Commonwealth Nations, 17 October 1991
Zahvalno pismo Milana Kučana papežu Janezu Pavlu II ob mednarodnem priznanju Vatikana Sloveniji, 13 Junuary 1992

Published documents and collections of archival materials:

Kardelj, Edvard, 'Historical Roots of Non-Alignment (8 September 1975)', in *Yugoslavia in the Contemporary World* (Belgrade: Federal Committee for Information, 1976), pp.71–107.
Klemenčič, Matjaž, Samo Kristen, Katalin Munda Hirnök, Milica Trebše Štolfa and Janez Stergar (eds), *Viri o demokratizaciji in osamosvojitvi Slovenije – IV del: Slovenci v zamejstvu in po svetu* (Ljubljana: Arhivsko društvo Slovenije, 2005)
Repe, Božo (ed), *Viri o demokratizaciji in osamosvojitvi Slovenije – I del: Opozicija in oblast* (Ljubljana: Modrijan Založba, 2002)
Available at: http://www.arhivsko-drustvo.si/publikacije/viri/Viri_17.PDF
———, *Viri o demokratizaciji in osamosvojitvi Slovenije – II del: Slovenci in federacija* (Ljubljana: Arhivsko društvo Slovenije, 2003)
———, *Viri o demokratizaciji in osamosvojitvi Slovenije – III del: Osamosvojitev in mednarodno priznanje* (Ljubljana: Arhivsko društvo Slovenije, 2004)
Tito, Josip Broz, 'Address to the Conference on European Security and Cooperation in Helsinki (31 July 1975)', in *Yugoslavia in the Contemporary World* (Belgrade: Federal Committee for Information, 1976), pp.54–61.

Newspapers, Magazines and News Agencies

Ameriška domovina
Borba
Corriere della Sera
Delo
Družina
The Economist
Financial Times
Foreign Broadcast Service

Frankfurter Allgemeine Zeitung
Fraternalist
Glas Koncila
The Guardian
Kirche in Not
Le Monde Diplomatique
Naš tednik
National
The National Review
The New York Times
Nova Revija
The Observer
L'Osservatore Romano
Otpor
Primorski dnevnik
Prosveta
La Repubblica
Slovenski vestnik
Der Standard
Time
The Times
The United Press International
Večernji list
Vjerske zajednice u Jugoslaviji
Wilmington Morning Star
Die Zeit

Television and Radio

Cable News Network (CNN)
Radio Free Europe
Televizija Beograd (TVB)
Televizija Ljubljana (TVL)
Zweites Deutsches Fernsehen (ZDF)

Selected Interviews

Mons. Remigio Musaragno, Rome, June-August 2004
Cardinal Camillo Ruini, Rome, December 2004
HE Lidija Topić, Bosnian diplomat and policy advisor, Brussels, summer 2005
Professor Barbara Delcourt, academic and policy advisor, Brussels, October 2006
Dr Janez Drnovšek, Slovenian politician, Ljubljana, summer 2007

Professor Jovan Živković, academic, Kosovo, summer 2007
HE Jaško Paro, Croatian diplomat, London, November 2007
HE Tanja Milašinović, Bosnian diplomat, London, November 2007
HE Muhamed Halili, Macedonian diplomat, London, November 2007
Mr Karsten Geier, German diplomat, Belgrade, December 2007
Dr Ivan Vejvoda, diplomat and advisor, Belgrade, December 2007
HE Stephen J. Wordsworth, British diplomat, Belgrade, December 2007
Professor Robert Hayden, academic, Pittsburgh, April 2008
Professor Željko Ivaniš, military expert and academic, Belgrade, June 2008
Professor Radmila Nakarada, academic, Belgrade, June 2008
Professor Ivo Visković, academic and diplomat, Belgrade, June 2008
Bogdan Tirnanić, journalist, Belgrade, June 2008
HE Dragan Županjevac, Serbian diplomat, London, November 2008
Marko Lopušina, diaspora expert, Belgrade, July 2009
Miloslav Samardžić, historian, Belgrade, July 2009
Veran Matić, Chief executive officer – Radio B92, Belgrade, August 2009
Aleksandar Tijanić, Chief executive officer – RTS, Belgrade, August 2009

Books, Pamphlets, Chapters and Articles

Adamič, Louis, *The Eagle and the Roots* (Garden City, NY: Doubleday & Company, 1952).
——, *My Native Land* (New York, NY: Harper & Brothers, 1943).
——, *The Native's Return. An American Immigrant Visits Yugoslavia and Discovers his Old Country* (New York, NY: Harper & Brothers, 1934).
Akmadža, Miroslav, 'Uzroci prekida diplomatskih odnosa izmedju Vatikana i Jugoslavije 1952. godine', *Croatica Christiana*, Vol.XXVII (2003), pp.171–202.
Alexander, Stella, *Church and State in Yugoslavia since 1945* (Cambridge: Cambridge University Press, 1979).
Allcock, John B., *Explaining Yugoslavia* (London and New York, NY: C. Hurst and Co. and Columbia University Press, 2000).
Almond, Mark, *Europe's Backyard War: The War in the Balkans* (London: William Heinemann Ltd., 1994).
Anderson, Benedict, 'Exodus', *Critical Inquiry*, Vol.20, No.1 (1994), pp.314–327.
——, *Long-Distance Nationalism: World Capitalism and the Rise of Identity Politics* (Amsterdam: Centre for Asian Studies, 1992).
Andreev, Svetlozar A., 'Path dependence and external shocks: the dynamics of the EU enlargement eastwards', in Finn Laaursen (ed), *Comparative Regional Integration: Theoretical Perspectives* (Hampshire: Ashgate, 2003), pp.251–272.
Arfi, Badredine, *International Change and the Stability of Multiethnic States* (Bloomington, IN: Indiana University Press, 2005).

Artisien, Patrick F. R. and Stephen Holt, 'Yugoslavia and the EEC in the 1970s', *Journal of Common Market Studies*, Vol.18, No.4 (1980), pp.355–369.
Arts, Bas, Math Noortmann and Bob Reinalda, *Non-state Actors in International Relations* (Aldershot: Ashgate, 2001).
Auty, Phyllis, 'The post-War period', in Stephen Clissold and Henry Clifford Darby (eds), *A Short History of Yugoslavia from Early times to 1966* (Cambridge: Cambridge University Press, 1968), pp.236–264.
———, *Yugoslavia* (London: Thames and Hudson, 1965).
Bahovec, Tina (ed), *Eliten und Nationwerdung: die Role der Eliten bei der Nationalisierung der Kärntner Slovenen* (Klagenfurt: Hermagoras, 2003).
Baker, James, *The Politics of Diplomacy: Revolution, War and Peace, 1989–1992* (New York, NY: G. P. Putnam and Sons, 1995).
Bakić, Jovo and Gazela Pudar, 'The Yugoslav succession wars and the war for symbolic hegemony', in Pål Kolstø (ed), *Media Discourse and the Yugoslav Conflicts: Representation of Self and Other* (Burlington: Ashgate, 2009), pp.105–127.
Ballinger, Pamela, *History in Exile: Memory and Identity at the Borders of the Balkans* (Princeton, NJ: Princeton University Press, 2003).
Banac, Ivo, 'Yugoslavia', *The American Historical Review*, Vol.97, No.4 (1992), pp.1084–1104.
Bellamy, Alex J., *The Formation of Croatian National Identity: A Centuries-old Dream?* (Manchester and New York, NY: Manchester University Press, 2003).
Bennett, Christopher, *Yugoslavia's Bloody Collapse: Causes, Course and Consequences* (Washington Square, NY: New York University Press, 1995).
Bethlehem, Daniel and Marc Weller (eds), *The Yugoslav Crisis in International Law* (Cambridge: Cambridge University Press, 1997).
Blagojević, Marina, 'War on Kosovo: a victory for the media?' in Florian Bieber and Zidas Daskalovski (eds), *Understanding the War in Kosovo* (London and Portland, OR: Frank Cass, 2003), pp.166–183.
Bogetić, Dragan, *Jugoslavija i Zapad 1952–1955: Jugoslovensko približavanje NATO-u* (Beograd: Službeni list SRJ, 2000).
Bojičić, Vesna, 'The disintegration of Yugoslavia: causes and consequences of dynamic inefficiency in semi-command economics', in David A. Dyker and Ivan Vejvoda (eds), *Yugoslavia and After: A Study in Fragmentation, Despair and Rebirth* (London and New York, NY: Longman, 1996), pp.28–47.
Bookman, Milica Z., 'Economic aspects of Yugoslavia's disintegration', in Raju G. C. Thomas (ed), *Yugoslavia Unraveled: Sovereignty, Self-Determination, Intervention* (USA: Lexington Books, 2003), pp.117–138.
Borowiec, Andrew, *Yugoslavia After Tito* (New York, NY: Praeger Publishers, 1977).
Both, Norbert, *From Indifference to Entrapment: The Netherlands and the Yugoslav Crisis, 1990–1995* (Amsterdam: Amsterdam University Press, 2000).
Bowman, Glenn, 'Constructive violence and the nationalist imaginary: the making of "The People" in Palestine and former Yugoslavia,' in Francisco

BIBLIOGRAPHY 233

Panizza (ed), *Populism and the Mirror of Democracy* (London and New York: Verso, 2005), pp.118–143.
Brenner, Michael J., 'EC: confidence lost', *Foreign Policy*, No.91 (1993), pp.24–43.
Buden, Boris, 'Europe is a whore', in Nena Skopljanac Brunner, Stjepan Gredelj, Alija Hodžić and Branimir Krištofić (eds), *Media & War* (Zagreb and Belgrade: Centre for Transition and Civil Society Research and Agency Argument, 2000), pp.53–62.
Bulajić, Milan, *Tudjman's "Jasenovac Myth": Genocide against Serbs, Jews and Gypsies* (Beograd: Stručna knjiga, 1994).
———, *The Role of the Vatican in the Break-up of the Yugoslav State* (Belgrade: Ministry of Information of the Republic of Serbia, 1993).
Burg, Steven L., *Conflict and Cohesion in Socialist Yugoslavia: Political Decision Making Since 1966* (Prineton, NJ: Princeton University Press, 1983).
Burg, Steven L. and Paul S. Shoup, *The War in Bosnia-Herzegovina: Ethnic Conflict and International Intervention* (Armonk, NY: M. E. Sharpe, 1999).
Burg, Steven L. and Michael L. Berbaum, 'Community, integration, and stability in multinational Yugoslavia', *The American Political Science Review*, Vol.83, No.2 (1989), pp.535–554.
Busch, Brigitta, 'Shifting political and cultural borders: language and identity in the border region of Austria and Slovenia', *European Studies: An Interdisciplinary Series in European Culture, History and Politics*, Vol.19 (2003), pp.125–144.
Buzan, Barry and Ole Wæver, *Regions and Powers: The Structure of International Security* (Cambridge: Cambridge University Press, 2003).
Byrnes, Robert F., 'The dispute: historical background', in Vaclav L. Benes, Robert F. Byrnes and Nicolas Spulber (eds), *The Second Soviet-Yugoslav Dispute* (Bloomington, IN: Indiana University Publications, 1959), pp.xi-xvi.
Byrnes, Timothy A., *Transnational Catholicism in Postcommunist Europe* (Lanham, MD: Rowman & Littlefield, 2001).
Caplan, Richard, *Europe and the Recognition of New States in Yugoslavia* (Cambridge: Cambridge University Press, 2005).
———, Richard, *International Governance of War-Torn Territories* (Oxford: Oxford University Press, 2005).
Carter, Sean, 'The geopolitics of diaspora', *Area*, Vol.37, No.1 (2005), pp.54–63.
Casaroli, Agostino, *Il martirio della pazienza: La Santa Sede e i paesi comunisti, 1963–89* (Torino: Einaudi, 2000).
Cattell, David T., 'The politics of the Danube Commission under Soviet control', *American Slavic and East European Review*, Vol.19, No.3 (1960), pp.380–394.
Checkel, Jeffrey T. and Peter J. Katzenstein, 'The politicization of European identities', in Jeffrey T. Checkel and Peter J. Katzenstein (eds), *European Identity* (Cambridge: Cambridge University Press, 2009), pp.1–25.

Christian Democratic Union of Central Europe (eds), *Freedom: Prerequisite to lasting Peace* (New York, NY: Christian Democratic Union of Central Europe, 1957).

Cigar, Norman, *Genocide in Bosnia: The Policy of "Ethnic Cleansing"* (College Station, TX: Texas A&M University Press, 1995).

Cohen, Lenard J., *Broken Bonds: Yugoslavia's Disintegration and Balkan Politics in Transition* (Boulder, CO: Westview Press, 1995).

Cohen, Lenard J. and Paul Warwick, *Political Cohesion in a Fragile Mosaic: The Yugoslav Experience* (Boulder, CO: Westview Press, 1983).

Collier, Paul and Nicholas Sambanis, *Understanding Civil War* (Washington DC: World Bank, 2005).

Comisso, Ellen, 'State structures and political processes outside the CMEA: a comparison', *International Organization*, No.40 (1986), pp.577–598.

Connolly, Paul, 'Playing if by the rules: the politics of research in "race" and education', *British Educational Research Journal*, No.18, Vol.2 (1992), pp.133–148.

Conversi, Daniele, 'Germany and the recognition of Slovenia and Croatia', in Brad K. Blitz (ed), *War and Change in the Balkans: Nationalism, Conflict and Cooperation* (Cambridge: Cambridge University Press, 2006), pp.57–75.

——, 'German-bashing and the breakup of Yugoslavia', *Donald W. Treadgold Papers in Russian, East European and Central Asian Studies*, Vol.16 (1998), pp.1–82.

'Council of Europe', *International Organization*, Vol.7, No.4 (1953), pp.595–608.

Ćosić, Dobrica, *Kosovo* (Beograd: Novosti, 2004).

Cox, John K., *Slovenia: Evolving Loyalties* (London: Routledge, 2005).

Cox, Robert W. and Timothy J. Sinclair (eds), *Approaches to World Order* (Cambridge: Cambridge University Press, 1996).

Craven, Matthew C. R., 'The European Community Arbitration Commission on Yugoslavia', *British Yearbook of International Law*, Vol.66 (1995), pp.333–413.

Crnobrnja, Mihailo, *The Yugoslav Drama* (London: I. B. Tauris Publishers, 1996).

Crawford, Beverly, 'Explaining defection from international cooperation: Germany's unilateral recognition of Croatia', *World Politics*, Vol.48, No.4 (1996), pp.482–521.

Curran, James, *Media and Power* (London: Routledge, 2002).

Daianu, Daniel, 'Transition failures: how does Southeast Europe fit in?', in Daniel Daianu and Thanos Veremis (eds), *Balkan Reconstruction* (London and Portland, OR: Frank Cass, 2001), pp.88–113.

Della Rocca, Roberto M., 'La vita cristiana nella Jugoslavia communista', in Luciano Vaccaro (ed), *Storia religiosa di Croazia e Slovenia* (Gazzada: Fondazione Ambrosiana Paolo VI, 2008), pp.449–464.

Delors, Jacques, *Our Europe: The Community and National Development* (London: Verso, 1992).

BIBLIOGRAPHY

Denitch, Bogdan, *Ethnic Nationalism: The Tragic Death of Yugoslavia* (Minneapolis, MN: University of Minnesota Press, 1996).

Dimitrijević, Vojin, 'The 1974 constitution and constitutional process as a factor in the collapse of Yugoslavia', in Payam Akhavan and Robert Howse (eds), *Yugoslavia, the Former and Future: Reflections by Scholars from the Region* (Washington, DC: Brookings Institution Press, 1995), pp.45–74.

Dinan, Desmond, *Europe Recast* (Basingstoke: Palgrave, 2004).

Djilas, Aleksa, 'Germany's policy toward the disintegration of Yugoslavia', in Stephen E. Hanson and Willfried Spohn (eds), *Can Europe Work? Germany & the Reconstruction of Post-communist Societies* (Seattle, WA: University of Washington Press, 1995), pp.151–168.

Djurić, Ivana and Vladimir Zorić, 'Foreclosing the other, building the war: a comparative analysis of Croatian and Serbian press discourses during the conflict in Croatia', in Pål Kolstø (ed), *Media Discourse and the Yugoslav Conflicts: Representation of Self and Other* (Burlington: Ashgate, 2009), pp.61–82.

Dragović-Soso, Jasna, 'Why did Yugoslavia disintegrate? An overview of contending explanations', in Lenard J. Cohen and Jasna Dragović-Soso (eds), *State Collapse in South-Eastern Europe: New Perspectives on Yugoslavia's Disintegration* (West Lafayette, IN: Purdue University Press, 2007), pp.1–39.

——, *Saviors of the Nation: Serbia's Intellectual Opposition and the Rise of Nationalism* (London: C. Hurst & Co., 2002).

Duncan, Raymond W., 'Yugoslavia's break-up', in Raymond W. Duncan and Paul G. Holman, Jr. (eds), *Ethnic Nationalism and Regional Conflict: The Former Soviet Union and Yugoslavia* (Boulder, CO: Westview Press, 1994), pp.19–51.

Dunn, Larry A., 'The roles of religion in ronflicts in the former Yugoslavia', *Religion in Eastern Europe*, Vol.16, No.1 (1996), pp.13–27.

Dyker, David A., *Yugoslavia: Socialism, Development and Debt* (London: Routledge, 1990).

Esman, Milton J., *Diasporas in the Contemporary World* (Cambridge: Polity Press, 2009).

Eyal, Jonathan, *Europe and Yugoslavia: Lessons From a Failure* (London: Royal United Services Institute for Defence Studies, 1993).

Fabinc, Ivo, 'Federalism: the Crossroads', in George Macesich (ed), *Yugoslavia in the Age of Democracy* (Westport, CT: Praeger Publishers, 1992), pp.87–99.

Fox, Jonathan, 'Religion as an overlooked element of international relations', *International Studies Review*, Vol.3, No.3, (2001), pp.53–73.

Fukuyama, Francis, *The End of History and the Last Man* (New York, NY: Free Press, 2006).

Gagnon, Valere Philip Jr., *The Myth of Ethnic War: Serbia and Croatia in the 1990s* (Ithaca, NY: Cornell University Press, 2004).

Galtung, Johan, 'Reflections on the peace prospects for Yugoslavia', in Tonči Kuzmanić and Arno Truger (eds), *Yugoslavia War* (Ljubljana: Peace Institute, 1992), pp.19–34.

Geertz, Clifford, *The Interpretation of Culture* (New York, NY: Basic Books, 1973).
Genscher, Hans-Dietrich, *Rebuilding a House Divided: A Memoir by the Architect of Germany's Reunification* (New York, NY: Broadway Books, 1998).
Gerolymatos, André, *The Balkan Wars: Conquest, Revolution and Retribution from the Ottoman era to the Twentieth Century and Beyond* (Staplehurst: Spellmount, 2004).
Glenny, Misha, *The Fall of Yugoslavia: The Third Balkan War* (London: Penguin Books, 1993).
Goldstein, Ivo, *Croatia: A History* (London: Hurst & Co., 1999).
Gow, James, *The Serbian Project and Its Adversaries: A Strategy of War Crimes* (London: C. Hurst & Co., 2003).
——, *Triumph of the Lack of Will: International Diplomacy and the Yugoslav War* (London: C. Hurst & Co., 1997).
——, 'After the flood: literature on the context, causes, and course of the Yugoslav war – reflections and refractions', *Slavonic and East European Review*, Vol.75, No.3 (1997), pp.446–484.
Gow, James and Cathie Carmichael, *Slovenia and the Slovenes: A Small State and the New Europe* (London: C. Hurst & Co., 2000).
Grant, Thomas D., *The Recognition of States: Law and Practice in Debate and Evolution* (Westport, CT: Praeger Publishers, 1999).
Gredelj, Stjepan, 'The media's role in producing conflict', in Svetlana Slapšak *et al.* (eds), *The War Started at Maksimir: Hate Speech in the Media* (Belgrade: Media Center, 1997), pp.195–231.
Haas, Ernst B., *The Uniting of Europe: Political, Social and Economic Forces, 1950–1957* (Stanford, CA: Stanford University Press, 1968).
Habermas, Jürgen, *Europe: The Faltering Project* (Cambridge: Polity Press, 2009).
Hadžić, Miroslav, 'The controversies of Euro-Atlantic interventionism in the Balkans," in Peter Siani-Davis (ed), *International Intervention in the Balkans since 1995* (London: Routledge, 2003), pp.59–67.
Hammersley, Martyn, 'Ethnography: problems and prospects', *Ethnography and Education*, Vol.1, No.1 (2006), pp.3–14.
Hanson, Alan, 'Croatian independence from Yugoslavia, 1991–1992', in Melanie Greenberg, John H. Barton and Margaret E. McGuinness (eds), *Words Over War: Mediation and Arbitration to Prevent Deadly Conflict* (Lanham, MD: Rowman & Littlefield Publishers, 2000), pp.76–108.
Hayden, Robert M., *Blueprints for a House Divided: The Constitutional Logic of the Yugoslav Conflicts* (Ann Arbor, MI: University of Michigan Press, 1999).
Hitchcock, William I., *The Struggle for Europe: The History of the Continent since 1945* (London: Profile Books Ltd, 2004).
Hockenos, Paul, *Homeland Calling: Exile Patriotism and the Balkan Wars* (Ithaca, NY: Cornell University Press, 2003).
Hoffmann, Stanley, 'Yugoslavia: implications for Europe and for European institutions', in Richard H. Ullman (ed), *The World and Yugoslavia's Wars* (New York, NY: Council on Foreign Relations, 1996), pp.97–122.

———, *The European Sisyphus: Essays on Europe, 1964–1994* (Boulder, CO: Westview Press, 1995).
Holmes, Douglas R., 'Experimental identities (after Maastricht)', in Jeffrey T. Checkel and Peter J. Katzenstein (eds), *European Identity* (Cambridge: Cambridge University Press, 2009), pp.52–80.
Hughes, Barry and Thomas Volgy, 'Distance in foreign policy behaviour: a comparative study of Eastern Europe', *Midwest Journal of Political Science*, Vol.14, No.3 (1970), pp.459–492.
Huntington, Samuel P., *The Clash of Civilizations and the Remaking of World Order* (London: Free Press, 2002).
Irwin, Zachary T., 'Yugoslavia's relations with European states', in Sabrina P. Ramet and Ljubiša S. Adamovich (eds), *Beyond Yugoslavia: Politics, Economics, and Culture in a Shattered Community* (Boulder, CO: Westview Press, 1995), pp.349–392.
Jambrek, Peter, *Development and Social Change in Yugoslavia: Crises and Perspectives of Building a Nation* (Farnborough: Saxon House, 1975).
Johnson, Ross A., 'Yugoslavia: in the twilight of Tito', *The Washington Papers*, Vol.2, Wash DC, Beverly Hills/London: Sage Publications, (1974), pp.1–67.
Johnstone, Diana, 'Seeing Yugoslavia through a dark glass: politics, media, and the ideology of globalization', *Covert Action Quarterly*, No.65 (1998), pp.47–57.
Jović, Dejan, *Yugoslavia: A State that Withered Away* (West Lafayette, IN: Purdue University Press, 2009).
———, 'The Slovenian-Croatian confederal proposal: a tactical move or an ultimate solution?', in Lenard J. Cohen and Jasna Dragović-Soso (eds), *State Collapse in South-Eastern Europe: New Perspectives on Yugoslavia's Disintegration* (West Lafayette, IN: Purdue University Press, 2007), pp.249–280.
———, 'The disintegration of Yugoslavia: a critical review of explanatory approaches', *European Journal of Social Theory*, Vol.4, No.1 (2001), pp.101–120.
Jusić, Tarik, 'Media discourse and the politics of ethnic conflict: the case of Yugoslavia', in Pål Kolstø (ed), *Media Discourse and the Yugoslav Conflicts: Representation of Self and Other* (Burlington: Ashgate, 2009), pp.21–38.
Kaldor, Mary, *New and Old Wars* (London: Polity Press, 2006).
Kintis, Andreas G., 'Between ambition and paralysis: the European Union's Common Foreign and Security Policy and the war in the former Yugoslavia', in Carl C. Hodge (ed), *Redefining European Security* (New York, NY: Garland Publishing, 1999), pp.273–298.
Klemenčič, Matjaž, 'The international community and the FRY/Belligerents, 1989–1997', in Charles Ingrao and Thomas A. Emmert (eds), *Confronting the Yugoslav Controversies: A Scholars' Initiative* (West Lafayette, IN: Purdue University Press, 2009), pp.153–198.
———, 'Slovenes as immigrants, members of autochthonous minorities in neighboring countries and members of multiethnic states (1500–1991)', in Ann

Katherine Isaacs (ed), *Languages and Identities in Historical Perspective* (Pisa: Pisa University Press, 2005), pp.97–124.

———, 'Slovenia as a part of a united Europe in the political philosophy of Slovene emigrants from Louis Adamič to Miha Krek', in Irena Gantar Godina (ed), *Intellectuals in Diaspora* (Ljubljana: Založba ZRC, 1999), pp.43–58.

Kolstø, Pål (ed), *Media Discourse and the Yugoslav Conflicts: Representation of Self and Other* (Burlington: Ashgate, 2009).

Kosin, Marko, 'Slovenska manjšina v slovensko-italijanskih odnosih', *Razprave in gradivo*, Vol.33 (1998), pp.57–97.

Koslowski, Rey, *Migrants and Citizens: Demographic Change in the European State System* (Ithaca, NY: Cornell University Press, 2000).

Krieger, Wolfgang, 'Toward a Gaullist Germany?', *World Policy Journal*, Vol.11 (1994), pp.1–30.

Kroeber-Riel, Werner and Jürgen Hauschildt, 'Decision making', in Jessica Kuper (ed), *Political Science and Political Theory* (London: Routledge, 1987), pp.45–49.

Kučan, Jakša, *Bitka za Novu Hrvatsku* (Rijeka: Otokar Keršovani, 2000).

Kurspahić, Kemal, *Prime Time Crime: Balkan Media in War and Peace* (Washington, DC: United States Institute of Peace Press, 2003).

Lak, Marteen, 'The involvement of the European Community in the Yugoslav crisis during 1991', in Martin van den Hauvel and Jan G. Siccama (eds), *The Disintegration of Yugoslavia* (Amsterdam and Atlanta, GA: Rodopi, 1992), pp.175–186.

Lampe, John R., *Yugoslavia as History: Twice there Was a Country* (Cambridge: Cambridge University Press, 2000).

Lampe, John R., Prickett O. Russell and Ljubiša S. Adamović, *Yugoslav-American Economic Relations since World War II* (Durham, NC: Duke University Press, 1990).

Lane, Ann, *Yugoslavia: When Ideals Collide* (London: Palgrave Macmillan, 2003).

Lantis, Jeffrey S., *Strategic Dilemmas and the Evolution of German Foreign Policy since Unification* (Santa Barbara, CA: Greenwood Press, 2002).

Le Gloannec, Anne-Marie (ed), *Non-State Actors in International Relations: The Case of Germany* (Manchester: Manchester University Press, 2007).

Libal, Michael, *Limits of Persuasion: Germany and the Yugoslav Crisis, 1991–1992* (Westport, CT: Greenwood Publishing Group, 1997).

Liotta, P. H., 'Religion and war: fault lines in the Balkan enigma', in Raju G. C. Thomas (ed), *Yugoslavia Unraveled: Sovereignty, Self-Determination, Intervention* (USA: Lexington Books, 2003), pp.87–116.

———, *Dismembering the State: The Death of Yugoslavia and Why it Matters* (Lanham, MD: Lexington Books, 2001).

Longinović, Tomislav Z., 'Yugoslavism and its discontents: a cultural post-mortem', in John Burt Foster Jr. and Wayne Jeffrey Froman (eds), *Thresholds of Western Culture: Identity, Postcoloniality, Transnationalism* (London: Continuum International Publishing Group, 2002), pp.146–169.

BIBLIOGRAPHY 239

Lucarelli, Sonia, *Europe and the Breakup of Yugoslavia: A Political Failure in Search of a Scholarly Explanation* (Leiden: Brill, 2000).
Lukić, Reneo and Alen Lynch, *Europe from the Balkans to the Urals: The Disintegration of Yugoslavia and the Soviet Union* (Oxford: Oxford University Press, 1996).
Lyons, Terrence, 'Diasporas and Homeland Conflict', paper presented at the George Mason University workshop on Contentious Politics, April 2004, Available at: http://www.bsos.umd.edu/gvpt/davenport/dcawcp/paper/mar0304.pdf, (1/10/2009).
Magaš, Branka, *The Destruction of Yugoslavia: Tracking Yugoslavia's Break-up, 1980–1992* (London: Verso, 1992).
Malešević, Siniša, *Ideology, Legitimacy and the New State: Yugoslavia, Serbia and Croatia* (London: Routledge, 2002).
Maresceau, Marc, 'The European Community, Eastern Europe and the URSS', in John Redmond (ed), *The External Relations of the European Community: The Internal Response to 1992* (New York, NY: St. Martin's Press, 1992), pp.93–119.
Marković, Ljubisav, 'Socialism: illusion and reality', in George Macesich (ed), *Yugoslavia in the Age of Democracy* (Westport, CT: Praeger Publishers, 1992), pp.27–38.
Mastnak, Tomaz, 'From the new social movements to political parties', in James Simmie and Jože Dekleva (eds), *Yugoslavia in Turmoil: After Self-management?* (London: Pinter Publishers, 1991), pp.45–64.
Mates, Leo, *Medjunarodni odnosi socijalističke Jugoslavije* (Beograd: Nolit, 1976).
McAllister, Richard, *From EC to EU: An Historical and Political Survey* (London: Routledge, 1997).
McFarlane, Bruce, *Yugoslavia: Politics, Economics and Society* (London and New York, NY: Pinter Publishers, 1988).
McGoldrick, Dominic, 'The tale of Yugoslavia: lessons for accommodating national identity in national and international law', in Stephen Tierney (ed), *Accommodating National Identity: New Approaches in International and Domestic Law* (Leiden: Brill, 2000), pp.13–64.
Meier, Viktor, *Yugoslavia: A History of Its Demise* (London and New York, NY: Routledge, 1999).
——, 'Yugoslav Communism', in William E. Griffith (ed), *Communism in Europe: European Communism and Sino-Soviet Rift* (Cambridge, MA: MIT Press, 1964), pp.58–72.
Menz, Georg, *The Political Economy of Managed Migration: Non-State Actors, Europeanization and the Politics of Designing Migration Policies* (Oxford: Oxford University Press, 2009).
Mesa-Lago, Carmelo, 'Unemployment in a socialist economy: Yugoslavia', *Industrial Relations*, Vol.10, No.1 (1971), pp.49–69.
Michas, Takis, *Unholy Alliance: Greece and Milosevic's Serbia* (College Station, TX: Texas A & M University Press, 2002).
Mihelj, Sabina, Veronika Bajt and Miloš Pankov, 'Reorganizing the identification matrix: televisual construction of collective identities in the early

phase of Yugoslav disintegration', in Pål Kolstø (ed), *Media Discourse and the Yugoslav Conflicts: Representation of Self and Other* (Burlington: Ashgate, 2009), pp.39–59.

Miller, Benjamin, *When Opponents Cooperate: Great Power Conflict and Collaboration in World Politics* (Ann Arbor, MI: University of Michigan Press, 2002).

Minahan, James, *Miniature Empires: A Historical Dictionary of the Newly Independent States* (Westport, CT: Greenwood Press, 1998).

Mitrany, David, 'The functional approach to world organization', *International Affairs*, Vol.24, No.3 (1948), pp.350–363.

Mojzes, Paul, *Yugoslavian Inferno: Ethnoreligious Warfare in the Balkans* (New York, NY: Continuum, 1994).

Monnet, Jean, *Memoirs* (Glasgow: Collins, 1978).

Mutz, Diana C., *Impersonal Influence: How Perceptions of Mass Collectives Affect Political Attitudes* (Cambridge: Cambridge University Press, 1998).

Mutz, Diana C., Paul M. Sniderman and Richard A. Brody, 'Political persuasion: the birth of a field of study', in Diana C Mutz, Paul M. Sniderman and Richard A. Brody (eds), *Political Persuasion and Attitude Change* (Ann Arbor, MI: University of Michigan Press, 1996), pp.1–16.

Nakarada, Radmila, *Raspad Jugoslavije: Problemi tumačenja, suočavanja i tranzicije* (Beograd: Službeni glasnik, 2008).

Newhouse, John, 'Bonn, der Westen und die Auflösung Jugoslawiens: das Versagen der Diplomatie. Chronik eines Skandals', *Blätter für deutsche und internationale Politik*, No.10 (1992), pp.1184–1198.

Nicoll, William and Trevor C. Salmon, *Understanding the New European Community* (Hemel Hampstead: Harvester Wheatsheaf, 1994).

Niemeyer, Ralph Thomas, *The Verdict: When A State Is Hijacked* (Bloomington, IN: iUniverse, 2003).

Nobilo, Mario, *Hrvatski Feniks* (Zagreb: Globus, 2000).

Ottaway, Marina, 'Rebuilding state institutions in collapsed states', in Jennifer Milliken (ed), *State Failure, Collapse and Reconstruction* (Malden, MA: Blackwell Publishing, 2003), pp.245–266.

Owen, David, *Balkan Odyssey* (Orlando, FL: Harcourt Brace & Co., 1995).

Palmer, Peter, 'The Churches and the conflict in former Yugoslavia', in Ken R. Dark (ed), *Religion and International Relations* (New York, NY: Palgrave, 2000), pp.83–99.

Papini, Roberto, *The Christian Democrat International* (Lanham, MD: Rowman & Littlefield Publishers, 1997).

Paterson, William, 'The German Christian Democrats', in John Gaffney (ed), *Political Parties and the European Union* (London: Routledge, 1996), pp.53–70.

Patterson, Patrick H., 'On the edge of reason: the boundaries of Balkanism in Slovenian, Austrian, and Italian discourse', *Slavic Review*, Vol.62, No.1 (2003), pp.110–141.

Paul, Rachel, 'Serbian-American mobilization and lobbying: the relevance of Jasenovac and Kosovo to contemporary grassroots efforts in the United

BIBLIOGRAPHY

States', in Thomas Ambrosio (ed), *Ethnic Identity Groups and U.S. Foreign Policy* (Westport, CT: Praeger Publishers, 2002), pp.93–114.

Pavković, Aleksandar, *The Fragmentation of Yugoslavia: Nationalism and War in the Balkans* (London: Palgrave Macmillan, 2000).

Pavković, Aleksandar and Peter Radan, *Creating New States: Theory and Practice of Secession* (Surrey: Ashgate, 2007).

Pavlowitch, Stevan K., 'Yugoslavia: why did It collapse?', in Vassilis K. Fouskas (ed), *The Politics of Conflict* (London: Routledge, 2007), pp.147–154.

——, *The Improbable Survivor: Yugoslavia and its Problems, 1918–1988* (London: C. Hurst & Co., 1988).

——, *Yugoslavia* (New York, NY: Praeger, 1971).

Perica, Vjekoslav, *Balkan Idols: Religion and Nationalism in Yugoslav States* (USA: Oxford University Press, 2004).

Pleština, Dijana, *Regional Development in Communist Yugoslavia: Success, Failure, and Consequences* (Boulder, CO: Westview Press, 1992).

Pocock, John Greville A., 'Deconstructing Europe', in Peter Gowan and Penny Anderson (eds), *The Question of Europe* (London: Verso, 1997), pp.297–317.

Pomfret, Richard, 'The European Community's relations with the Mediterranean countries', in John Redmond (ed), *The External Relations of the European Community: The International Response to 1992* (New York, NY: St. Martin's Press, 1992), pp.77–92.

Popović, Jovan P., 'Sukcesija arhiva na prostorima bivše SFRJ', in Kosta Mihailović (ed), *Sukcesija i kontinuitet Savezne Republike Jugoslavije* (Beograd: Institut za medjunarodnu politiku i privredu, 2000), pp.146–151.

Potter, Jonathan and Margaret Wetherell, *Discourse and Social Psychology* (London: Sage, 1987).

Pratt, Jeff, *Class, Nation and Identity: The Anthropology of Political Movements* (London: Pluto Press, 2003).

Pribičević, Branko, 'Relations with the superpowers', in Sabrina P. Ramet and Ljubiša S. Adamovich (eds), *Beyond Yugoslavia: Politics, Economics, and Culture in a Shattered Community* (Boulder, CO: Westview Press, 1995), pp.331–348.

Prpić, Jure, *Hrvati u Americi* (Zagreb: Hrvatska matica iseljenika, 1997).

Ra'anan, Gavriel D., *Yugoslavia after Tito: Scenarios and Implications* (Boulder, CO: Westview Press, 1977).

Radan, Peter, *The Break-up of Yugoslavia and International Law* (London: Routledge, 2002)

Ragazzi, Francesco, 'The invention of the Croatian diaspora: unpacking the politics of "diaspora" during the war in Yugoslavia', *Working Paper No. 10*, George Mason University, VA: Center for Global Studies, 2009, pp.1–10.

Ramet, Sabrina P., 'The way we are – and should be again: European Orthodox Churches and the "idyllic past"', in Timothy A. Byrnes and Peter J. Katzenstein (eds), *Religion in an Expanding Europe* (Cambridge: Cambridge University Press, 2006), pp.148–175.

———, *Thinking about Yugoslavia: Scholarly Debates about the Yugoslav Breakup and the Wars in Bosnia and Kosovo* (Cambridge: Cambridge University Press, 2005).

———, *Balkan Babel: The Disintegration of Yugoslavia from the Death of Tito to the Fall of Milošević* (Boulder, CO: Westview Press, 2002).

———, *Nationalism and Federalism in Yugoslavia, 1962–1991* (Bloomington, IN: Indiana University Press, 1992).

Ramet, Pedro, 'Factionalism in Church-State interaction: the Croatian Catholic Church in the 1980s', *Slavic Review*, Vol.44, No.2 (1985), pp.298–315.

———, 'Catholicism and politics in socialist Yugoslavia', *Religion in Communist Lands*, Vol.10, No.3 (1982), pp.256–274.

Reuter, Jens, 'Yugoslavia's role in changing Europe', in D. Muller *et al.* (eds), *Veranderungen in Europa – Vereinigung Deutchlands: Perspektiven der 90er Jahre* (Belgrade: Institute for International Politics and Economy, 1991).

Roberts, Walter R., 'The tragedy in Yugoslavia could have been averted', in Raju G. C. Thomas and H. Richard Friman (eds), *The South Slav Conflict* (New York, NY: Garland Publishing, 1996), pp.363–374.

Rosamond, Ben, *Theories of European Integration* (Hampshire: Palgrave Macmillan, 2000).

Rosenberger, Sieglinde K., 'Political parties and religion', in Günter Bischof, Anton Pelinka and Hermann Denz (eds), *Religion in Austria* (New Brunswick, NJ: Transaction Publishers, 2005), pp.63–80.

Rusinow, Dennison, *The Yugoslav Experiment, 1948–1974* (London: C. Hurst & Co., 1977).

Sabl, Andrew, 'Governing pluralism', in Denis Saint-Martin and Fred Thompson (eds), *Public Ethics and Governance: Standards and Practices in Comparative Perspective* (Stamford, CT: JAI Press, 2006), pp.243–256.

Sadkovich, James J., 'Franjo Tudjman: A Political and Intellectual Biography', research presented at George Mason University, 2006,
Available at: http://www.irex.org/programs/stg/research/05/sadkovich.pdf, (1/2/2008).

Safran, William, 'Diasporas in modern societies: myths of homeland and return', *Diaspora*, Vol.1, No.1 (1991), pp.83–99.

Schloer, Wolfgang, 'Germany and the break-up of Yugoslavia', in Raju G. C. Thomas and Richard H. Friman (eds), *The South Slav Conflict* (New York, NY: Garland Publishing, 1996), pp.315–330.

Seers, Dudley and Constantine Vaitsos (eds), *The Second Enlargement of the EEC The Integration of Unequal Partners* (Basingstoke: Macmillan, 1986).

Sekulić, Duško, Garth Massey and Randy Hodson, 'Who were the Yugoslavs? Failed sources of a common identity in the former Yugoslavia', *American Sociological Review*, Vol.59, No.1 (1994), pp.83–97.

Sheffer, Gabriel, *Diaspora Politics: At Home Abroad* (Cambridge: Cambridge University Press, 2006).

Sheffer, Gabriel (ed), *Modern Diasporas in International Politics* (London and Sydney: Croom Helm, 1986).

Shonfield, Andrew, *Europe: Journey to an Unknown Destination* (London: Allen Lane, 1973).
Shoup, Paul, 'The disintegration of Yugoslavia and Western foreign policy in the 1980s', in Lenard J. Cohen and Jasna Dragović-Soso (eds), *State Collapse in South-Eastern Europe: New Perspectives on Yugoslavia's Disintegration* (West Lafayette, IN: Purdue University Press, 2007), pp.333–364.
——, *Communism and the Yugoslav National Question* (New York, NY: Columbia University Press, 1968).
Silber, Laura and Allan Little, *The Death of Yugoslavia* (London: BBC Books, 1995).
Skrbiš, Zlatko, 'The mobilized Croatian diaspora: its role in homeland politics and war', in Hazel Smith and Paul Stares (eds), *Diasporas in Conflict: Peace-makers or Peace-wreckers?* (Tokyo, New York and Paris: United Nations University Press, 2007), pp.218–238.
——, '"The First Europeans" fantasy of Slovenian Venetologists: emotions and nationalist imaginings', in Maruška Svašek (ed), *Postsocialism: Politics and Emotions in Central and Eastern Europe* (Oxford: Berghahn Books, 2007), pp.138–158.
——, 'The emotional historiography of Venetologists: Slovene diaspora, memory, and nationalism', *European Journal of Anthropology*, No.39 (2002), pp.41–55.
——, 'Nationalism in a transnational context: Croatian diaspora, intimacy and nationalist imagination', *Revija za Sociologiju*, Vol.32, No.2–3 (2001), pp.133–146.
——, *Long-Distance Nationalism: Diasporas, Homelands, and Identities* (Sydney: Ashgate, 1999).
Smith, Hazel, 'Diasporas in International Conflict', in Hazel Smith and Paul Stares (eds), *Diasporas in Conflict: Peace-makers or Peace-wreckers?* (Tokyo, New York and Paris: United Nations University Press, 2007), pp.3–16.
Sofos, Spyros, 'Culture, media and the politics of disintegration and ethnic division in former Yugoslavia', in Tim Allen and Jean Seaton (eds), *The Media of Conflict: War Reporting and Representations of Ethnic Violence* (London: Zed Books, 1998), pp.162–174.
Sparks, Colin, 'Media theory after the fall of European communism', in James Curran and Myung-Jin Park (eds), *De-Westernizing Media Studies* (London: Routledge, 2000), pp.35–49.
Stark, Hans, 'Dissonances franco-allemandes sur fond de guerre serbo-croate', *Politique etrangere*, Vol.57, No.2 (1992), pp.339–347.
Stehle, Hansjakob, *Eastern Politics of the Vatican, 1917–1979* (Athens, OH: Ohio University Press, 1981).
Stokes, Gale, John Lampe, Dennison Rusinow and Julie Mostov, 'Instant history: understanding the wars of Yugoslav succession', *Slavic Review*, Vol.55, No.1 (1996), pp.136–160.
Sörensen, Jens Stilhoff, *State Collapse and Reconstruction in the Periphery: Political Economy, Ethnicity and Development in Yugoslavia, Serbia and Kosovo* (Oxford: Berghahn Books, 2009).

Tanner, Marcus, *Croatia: A Nation Forged in War* (New Haven, CT: Yale University Press, 1997).

Tenšek, Tomislav Zdenko, 'L'ecumenismo cattolico: dal "Glas Koncila" alla ricerca della riconciliazione dopo la guerra nella ex Jugoslavia', in Luciano Vaccaro (ed), *Storia religiosa di Croazia e Slovenia* (Milano: Centro Ambrosiano, 2008), pp.465–486.

Therborn, Göran, 'Europe in the twenty-first century: the world's Scandinavia', in Peter Gowan and Penny Anderson (eds), *The Question of Europe* (London: Verso, 1997), pp.357–384.

Thomas, Raju G. C., 'Sovereignty, self-determination, and secession: principles and practice', in Raju G. C. Thomas (ed), *Yugoslavia Unraveled: Sovereignty, Self-Determination, Intervention* (USA: Lexington Books, 2003), pp.3–40.

Thompson, Mark, *Forging War: The Media in Serbia, Croatia and Bosnia-Herzegovina* (Luton: University of Luton Press, 1999).

——, *A Paper House: The Ending of Yugoslavia* (London: Hutchinson Radius, 1992).

Tindemans, Leo *et al.*, *Unfinished Peace: Report of the International Commission on the Balkans* (Washington, DC: Carnegie Endowment for International Peace, 1996).

Tomac, Zdravko, *The Struggle for the Croatian State: Through Hell to Democracy* (Zagreb: Profikon, 1993).

Tomanić, Milorad, *Srpska crkva u ratu i ratovi u njoj* (Beograd: Medijska knjižara Krug, 2001).

Toš, Niko, 'Nove vrednote v funkciji deblokade družbenega razvoja', in Niko Toš *et al.* (eds), *Slovenski utrip. Slovensko javno mnenje 1988–89* (Ljubljana: Center za raziskovanje javnega mnenja, 1989), pp.14–32.

Touval, Saadia, *Mediation in the Yugoslav Wars: The Critical Years, 1990–95* (New York, NY: Palgrave, 2002).

Trifunovska, Snežana (ed), *Former Yugoslavia through Documents: From its Dissolution to Peace Settlement* (Dordrecht: Martinus Nijhoff Publishers, 1999).

——, *Yugoslavia through Documents: From its Creation to its Dissolution* (Dordrecht: Martinus Nijhoff Publishers, 1994).

Tully, James (ed), *Meaning and Context: Quentin Skinner and his Critics* (Princeton, NJ: Princeton University Press, 1988).

Ullman, Richard H. (ed), *The World and Yugoslavia's Wars* (New York, NY: Council on Foreign Relations, 1996).

Van Schendelen, Rinus, *Machiavelli in Brussels: The Art of Lobbying the EU* (Amsterdam: Amsterdam University Press, 2005).

Vertovec, Steven, 'Three meanings of "Diaspora", exemplified among South Asian religions," *Diaspora*, Vol.6, No.3 (1997), pp.277–330.

Vlajki, Emil, *Demonization of Serbs: Western Imperialism and Media War Criminals* (Ottawa: Revolt, 2001).

Vodopivec, Janez, *Ekumenizam je ipak počeo* (Zagreb: Kršćanska sadašnjost, 1968).

BIBLIOGRAPHY 245

Vojnić, Dragomir, 'Reforms in retrospect', in George Macesich (ed), *Yugoslavia in the Age of Democracy* (Westport, CT: Praeger Publishers, 1992), pp.17–26.

Vukadinović, Radovan, 'Yugoslavia and the East: from non-alignment to disintegration', in Martin van den Heuvel and Jan G. Siccama (eds), *The Disintegration of Yugoslavia* (Amsterdam: Rodopi, 1992), pp.147–173.

Wachtel, Andrew, *Making a Nation, Breaking a Nation: Literature and Cultural Politics in Yugoslavia* (Stanford, CA: Stanford University Press, 1998).

Wallace, William, 'National inputs into European Political Cooperation', in David Allen, Reinhardt Rummel and Wolfgang Wessels (eds), *European Political Cooperation: Towards a foreign policy for Western Europe* (Bonn: Institut für Europaische Politik, 1982), pp.46–59.

Watson, Adam, *Diplomacy: The Dialogue between States* (London: Eyre Methuen, 1982).

Weithmann, Michael W., 'Renaissance der Religion auf dem Balkans', *Gewerkschaftliche Monatshefte*, No.46 (1995), pp.753–768.

Weller, Marc, 'The international response to the dissolution of the Socialist Federal Republic of Yugoslavia', *The American Journal of International Law*, Vol.86, No.3 (1992), pp.569–607.

Wengraf, Tom, *Qualitative Research Interviewing: Semi-Structured, Biographical and Narrative Methods* (London: Sage Publications, 2001).

Winland, Daphne N., *We Are Now a Nation: Croats Between Home and Homeland* (Toronto: University of Toronto Press, 2007).

——, 'Croatian diaspora', in Marvin Ember, Carol R. Ember and Ian Skoggard (eds), *Encyclopedia of Diasporas: Immigrant and Refugee Cultures around the World* (USA: Springer, 2005), pp.76–84.

Wodak, Ruth, 'Fragmented identities: redefining and recontextualizing national identity', in Paul A. Chilton and Christina Schäffner (eds), *Politics as Text and Talk: Analytical Approaches to Political Discourse* (Amsterdam: John Benjamins, 2002), pp.143–172.

Woodward, Susan L., 'The West and the international organisations', in David A. Dyker and Ivan Vejvoda (eds), *Yugoslavia and After: A Study in Fragmentation, Despair and Rebirth* (London and New York, NY: Longman, 1996), pp.155–176.

——, *Balkan Tragedy: Chaos and Dissolution after the Cold War* (Washington, DC: Brookings Institution Press, 1995).

——, *Socialist Unemployment: The Political Economy of Yugoslavia, 1945–1990* (Princeton, NJ: Princeton University Press, 1995).

Zeitler, Klaus P., *Deutschlands Rolle bei der völkerrechtlichen Anerkennung der Republik Kroatien unter besonderer Berücksichtigung des deutschen Außenministers Genscher* (Marburg: Tectum Verlag, 2000).

Zimmermann, Warren, *Origins of a Catastrophe: Yugoslavia and Its Destroyers – America's Last Ambassador Tells What Happened and Why* (New York, NY: Times Books, 1996).

Zimmerman, William, *Open Borders, Nonalignment, and the Political Evolution of Yugoslavia* (Princeton, NJ: Princeton University Press, 1977).

——, 'Hierarchical regional systems and the politics of system boundaries', *International Organization*, Vol.26, No.1 (1972), pp.18–36.

Žižek, Slavoj, 'Eastern Europe's republics of Gilead', *New Left Review*, No.183 (1990), pp.50–62.

Zucconi, Mario, 'The European Union in the former Yugoslavia', in Abram Chayes and Antonia Handler (eds), *Preventing Conflict in the Post-communist World* (Washington, DC: Brookings Institution Press, 1996), pp.237–280.

INDEX

Note: *n* attached to a page number denotes an endnote, with appropriate number.

Action Committee for a United and Sovereign Slovene State 97, 98
Adamič, Louis 97
agriculture 54, 56, 79–80
Akmadža, Miroslav 148
Albanian population, Kosovo 75–6
Alexander, Stella 149
Allcock, John 20
Alps-Adriatic Work Community 18, 111
Anderson, Benedict 104
Andreev, Svetlozar 163
Andreotti, Giulio 117
archives 9, 177–8*n*30
Artisien, Patrick 57, 60, 62
Austria
    Alps-Adriatic Work Community 18, 111
    Austrian People's Party 161
    Carinthian Slovenes 111–12, 114–15, 119–20, 208*n*71
    Croat emigré terrorists 58
    Croatia as buffer state 115
    EC membership application 110–111

    recognition of Slovenia and Croatia 30, 115, 120, 136–7, 172
    religious dimension 161, 162
    and Slovenia 112–15
    Slovenian diaspora 111–16
    Vatican embassy 157–8

Badinter Commission 27–8, 145, 171
Baker, James 132–3
Banac, Ivo 150
Bellamy, Alex 161–2
Bennett, Christopher 24
Bettiza, Enzo 65, 68–9
Bilandzich, N. 101
Blagojević, Marina 35
Bosnia-Herzegovina
    Badinter Commission recommendation 28
    EC assistance 138
    economic underperformance 19
    Republika Srpska 28
    and the Vatican 158
    war 12
Both, Norbert 30–31

Brenner, Michael 143, 172
Brioni Agreement 18, 32, 170, 182*n*30
Buden, Boris 129
Bulajič, Milan 160
Busch, Brigitta 107
Busek, Erhard 136–7, 161
Buzan, Barry 25
Byrnes, Timothy 166

Canada, Croatian diaspora in 34, 102–3
Caplan, Richard 27
Carinthian Slovenes 111–12, 114–15, 119–20, 208*n*71
Carmichael, Cathie 33
Carrington, Peter, Lord 141
Carter, Sean 106
Casaroli, Agostino 151–2, 153, 155
Catholic Church *see* Roman Catholic Church
Charter of Fundamental Rights 173
Checkel, Jeffrey 160, 161
Christian Democratic Union of Central Europe (CDUCE) 97–8, 204*n*11
Christian Social Union of Bavaria (CSU) 7, 161, 163, 168
Cohen, Lenard 21, 29
Cold War 44, 45
COMECON (Council for Mutual Economic Assistance) 47, 77
Comisso, Ellen 79, 87
Common Foreign and Security Policy (CFSP) 141
Conversi, Daniele 31, 35, 158
Cooperation Agreement (1980)
   adoption and terms 71–5, 78, 79
   suspension of 87
   see also Financial Protocols
Cooperation Council 81, 91, 197*n*21
Corriere della Sera 127, 134
Ćosić, Dobrica 53
Council of Europe 49
Crawford, Beverly 30, 106
Crnobrnja, Mihailo 1
Croatia

Alps-Adriatic Work Community 18, 111
bishops' letter 159
Brioni Agreement 18, 32, 170, 182*n*30
and Catholic Church 151–2, 153, 157, 159–60, 162
conflict 135, 142, 161
Croatian Spring (1971) 151
diaspora *see* Croatian diaspora
foreign support sought 25
independence for 105
Krajina 28, 125
media coverage 35–6, 123–4, 125, 128, 136, 138
recognition debate 6–7, 27–8, 30–32, 104–5, 144–5, 168
recognition as independent state 32, 120, 165, 171
referendum (1991) 128, 160
and religion 150, 156–7
Serbian Democratic Party in Croatia (SDS) 125
Serbian population 17, 125, 128–9, 140–41, 142–3, 157, 180*n*12
Vatican support 8, 158–9, 160
wartime *Ustasha* regime 102, 148, 157
and Yugoslav disintegration 16–17
see also Tudjman, Franjo
Croatian Democratic Union (HDZ) 103–5, 157
Croatian diaspora
   activism 34, 100–105
   arms support 104
   divided aims 34, 119
   effectiveness 6–7, 34, 106
   financial support 103–4
   in Germany 6–7, 34, 104, 105, 106
   mixed Serb/Croat marriages 106, 119
   in North America 34, 102–3, 104
   and voting rights 105
Čuk, Marij 116

Danube Commission 56, 192–3*n*70
De Clercq, Willy (Viscount) 70

INDEX

de Gaulle, Charles 53
de Michelis, Gianni 32, 117, 127
Declarations on Yugoslavia (1991) 27,
    133–5, 140, 142
Delors, Jacques 45, 81
Denitch, Bogdan 16, 16–17
Der Standard 127, 134
diaspora 58, 95, 96, 109
diasporas, *see also* Croatian diaspora;
    Slovenian diaspora
Die Zeit 127, 128, 141
Dimitrijevič, Vojin 122
Dizdarević, Raif 80, 81
Djilas, Aleksa 142
Dular, Janez 119–20
Dumas, Roland 170
Duncan, Raymond 22

Eagleburger, Lawrence 21
Economic and Social Committee 78–9, 89
EEC (European Economic Community)
    see European Community (EC)
enlargement
    Greek accession 57, 72, 76, 81
    religious affiliation of future states 173–4
    Slavic possibility 129
    Slovenian possibility 127–8, 131
    and Yugoslav guest-workers 90
European Community (EC)
    Catholic background 160–61, 163, 168
    changing attitudes towards Yugoslav unity 5–6
    criticised for lack of knowledge 22–3, 24, 116, 130
    criticised for lack of policy 51, 109, 115, 133, 170, 172
    criticism of policies 62–3, 140–41
    Declarations on Yugoslavia (1991) 27, 133–5, 140, 142
    and developing countries 49–50
    diplomatic relations with Yugoslavia 4, 56–7
    and Eastern bloc countries 55
    EC Conference on Yugoslavia (EC-COY) 27
    economic integration 47
    economic response to crisis 137–8
    and ethnic tensions 140–41, 143
    exclusivity as an institution 46
    external relations 45–6
    external sources of information 22, 105–6, 113–14, 126, 157–8
    financial support for Yugoslavia 42, 43–4, 63, 65
    and human rights 165
    media influence on policy 133–5, 137, 138, 144–5
    monitoring mission 135, 143–4, 201–2*n*92
    political cooperation 23, 42, 56–8, 64–5, 66, 74, 75–8, 81–2
    positive view of SFRY 79
    press and information centres 125–6
    press releases show confusion 131–2
    recognition policy 26, 27–8, 30–32, 120, 142, 170–71
    recognition of Slovenia and Croatia 32, 120
    response to crisis 27, 87–8, 91–2, 133–5, 137–8, 140, 142, 201–2*n*92
    Serbia's lack of interest in influencing 129–30
    support for Tito and communists 23
    traditional ties with Yugoslavia 132
    uncertainty over future of federation 87–8
    and Yugoslav EC membership 21, 70
    and Yugoslav identity 151
    Yugoslavia's reaction to establishment of 51–3
European Free Trade Association (EFTA) 47
European Investment Bank 63, 71–2, 78, 138

European Parliament
  Christian Social Union of Bavaria 163
  and guest-workers 88
  and Kosovo 75–6
  links with Yugoslav Federal
    Assembly 74, 77
  on Yugoslav problem 65, 68–9, 69,
    70, 82, 159
  Yugoslav trade 77

Ferletič, Maria 118
Financial Protocols
  first 71, 81
  second 78, 79, 80, 81, 138, 200*n*60
  third 87, 137
Fox, Jonathan 146, 147
France, and Serbian forces 31
Frankfurter Allgemeine Zeitung (FAZ) 36,
  128, 134
Fukuyama, Francis 15

Gagnon, Valere 125, 129–30
Genscher, Hans-Dietrich 26, 32,
  163–4, 172
Germany
  Christian Social Union of Bavaria
    (CSU) 7, 161, 163, 168
  and Croatian diaspora 6–7, 34, 104,
    105, 106
  and ethnic groups 142
  fears over trade agreement 75
  guest-workers 91
  media coverage 127–8, 134, 137, 138,
    144–5
  recognition of Slovenia and Croatia
    6–7, 30–32, 104, 143–4, 144–5,
    164, 172
  religious dimension 161, 162
  and the Vatican 163–4
Glas Koncila 164
Glenny, Misha 167, 180*n*12
Gow, James 33
Granfil, Toma 58
Greater Serbia 105, 155, 180–81*n*19

Greece
  accession to EC 57, 72, 76, 81
  joins NATO 48–9
  and Macedonia 30
  recognition debate 32
  transit links 76, 195*n*106, 199*n*42
  Greek Orthodox Church 8, 36, 147
  guest-workers
    in Europe 4, 60–61, 67, 88–91
    statistics 74, 194*n*96

Habermas, Jürgen 144
Hague Peace Conference (1991) 91–2,
  139–40, 141–2
Hanson, Alan 32
Hauschildt, Jürgen 6
Hayden, Robert 14
Helsinki Final Act (1975) 26
Hinsley, Harry, Sir 133
Hockenos, Paul 34, 100, 104–5
Hoffmann, Stanley 28–9
Holmes, Douglas 160, 161, 163
Holt, Stephen 57, 61, 62
human rights 30–31, 75–6, 165

IMF (International Monetary Fund) 20,
  85, 182*n*40
International Conference on the Former
  Yugoslavia (ICFY) 27
Italy
  and 1980 Cooperation Agreement 75
  Alps-Adriatic Work Community
    18, 111
  indirect threat from Yugoslav army
    117–18
  recognition debate 32, 120
  recognition of Slovenia and Croatia
    120, 172
  religious dimension 161, 162
  and Slovenia 127
  Slovenian diaspora 116–18, 120
  Trieste 190*n*30
  and Yugoslavia 49
  see also Vatican

INDEX

251

Jančar, Matjaž 207n54
JNA *see* Yugoslav People's Army (JNA)
John Paul II, Pope 164, 165, 166
John XXIII, Pope 149
Johnson, Ross 58, 62
Johnstone, Diana 128
Jusič, Tarik 122

Kardelj, Edvard 51, 52, 55
Katzenstein, Peter 160, 161
Khol, Andreas 112
Kintis, Andreas 131–2
Klemenčič, Matjaž 111
Kosin, Marko 117
Kosovo 19, 28, 54, 75–6, 113, 155
Kovač, Oskar 80, 81
Krajina 28, 125
Krek, Miha 97
Krizni štab Slovencev v Italiji 117
Kroeber-Riel, Werner 6
Kučan, Milan 107–8

Lane, Ann 19–20, 44, 57
Le Monde Diplomatique 134
Levi Sandri, Lionello 71
Libal, Michael 133
Likar, Ivan 154
Ljubljana Program (1958) 51, 52
Lončar, Budimir 82–4, 85–6
Lucarelli, Sonia 137, 178n4

Maastricht Treaty, negotiations 32
McAllister, Richard 46
Macedonia 19, 30, 54, 92, 138, 155, 190n30
Magaš, Branka 34–5, 128
Major, John 32
Malcolm, Noel 136
Malešević, Siniša 16
Marković, Ante 84–5
Mates, Leo 47
Matič, Veran 141
media 121–45
American 126

and Croatia 35–6, 123–4, 125, 128–9, 136, 138
EC policies criticized 133, 140–41
encouraged and sustained the conflict 7, 34–5
focus on Western audiences 35–6
German influence on policy 127–8, 134, 137, 138, 144–5
influence on EC policy 133–5, 137, 138, 144–5
and persuasion 139
polarized representation 121–2
and Serbia 7, 35, 123–4, 129–30, 142–3, 156
and Slovenia 35–6, 124, 125, 126–8, 135–6, 138
Yugoslav 121, 123–6
Meier, Viktor 4–5, 18, 24, 114
Member States
discord within 172–3
reluctance to support independence 116–17
Memorandum on Yugoslav economic reforms (1989) 84–5
methodology 8–10
migrant workers *see* guest-workers
Milošević, Slobodan
early Western views of 23–4
Hague Conference 141
and Kosovo Serbs 156
media representation of 123, 138
no religious views 147
US view of 21
and Yugoslav destruction 15–16
Mitterand, François 32
Mock, Alois 112, 114, 137, 161
Mojzes, Paul 156, 157
Monnet, Jean 49
Montenegro 19, 92, 169
Mutz, Diana 34

nationalism 15, 179n12
NATO (North Atlantic Treaty Organization) 49

Netherlands 31, 32
New York Times 21–2
Nicoll, William 53
Nobilo, Mario 17, 164
Nova Revija (magazine) 125

Observateur 52
Observer 15
Osimo Agreements 118, 210*n*95
Owen, David 15

Paris Summit (1989) 84
Pavle, Patriarch of Serbia 165–6
Pavlowitch, Stevan 23, 24, 45, 49, 50, 51, 53–4
Perič, Ratko 160
Perica, Vjekoslav 152, 156, 157
Phare 87, 200*n*73
Pipp, Marijan 114
Planinc, Milka 155
Pocock, John 26
political cooperation 23, 42, 56–8, 64–5, 66, 74, 75–8, 81–2
Pomfret, Richard 75
Poos, Jacques 25, 117

Radan, Peter 24–5
Ramet, Pedro 153, 154
Ranković, Aleksandar 51, 55
Reismüller, Johann Georg 128
religion 146–68
  in future EC member states 173–4
  and identity 7–8, 36
  and politics 156–7, 167–8
  religious education 148, 154
  source of political legitimacy 146–7
  see also Greek Orthodox Church; Roman Catholic Church; Serbian Orthodox Church; Vatican
Republika Srpska 28
Roman Catholic Church
  and Communist Party 148–9, 153
  in Croatia 159–60
  EC cultural background 160–61, 163, 168

election of clergy 150
humanitarian support 158
priests' associations 148–9
religious press 188*n*121
sermons on Slovenia and Croatia 162, 163
support for Slovenia and Croatia 8, 36
and Yugoslav government 148–54
see also Vatican
Ruehe, Volke 133
Rühe, Volker 133, 143–4
Rupel, Dimitrij 112

Salmon, Trevor 53
Serbia
  armed response to protesters 31
  Austrian media portrayal 142–3
  Belgrade anti-war protests 31
  German media portrayal of 127–8
  Greater Serbia 105, 155, 180–81*n*19
  and Greek Orthodox Church 8, 36, 147
  media coverage 7, 35, 123–4, 129–30, 142–3, 156
  reaction to Vatican decision 165
  responsibility for wars 169
  and Russian support 25
  see also Croatia, Serbian population; Milošević, Slobodan
Serbian Academy of Sciences and Arts, *Memorandum* 156
Serbian League of Communists 23
Serbian Orthodox Church 8, 156, 159, 165–6
Skrbiš, Zlatko 95–6, 99, 104
Slovenia
  Alps-Adriatic Work Community 18, 111
  archival sources 9, 107
  Austrian support for 112–13
  Brioni Agreement 18, 32, 170, 182*n*30
  Communist support for autonomy 157

INDEX

desire for self-determination 108–110
diaspora *see* Slovenian diaspora
EC membership aspirations 127–8, 131
foreign support sought 25
growing nationalism 99
Information Ministry 127
and Italy 127
media coverage 35–6, 124, 125, 126–8, 135–6, 138
recognition debate 27–8, 30–32, 120, 135–6, 144–5, 168
recognition as independent state 32, 120, 165, 171
and religion 150, 153–4, 156
responsibility for conflict 16–17
Television Slovenia (TVS) 135
Ten-Day War 108, 115–16, 132–3, 135–6
and Vatican 165
Slovenian diaspora
activism 33–4, 97–9, 107–8, 116–18
in Austria 111–16
Carinthian Slovenes 111–12, 114–15, 119–20, 208*n*71
financial assistance 118
in Italy 116–18
Unity List 115–16
in US 207*n*54
and the Vatican 98
Slovenian World Congress 33–4, 99, 107, 118
Slovenski narodni odbor 97–8
Smolle, Karel 113
Sofos, Spyros 123
Soviet Union
concern over Yugoslav crisis 91
and European Community 53
and Yugoslavia 44, 47, 50–51, 62, 190*n*28
Stabilization and Association Agreements (SAA) 86
Stark, Hans 34
Stehle, Hansjakob 152–3

Stepinac, Alojzije 148, 149, 150
Stergar, Janet 113
Süddeutsche Zeitung 128
Šušak, Gojko 205–6*n*38
Svet slovenskih organizacij 117, 118

Television Slovenia (TVS) 135
Thomas, Raju 26
Times, The 133
Tito, Josip Broz
career 180*n*17
and Catholic Church 152
foreign policy 48
ideological communist links 16, 19
illness 62
third world links 49
and the West 51
Titoism 44–5, 180*n*17
trade
1970s agreements 58–60
agriculture 56, 79–80
beef and veal exports 60, 76
Cooperation Agreement (1980) 71–5, 78, 79, 87
imbalance/balance 52, 64–5
negotiations 47–8, 54, 56, 81
preferential arrangements 137, 138
Yugoslav-COMECON 77
Trieste 190*n*30
Tudjman, Franjo
appreciation of 181*n*20
and Catholic Church 8
and Croatian Democratic Union 157
and Croatian diaspora 102–4
in Croatian media 123
electoral campaign 34
Hague Conference 141
religious views 147
and Serbians in Croatia 17, 180*n*12
and the Vatican 160, 161–2
and Yugoslav disintegration 16
Turkey
joins NATO 48–9
and Yugoslavia 49, 190*n*30

United Kingdom, and Serbian forces 31
United States
 Croatian diaspora in 34, 102–3, 104
 and Hague agreement 91
 and neutral stance 21–2, 183*n*52, 184*n*56
 recognition policy 21–2, 26
 responsibility for conflict 116
 and Slovenian diaspora 207*n*54
 source of information for EC 105–6, 126
 and worsening situation 132–3
Unity List 115–16
Ustasha regime 102, 148, 157

Van den Broek, Hans 31, 132–3
Vatican
 and Bosnia-Herzegovina 158
 criticized by Serbian Orthodox Church 165–6
 and Croatia 8, 158–9, 160, 164, 168
 and Croatian clergy 148–9
 diplomatic relations with Yugoslavia 149–50, 152–3
 and EC officials 161
 global power of 162
 and human rights 165
 and Kosovo 155
 non-interference guarantee 152
 and Slovenian diaspora 98
 support for Slovenia and Croatia 30, 36, 164–7
 violence condemned 147
 and Yugoslavia 148–54, 157–8
Veres, Milan 165
Vogel, Hans-Jochen 133
Vospernik, Reginald 113
Vranitzky, Franz 111, 112, 120

Wachtel, Andrew 180*n*12
Wæver, Ole 25
Wakounig, Andrej 115–16
Watson, Adam 41
Weithmann, Michael 158–9

Wengraf, Tom 10
western Balkans 188*n*127
Winland, Daphne 101–2
Woodward, Susan 18–19, 23–4, 29, 111
World War II 102, 148, 157, 166

Yugoslav Federal Assembly 74, 77
Yugoslav People's Army (JNA)
 in Croatia 135, 142, 161
 EC criticism of 138–9, 141
 and EC policy 5, 24
 in Slovenia 5, 109, 115–16, 116
Yugoslavia
 ancient hatreds 15
 archives 9, 177–8*n*30
 and Catholic Church 148–9, 153, 155–6, 158–9
 Community policy criticised 62–3
 constitution (1974) 60, 195*n*97
 cultural diversities 15, 180*n*12
 diaspora *see* Croatian diaspora; diaspora; Slovenian diaspora
 diplomatic relations with EEC 4, 56–7
 economic dependence on the West 19–21, 43–4
 economic problems 18–21, 48, 75, 79
 economic reforms 53–4, 61, 82, 84–5, 192*n*60
 European Investment Bank loans 63, 71–2, 78
 fear of marginalization in Europe 82–3
 financial support 42, 43–4, 63–4, 65, 71–2, 78, 79
 Five-year plan (1947–51) 43, 189*n*3
 foreign policy 47–8, 49, 51–2, 56–7
 identity 15, 150–51
 internal causes of collapse 15–18
 Ljubljana Program (1958) 51, 52
 media 121, 123–6

Memorandum on Yugoslav economic reforms (1989) 84–5
non-aligned status 43–5, 46, 48, 51, 57, 58, 65–6, 71
political cooperation 23, 42, 56–8, 64–5, 66, 74, 75–8, 81–2
political democracy 85, 86–7
Program of the League of Communists of Yugoslavia (Ljubljana) 51, 52
recognition policy debate 26, 27–8, 30–32
regional development 68–9, 196*n*1
and Soviet Union 44, 47, 50–51, 62, 190*n*28
Titoism (socialism) 44–5, 180*n*17
trade *see* trade
transit link with Greece 76, 195*n*106, 199*n*42
and Turkey 49, 190*n*30
unemployment 54, 55, 61
Ustasha regime 102, 148, 157, 166
and the Vatican 148–54, 157–8
view of creation of EC 3, 51–2
see also Bosnia-Herzegovina; Croatia; Serbia; Slovenia
Yugoslavism 150–51

Zagari, Mario 69, 88
Žebot, Cyril 98
Zerzer, Janko 113
Zimmermann, Warren 17, 22, 25–6, 26, 106, 110, 147